THE TEXTUAL CULTURE OF ENGLISH
PROTESTANT DISSENT 1720–1800

The Textual Culture of English Protestant Dissent 1720–1800

TESSA WHITEHOUSE

OXFORD
UNIVERSITY PRESS

OXFORD
UNIVERSITY PRESS

Great Clarendon Street, Oxford, OX2 6DP,
United Kingdom

Oxford University Press is a department of the University of Oxford.
It furthers the University's objective of excellence in research, scholarship,
and education by publishing worldwide. Oxford is a registered trade mark of
Oxford University Press in the UK and in certain other countries

First Edition published in 2015

Impression: 1

Published in the United States of America by Oxford University Press
198 Madison Avenue, New York, NY 10016, United States of America

British Library Cataloguing in Publication Data
Data available

Library of Congress Control Number: 2015937495

ISBN 978–0–19–871784–3

Printed in Great Britain by
Clays Ltd, St Ives plc

Acknowledgements

Without the resources and staff of Dr Williams's Library, writing this book would have been impossible. Staff there (both current and past) helped me immeasurably and always shared their expertise with great cheerfulness, for which I thank them all. My thanks also to librarians and archivists at the British Library, the John Rylands University Library, the University of Manchester, the libraries of Harris Manchester and Brasenose Colleges, Oxford, the library of the Bristol Baptist College, the Library and Archives of the Society of Jesus, the Roderic Bowen Library, the University of Wales, Trinity St David's, Northampton Public Library, and Castle Hill United Reformed Church, Northampton. I gratefully acknowledge permission to quote from manuscripts in the possession of these libraries and archives.

Material in Chapter 1 first appeared in '"Upon Reading Over the Whole of this Letter I am Sensibly Struck": Affectionate Networks and Schemes for Dissenting Academies', in *Lives and Letters*, 3 (2011). My thanks to the editors for permission to reuse it in this book. The detailed account of the posthumous publication of Doddridge's *Family Expositor* was first published in my article '*The Family Expositor*, the Doddridge Circle and the Booksellers', in *The Library* seventh series, 11 (2010), 321–44 and I am grateful to Oxford Journals for permission to use it here. Part of Chapter 5 first appeared in 'Godly Dispositions and Textual Conditions: The Literary Sociology of International Religious Exchanges, c.1722–1740', in *History of European Ideas*, 39 (2013), 394–408. My thanks to Taylor and Francis Group (<www.tandfonline.com>) for permission to reproduce this material.

The research underpinning this book was enabled by an Arts and Humanities Research Council Collaborative Doctoral Award and support from the Trustees of Dr Williams's Library, for which I thank them. I am deeply grateful, of course, to both my doctoral supervisors. Isabel Rivers has been unfailingly generous with her time, knowledge, and attention, and her questions and guidance have opened up new paths for investigation and have enriched my understanding. David Wykes has shared his extensive knowledge of dissent in general and the holdings of Dr Williams's Library in particular. Searching questions and apposite suggestions from my examiners Karen O'Brien and Judith Hawley and the anonymous readers for Oxford University Press helped me improve my arguments immeasurably. Many thanks to Mark Burden, Stephen

Burley, Rose Dixon, Simon Dixon, Inga Jones, Simon Mills, Kyle Roberts, and Olivia Smith, who all read and responded to earlier versions of this material. I owe intellectual debts to, among others, Julia Boffey, Françoise Deconinck-Brossard, Jane Giscombe, N. H. Keeble, Anne Janowitz, Jim McLaverty, Jon Mee, Chris Reid, Alison Searle, John Seed, James Vigus, and Maurice Whitehead. I wish to thank them all. Members of the School of English and Drama at Queen Mary University of London welcomed me into their community in 2012 and since then have been delightful and generous colleagues whose commitment to teaching and scholarship is inspiring.

Despite varying degrees of bafflement as to why I would research Protestants, and nonconformist ones at that, my family has been a wonderful source of encouragement which I appreciate very much. For companionship and stimulating conversations, thanks to all my friends and most especially to Steve, with love.

Contents

List of Figure

Abbreviations

A Course of Lectures (1763)	Philip Doddridge, *A Course of Lectures on the Principal Subjects of Pneumatology, Ethics and Divinity*, ed. S. Clark (London, 1763)
A Course of Lectures (1794)	Philip Doddridge, *A Course of Lectures on the Principal Subjects of Pneumatology, Ethics and Divinity*, ed. A. Kippis, 2 vols (London, 1794)
Add. MS	Additional manuscript
AFSt/H	Archiv Franckesche Stiftungen, Halle
BBC	Bristol Baptist College
Biographia Britannica	*Biographia Britannica: or, the Lives of the Most Eminent Persons who have Flourished . . . from the Earliest Ages, to the Present Times*, 2nd edition, ed. A. Kippis, 5 vols (London, 1778–1795)
BL	British Library
Calendar	G. F. Nuttall, *A Calendar of the Correspondence of Philip Doddridge* (London, 1979)
CHCN	Castle Hill United Reformed Church, Northampton
CHBB, IV	*The Cambridge History of the Book in Britain Volume IV: 1557–1695*, ed. Lotte Hellinga, D. F. McKenzie, John Barnard, J. B. Trapp, and David McKitterick (Cambridge, 2002)
CHBB, V	*The Cambridge History of the Book in Britain Volume V: 1695–1830*, ed. Michael F. Suarez, SJ and Michael L. Turner (Cambridge, 2009)
Doddridge, *Works*	*The Works of the Rev. P. Doddridge, D.D.*, ed. E. Williams and E. Parsons, 10 vols (Leeds, 1802–1805)
DWL	Dr Williams's Library, London
HMCO	Harris Manchester College, Oxford
Humphreys	Philip Doddridge, *The Correspondence and Diary of Philip Doddridge*, ed. J. D. Humphreys, 5 vols (London, 1829–1831)
JRUL	The John Rylands University Library, the University of Manchester
MHS, *Proceedings*	Massachusetts Historical Society, *Proceedings*, second series, 20 vols (1884–1907), IX (1894–1895), 331–410
Monthly Repository	*The Monthly Repository of Theology and General Literature*

NCL	New College, London. The collection is now at Dr Williams's Library
ODNB	*Oxford Dictionary of National Biography*
OED	*Oxford English Dictionary*
Orton, *Memoirs*	Job Orton, *Memoirs of the Life, Character and Writings of the Late Philip Doddridge, D.D.* (Shrewsbury, 1766)
TNA: PRO	The National Archives: Public Record Office
Watts, *Works*	*The Works of the Late Reverend and Learned Isaac Watts, D.D.*, ed. P. Doddridge and D. Jennings, 6 vols (London, 1753)

A Note on Transcription

This book contains many quotations from manuscripts. These have been transcribed in such a way as to correspond to the original as closely as is feasible in the medium of type. Original spelling and punctuation, and crossings out as they appear in the manuscripts have been retained throughout. Words added as an afterthought above the original line of text have been given between carats in the form: ^word^. Words and letters missing through a tear or obscured by a blot are given in angle brackets. Contractions remain unexpanded, unless the meaning is unclear. In such cases, the missing letters in contracted words are supplied in square brackets, as are explanatory words.

A NOTE ON LETTERS

References to Doddridge's correspondence appear throughout this book. There are three printed sources: a selection of his letters, edited by Thomas Stedman and published in 1793, an edition of his correspondence published between 1829 and 1831 by his great-grandson John Doddridge Humphreys, and a calendar of his correspondence produced by G. F. Nuttall in 1979 (*Calendar*). The last of these is the most reliable source, and contains letters which do not appear in either of the earlier editions. Both Stedman's and Humphreys's editions conform to different editorial standards from those expected today. In particular, Humphreys sometimes changes dates of letters or merges two letters into one. For a study of Humphreys's changes to manuscript letters, see *Calendar*, Appendix I: 'Examples of variation in transcribing'. In this book I refer to manuscript letters whenever possible, but sometimes a printed edition of correspondence is the only extant source for a particular letter. In such cases, all available printed versions of the letter have been compared. In references, the letter number from Nuttall's *Calendar* is always given. If the quotation given is from either of the printed correspondence editions, an abbreviated reference to that work is provided.

Introduction

Religious Dissent and Textual Culture in the Eighteenth Century

With respect to admitting Pupills I find it Necessary to observe these Rules.

1) That I admit no Young man till I see him & Inform my self by Personal Conference of his turn of Genius & Proficience in former Studies.

2) That I wait for sufficient Recommendation of him as to Sobriety from Impartial & Competent Persons, (as to this I'm well Satisfy'd as to your son)

3) That I take None from other Academys excepting they are of such short standing that they'll be Content to begin with me anew or at least Joyn my Lowest Class If that can be done, because my Scheme is So particular, I can build upon no Mans Foundation.

John Jennings, letter to a parent, *c.*1720[1]

It is hoped the candid and moderate will meet with nothing to give them offence. It is true, that here, more than in any other of his writings, Mr. ORTON appears the strict *Dissenter.*

Samuel Palmer's preface to Job Orton,
Letters to Dissenting Ministers, 1806 (I, viii)

This book is about the textual, social, and pedagogical means by which a group of Protestant dissenters in the eighteenth century sought to develop a reputation of candour, moderation, and learning for their community and to avoid being perceived as 'strict *Dissenters*' by the world at large. They did this through their work as authors, educators, and editors, by which means they addressed the British nation and an international religious public

---

[1] For the original transcription see 'John Jennings's Description of his Academy' in *Dissenting Education and the Legacy of John Jennings c.1720–c.1729*, ed. Tessa Whitehouse (2nd edn, 2011). URL: <http://www.english.qmul.ac.uk/drwilliams/pubs/jennings%20legacy.html>.

sphere. This group of men were all dissenting ministers who had been educated at dissenting academies. Many were also tutors at these academies: among these were John Jennings, who taught Philip Doddridge, later also a tutor who in turn taught Job Orton, Andrew Kippis, and Caleb Ashworth, himself tutor to the biographer Samuel Palmer.[2] Indeed, the existence of dissenting academies was crucial to the development of this textual, educational culture. These academies played an important role in shaping the minds of young men of England, not all of them dissenters. They were sites for social and cultural transmission, for inculcating traditions, and for promoting philosophies and pedagogies which, through print, reached audiences beyond the students for whom the texts were originally intended. The academies' contribution to discourses of national identity and moral purpose was therefore a significant (if heterogeneous and not always respectable) alternative to those articulations coming from the political and religious establishment.

Isaac Watts was not an academy tutor but as the author of *Logick*, *The Art of Reading and Writing English*, and *The Knowledge of the Heavens and Earth made Easy*, he was a leading pedagogue of the period. He was a central figure in mid-eighteenth-century dissenting culture and close friends with Doddridge, who respected his works immensely and used them in his lectures. These two men were highly significant religious authors of the eighteenth century, but to understand the range of their work and the roles they played in educational, religious, and cultural life within and beyond the dissenting world, it is important to look also at the activities of their friends. This was an associative, supportive community whose members strove to combine social action and intellectual endeavour. The younger men in their network read books written by the older men and attended lectures given by them. Later, they delivered lectures of their own modelled on those of their tutors, and edited the texts of their mentors. The men who preceded, succeeded, and worked with Watts and Doddridge identified themselves as participants in the same endeavours. They worked together (often invisibly) to produce textual testaments to dissenting learning, candour (in the eighteenth-century sense of generous openness), and social activism. Such texts acted both as memorials and celebrations of a moderate, learned dissenting tradition and as a spur and guide to future generations.

These activities were important because Protestant dissenters lacked any secure place within the English political, legal, and educational establishment and therefore cultivated alternative institutions through which their

---

[2] For the life-dates of these men, see Figure 1, p. 24. For further information about them and other figures in this book, see the Appendix: Biographical Notes.

traditions were sustained. This was effected primarily through their textual and educational culture. Dissenters' ideas did not develop or circulate in isolation, however: though they participated in a variety of cross-denominational engagements and used print to express their patriotism and nationalist commitments very strongly, the channels by which their ideas and practices spread have not been especially well understood. To redress this, it is necessary both to chart the circulation of texts they produced and to examine the educational and social contexts in which these texts and practices developed. What emerges is an enlightened, evangelical world of ecumenical projects, overlapping endeavours, friendship, and rivalry involving a great variety of individuals. Because the scene is a complex and relatively unfamiliar one, this book provides material histories and thorough descriptions of texts, people, and engagements to enable the fullest understanding of the diverse priorities and processes at work. My hope is that providing a strong contextual picture will bring into sharper focus not only these dissenters' intellectual community, but also the contribution they made to wider developments in eighteenth-century textual culture, particularly in the sphere of education.

Some striking features of the culture of moderate, orthodox dissent are evident in both the content and the form of the two extracts above. Personal encounters lay at the centre of the admissions procedures at the dissenting academy operated by John Jennings. The tutor assessed each student's aptitude, and personal testimonials counted for a great deal in determining the pupil's prior learning and good conduct. Significantly, Jennings did not impose religious tests for entry: rather than the capacity to recite doctrinal formulae, he sought students intellectually adventurous enough to participate in a completely new system and humble enough to start at the beginning of a post-grammar school educational programme. Personal communications were also the substance of the minister Samuel Palmer's edition of Job Orton's letters in the nineteenth century which were intended as models in content and style for young dissenting ministers and which attested to Orton's care for academies and ministerial students. The book of letters is filled with Palmer's notes about the present and recent state of dissenting academies and biographical references to notable dissenting educators, including Jennings. Palmer was certainly not alone in using paratexts to articulate a collective, contributive disposition for textual production, and the background to and implications of the importance of this editorial mode for dissenting publications are presented throughout this book.

Respectful adherence to the priorities and practices of the dissenting tradition are evident in both extracts. This tradition included a strong emphasis on individual judgement in intellectual endeavours, but also valued 'sobriety' so highly that it might be interpreted negatively: 'the strict *Dissenter*' was a stereotype of sobriety and piety taken to excess. The acts of organization detailed in these extracts take place within a relatively enclosed world peopled by those who have chosen to identify themselves among the dissenting community. Palmer assumes his readers will be familiar with Orton's work, but later in the preface expresses some concern over the informality of Orton's epistolary style on one hand and the strictness of the rules he presents for conduct on the other. Dissenters, it seems, could not be quite comfortable in public society despite 'the greatest ease and freedom' they privileged in their communications with one another.[3]

Jennings, writing to the parent of a prospective candidate for the dissenting ministry (a profession that was crucial to the ongoing existence of dissenting congregations), is confident about the innovations he brings to that training in the form of an entirely new sequence of academic lectures. Oscillation between intellectual confidence on one side and embattled appeals to shared culture and a significant (if increasingly distant) history on the other marked dissenters' discourse in the eighteenth century, and both the extracts here should be seen as interventions in an ongoing struggle to secure and improve dissent.

The personal and professional priorities of these men had significant implications both within dissenting culture and for a more widely configured Protestant international. To understand how this worked, it is necessary to consider their legal, educational, and social situation in its coterie, national, and international contexts. The connections dissenters created drew on their collective history and were characterized by self-reflexivity (as shown in Palmer's address to dissenting readers of Orton's letters); but they looked outwards too and imagined their community in broad terms. The crucial mechanism which enabled this historically grounded self-fashioning and address to international publics as well as personal associates was text.

The lives and work of these men, their relationships with each other, and their views on print, text, and literature will be explored thoroughly in the chapters to come. Here, I want to situate these interactions in a broader frame by explaining what I mean by 'textual culture' as an object of study, setting out the methods taken in its investigation, and introducing the key areas in the historiography of eighteenth-century culture in which this book intervenes.

---

[3] Samuel Palmer, 'Preface' in Job Orton, *Letters to Dissenting Ministers*, 2 vols (London, 1806), I, ix.

1. ASPECTS OF TEXTUAL CULTURE

The men who figure in this book all saw publishing as a central component of their work which they pursued while (and by) participating in
epistolary networks and exchanging manuscripts: this is understood as
their textual culture. Their publishing activities sought to promote practical piety, to consolidate the intellectual status of dissent, and to provide
educational models. Their teaching materials, which circulated in manuscript before being printed, also had these aims. Numerous manuscript
copies of lecture notes survive, and their circulation and recopying was
central to the continued influence of Philip Doddridge's educational
methods. Defining 'scribal publication', Harold Love has described 'a
more inclusive "weak" sense' of publication 'in which it is enough to
show that the text has ceased to be a private possession'.[4] In this sense,
some versions of academy lectures can be considered as publications; they
certainly attest to a lively scribal culture which existed in dissenting
academies until the late eighteenth century at least.[5] One of the aims of
this book is to consider the full variety of textual forms and publication
patterns by which these dissenters' ideas circulated. The relationship
between manuscript and print is complicated when considering educational culture, as Love has noted.[6] Surviving materials from dissenting
academies demonstrate that manuscript and print cannot be clearly
separated. Printed books were interleaved so that notes could be added,
lecture notes included summaries of and responses to printed texts,
volumes of lecture notes themselves contained a great deal of blank
space for future additions, and new material in a later edition of a printed
text could be copied into an earlier edition.[7] Letter-writers included

---

[4] Harold Love, *Scribal Publication in Seventeenth-Century England* (Oxford, 1993), 36.
[5] A similar culture in North America to the mid-eighteenth century is noted in Thomas
Knoles, Rick Kennedy, and Lucia Zaucha Knoles, *Student Notebooks at Colonial Harvard:
Manuscripts and Educational Practice* (Worcester, Mass., 2003). See also David McKitterick, *Print, Manuscript and the Search for Order* (Cambridge, 2003), 11.
[6] Love, *Scribal Publication*, 217–24.
[7] Watts's interleaved copy of John Wilkins's *Ecclesiastes* in which Watts has made
numerous notes survives in Dr Williams's Library, shelfmark 564.D.6: see William
E. Stephenson, 'Isaac Watts's Education for the Dissenting Ministry: A New Document',
Harvard Theological Review, 61 (1968), 263–81. Doddridge's theology lectures routinely
incorporate material from and discussion of printed books: see Chapter 2. Interleaved
copies of John Jennings's lecture notes with Doddridge's additions survive, including the
second part of Jennings's theology lectures, DWL MS 28.117. A copy of the 1776 edition
of Doddridge's *A Course of Lectures in the Principal Subjects of Pneumatology, Ethics and
Divinity* has the additional references from Andrew Kippis's edition of 1794 inserted by
hand: see BL, shelfmark 1601/9.

passages from printed texts in letters to friends and remarks on reading were a staple of letters, particularly in those from academy students to their mentors. Knowledge of these practices enables a fuller understanding of the educational culture of dissent, from which all their printed works emerged.

As David McKitterick has pointed out, 'print sits beside manuscript' in this period, and thinking about a textual culture invites us to consider relationships between forms as well as understanding texts as they existed in one form or another.[8] The term encourages emphasis on adaptation, transformation, fluidity, and *weave*: the human relationships that make the texts (including friendships, intellectual sharing, and business arrangements) must be approached with as much care as the content of the texts themselves. The diversity of the textual projects presented in this book means a flexible approach to their investigation is required.[9] The communicative, communal, multifaceted dimensions of textual culture are the central object of this study, and here Robert Darnton's 'communications circuit' and Richard B. Sher's work on Scottish authors have provided enabling methodologies.

Darnton's 'communications circuit' of participants in book production, distribution, and use placed book trade professionals such as compositors, wholesalers, binders, and authors in an endless loop of successive interactions. These agents and their relations are influenced by the 'economic and social conjuncture', 'intellectual influences and publicity', and 'legal sanctions' at the centre of the diagram.[10] The schema foregrounds the combination of personal engagements, professional responsibilities, and the larger social structures within which the participants operate. Leslie Howsam understands Darnton's model to make the book into a metonym: 'His *book* is as much an abstraction standing for those mediated relationships as it is a physical artefact.'[11] While there is a risk that the flexibility of the model means that it can be infinitely extended to all acts of communication and thereby loses sight of the specific purposes and powers of books, the emphasis on the relational nature of textual production is a powerful one. It guides the present study, which further finds that the very ideas for books and their writing (as well as the publishing, marketing, distribution, and use that form Darnton's circuit) often

---

[8] McKitterick, *Print, Manuscript and the Search for Order*, 20.

[9] The diversity of methodologies and objects of study that 'the history of the book' encompasses is demonstrated in *CHBB*, V and is discussed by Suarez in its 'Introduction', 1–35 (2).

[10] Robert Darnton, 'What is the History of Books?', *Daedalus*, 111 (1982), 65–82 (68).

[11] Leslie Howsam, *Old Books and New Histories: An Orientation to Studies in Book and Print Culture* (Toronto, 2007), 31.

developed collectively and out of conversation, epistolary exchange, the accumulation of teaching materials, and the modification of old books.

There are several elements of the 'communications circuit' that can be adjusted. It is by no means a one-directional circling: booksellers tell authors what kind of books they are likely to finance; shipments are returned to booksellers' warehouses from regional shops; books are sent by their owners to be rebound. This last example leads to a second important modification. The circuit is not an isolated one: it overlaps with the trade in second hand books and the persistent production and circulation of manuscripts. The educational culture of the men described in this book shaped their understanding of the intersections of these three (or more) textual channels. Doddridge, Watts, and their circle articulated the processes of textual creation and adaptation in terms of two fundamental principles of Protestant dissent: commitment to liberty of thought and encouragement of debate. But such an idealized understanding of their work as agents in interwoven circuits of communication did not necessarily make that work easy, and the frustrations and joys of human relationships (which are difficult to represent diagrammatically) shaped the routes taken by these channels of textual production.

Given the variations and repetitions of the paradigmatic 'communications circuit' found in many histories of particular books, it is unsurprising that Darnton's model has been contested.[12] A decade later, a new model was proposed by the bibliographers Thomas Adams and Nicolas Barker. Their model, of which Darnton himself approves, is (like his) founded on the belief that relations create books. Adams and Barker shift the focus onto the book rather than the people who contribute to its production, and present their model as a map (rather than a circuit that must be closed in order to function) which can be used to the trace the ongoing life of a book after the reader receives it and influences the author's next piece of writing.

The strength of the Adams/Barker model is its open-ended scheme for the reception, use, and influence of books which highlights survival as a factor affected by intellectual influences and social behaviour. The relationship between texts, behaviour, and taste is a complicated one: books, periodicals, lectures, letters, diaries, essays, and conversation reflect the intellectual and cultural trends of their time but also contribute to them. These patterns of influence are complex, and tracing them requires a flexible and diverse methodology in order to encompass the varieties of behaviour, experience, and response that can constitute evidence.

---

[12] Darnton surveys some responses in '"What is the History of Books?" Revisited', in *Modern Intellectual History*, 4 (2007), 495–508.

In what follows, I emphasize the role of friends and non-professional agents in almost every stage of the communications circuit. Using examples of collective composition, editing, revising, abridging, recommending, distributing, extracting, teaching, and rewriting, I want to put pressure on the idea of 'author' as a single individual. There is, of course, a long history to this debate. The idea that the printed book is the final version which embodies the author's intentions has been modified and contested from several angles: theoretical (including Roland Barthes and Michel Foucault); technical (such as D. F. McKenzie and Adrian Johns); and social (such as Margaret Ezell and Richard B. Sher). The present study draws particularly on the third of these modes. In *The Enlightenment and the Book*, Sher uses an empirical, evaluative methodology which looks at the physical appearance and content of successive editions of works by 115 authors of what he terms 'the mature Scottish Enlightenment' published and distributed in London, Ireland, and North America.[13] He emphasizes the personal and national bonds between authors and publishers, and the associative networks through which books came into existence. Many of the patterns he identifies can also be found among dissenting authors, suggesting that the eighteenth-century cultural world of print was conducive to sophisticated self-fashioning of both individual and corporate identities among peripheral groups. The argument here is that sustained social production of texts was both facilitated by and essential to the religious and educational environments in which dissent thrived.

It is clear, then, that texts emerge out of complex patterns of personal and professional association primarily among men and with only rare (though highly significant) participation from women.[14] But books are usually attributed to a single, named author and this contradiction requires consideration of the purpose of such designations. If Darnton's 'book' is metonymic of social relations then so too, I contend, is the idea of the 'author' for Protestant dissenters. Foucault's series of questions about the problems of and categories for a 'work' and its relationship to a known

---

[13] Richard B. Sher, *The Enlightenment and the Book: Scottish Authors and their Publishers in Eighteenth-Century Britain, Ireland, and America* (Chicago, 2007), 80. The list of authors is table 1.

[14] Nonconformist women's writing in this period was extremely rich, and its distinctive patterns of manuscript circulation and preservation require further study. The important collection of materials gathered and edited by Timothy Whelan is fundamental to this future work. See Timothy Whelan (ed.), *Nonconformist Women Writers 1720–1840*, 8 vols (London, 2011) and *Other British Voices: Women, Poetry and Religion 1766–1840* (Houndmills, Basingstoke, 2015); Marjorie Reeves, *Female Education and Nonconformist Culture, 1700–1900* (2nd edn, London, 2000); Sarah Prescott, 'Provincial Networks, Dissenting Connections, and Noble Friends: Elizabeth Singer Rowe and Female Authorship in Early Eighteenth-Century England', *Eighteenth-Century Life*, 25 (2001), 29–42.

'author' are useful for considering processes of cumulative, collective authorship. An author's name—'situated between a description and a designation'—serves 'a clarificatory function' that provides a framework within which the reader approaches a text.[15] Naming a particular author might allow a work (or body of work) to become the starting point or exemplar of a wider tradition. For Protestant dissenters eager to shed their lingering reputation as strange, rude, and inflexible (a stereotype which persisted from the seventeenth century), significant authors within their tradition could serve this function and were therefore highly prized. By producing substantial, impressive editions of scholarly works by Watts and Doddridge adorned with portraits, their editors and successors—including Job Orton, Andrew Kippis, Samuel Clark, Samuel Palmer, and, in the case of Watts, Doddridge himself—established these men as the 'authors' of a tradition within dissent that was learned, sociable, moderate, and orthodox, which was self-sustaining but outward looking and which generously embraced diversity: a tradition which was influenced by and could participate in the polite world of letters.[16] In order to secure this tradition in public consciousness, great care was devoted to the content, format, and distribution of works attributed to two such well-known and widely respected men as Watts and Doddridge.

In order to make sense of dissent's textual culture, this book pays great attention to not-printed texts. As exemplified in the work of Richard Sher, letters can be a vital source for book history, particularly for the light they shed on author–bookseller relations and a rich cache of correspondence with booksellers survives in the Doddridge manuscripts. But other aspects of non-print textual culture are also explored here, such as the circulation of lectures within an extensive but self-constituting sphere and collaborative writing and editing practices among groups of friends. In this respect, this book is methodologically aligned with work on familial networks which investigates dissent in later periods.[17] The comparable findings of the present work and those studies gives a sense of the duration and continuity of dissenting textual practice. It should enable new sets of connections to be made in future: between mid-century orthodox dissent,

---

[15] Michel Foucault, 'What is an Author?', in *The Foucault Reader*, ed. Paul Rainbow (Harmondsworth, 1984), 101–20 (105, 113).

[16] 'Author of a tradition' is Foucault's expression, see 'What is an Author?', 113.

[17] See Anne Janowitz, 'Amiable and Radical Sociability: Anna Barbauld's "Free Familiar Conversation"', in *Romantic Sociability: Social Networks and Literary Culture in Britain, 1770–1840*, ed. Gillian Russell and Clara Tuite (Cambridge, 2002), 62–81; Daniel E. White, *Early Romanticism and Religious Dissent* (Cambridge, 2006); Michelle Levy, *Family Authorship and Romantic Print Culture* (Houndmills, Basingstoke, 2007); and Felicity James and Ian Inkster (eds), *Dissent and the Aikin–Barbauld Circle* (Cambridge, 2011).

rational dissenters and Unitarians, and other figures often considered in
the context of literary Romanticism rather than religious history on one
hand, and between orthodox dissenters and Church of England evangelicals on the other. A rich and sustained textual culture that is confession-
ally situated but not sectarian or restricted in its scope can thereby be
delineated.

2. DISSENT IN EIGHTEENTH-CENTURY ENGLAND

It is difficult to overstate the importance of their religious identity to the
men discussed in this book. But what did it actually mean to be a dissenter
in eighteenth-century England? N. H. Keeble has observed that the labels
'nonconformist' and 'dissenter' incorporated a range of different religious
positions in this period, and John Seed contends, 'Dissenters remained . . .
a complex and disconnected set of groups and configurations.'[18] Some
general characteristics can nevertheless be noted. Those opposed to state
intervention in religious matters and who chose to exclude themselves
from the national religious establishment were known as dissenters, and
they made up approximately 6 per cent of the population.[19] Choosing to
be a dissenter had repercussions for one's political and educational circumstances: taking up municipal or state offices, matriculating at the
University of Oxford and graduating there and at Cambridge required
the public taking of oaths, which dissenters technically could not do. The
terms of the seventeenth-century legislation made them effectively second-
class citizens, and dissenters felt their exclusion sharply.

In such circumstances, the recent history of nonconformity was very
important to eighteenth-century dissenters. They considered their immediate antecedents to be the considerable number of clerics who lost their
livings as a consequence of the religious settlement which followed the
restoration of Charles II to the throne in 1660, and who faced persecution

[18] N. H. Keeble, *The Literary Culture of Nonconformity in Later Seventeenth Century
England* (Leicester, 1987), 41–4; John Seed, *Dissenting Histories: Religious Division and the
Politics of Memory in Eighteenth-Century England* (Edinburgh, 2008), 68.

[19] There were much larger concentrations in cities such as London, Manchester, and
Bristol. See Michael R. Watts, *The Dissenters*, 2 vols (Oxford, 1978–1997), I, 269–89.
Technically, 'dissenters' were Protestant nonconformists who agreed to subscribe to
thirty-six of the Thirty-Nine Articles and to take the oaths of Supremacy and Allegiance:
see Jeremy Black, *Eighteenth-Century Britain, 1688–1783* (2nd edn, 2008), 131. See also
Isabel Rivers and David L. Wykes, 'Dissenting Academies Historical Information:
Protestant Dissent', URL: <http://www.english.qmul.ac.uk/drwilliams/academies/protest
ant.html>.

until the accession of William III in 1688.[20] Eighteenth-century dissenters
still felt a close association with Restoration-era nonconformists, and this
was commonly expressed in personal, political, and intellectual terms.[21]
The example of Isaac Watts highlights the personal dimension of dissenters' self-definition. He was born in penal times and his father was
imprisoned for nonconformity. The image of young Isaac being suckled
by his mother on the steps of the prison in Southampton (which continues
to figure in biographical accounts) became symbolic of dissenters' familial
loyalty and fortitude in the face of persecution. Personal and community
stories were woven into national ones. The politico-religious resonances of
5 November were nationally important, and William of Orange's arrival
in England in 1688 and the thwarting of the Roman Catholic plot to burn
down Parliament in 1605 were marked by a fast day on which commemorative sermons which emphasized God's support for Protestant England
were preached.[22] Dissenters considered these events to have particular
significance for their godly community, especially because William III
took the throne promising toleration. Rich traditions of nonconformist
preaching and writing were celebrated and renewed throughout the period
of this book. Ministerial authors such as Richard Baxter were cherished by
moderate dissenters as intellectual and religious forebears, and preachers
including Edward Reynolds and William Bates were admired for combining piety with good style. In Hanoverian England, dissenters imagined
their familial, religious, and national identity in terms of a community that
reached from the seventeenth century to the present. They also continued
to express their identity in terms of their separation from the national
church while attempting to avoid the rancour that characterized
seventeenth-century religious disputes, partly to keep dissent as inclusive
a category as possible.[23]

i. Church of England, Dissenters, and Methodists

As a confessional state which tolerated different varieties of Protestantism,
religious commitment was an index for self-definition in eighteenth-
century England. The most numerous and active groups of Protestants

[20] Estimates of the numbers of clergy involved have varied considerably: see David
L. Wykes, 'To Revive the Memory of Some Excellent Men': Edmund Calamy and the Early
Historians of Nonconformity (London, 1997), 7–8, 21. In the eighteenth century, the number
was considered to be 2,000 or more. In 1924, A. G. Matthews calculated 1,760, a figure now
widely agreed upon.
[21] Seed, Dissenting Histories, ch. 2.
[22] Linda Colley, Britons: Forging the Nation (New Haven, 1992), 19–20.
[23] Seed, Dissenting Histories, 68.

were members of the Church of England (over 90 per cent of the population), dissenters from that church (most of whom belonged to the 'Three Denominations' of Presbyterians, Independents and Baptists, but also including Quakers), and, from the 1730s onwards, Methodists.[24] By the nineteenth century Methodism had become a variety of dissent, but it developed in the eighteenth century within the Church of England and most early Methodists (including the Wesley brothers) remained members of that church. Though these three broad divisions could be endlessly split into smaller groupings based on theological distinctions, religious practice, or regional interests, virtually all English Protestants would have identified themselves within one of the three groups. There was considerable cooperation across denominational divisions at all points on the theological spectrum. The friendships of rational dissenters Joseph Priestley and Unitarians such as Theophilus Lindsey (originally a Church of England clergyman) are comparable with collaborations among evangelical members of the established church who were low church Calvinists (such as John Newton, James Stonhouse, and Hannah More) and moderate dissenters committed to religious education and doctrinal orthodoxy such as David Jennings (who corresponded with Newton) and Job Orton (who knew Stonhouse through Doddridge).

It can be difficult to get a comprehensive view of the points of contact between different religious communities because religious history of the eighteenth century tends to consider denominations in isolation. This is partly because the strength of their group ties was reflected in the religious commitments of those writing their histories in the twentieth century. The sensitivity and deep historical understanding that religious historians brought to the study of their own denominations has been of enormous benefit to our understanding of how religious groups operated and the varieties of belief in eighteenth-century Christianity.[25] But the examples of Watts, Doddridge, Orton, and both Jennings brothers show that it is essential to consider interdenominational religious exchanges in order to develop a full picture of the activities undertaken under the banner of Christianity in the period. John Jennings took his students to hear ministers from the established church preach, Watts befriended Lutheran Pietists in England and Germany, Doddridge exchanged ideas with Anglicans, sought their friendship and directed his books towards them, and invited the Methodists George Whitefield and John Wesley to preach

---

[24] John Walsh, Colin Haydon, and Stephen Taylor (eds), *The Church of England, c.1689–c.1833: From Toleration to Tractarianism* (Cambridge, 1993). Quakers had a distinct culture and were not associated with the Three Denominations.

[25] Two important historians in this respect are G. F. Nuttall and W. R. Ward.

from his pulpit and Orton corresponded extensively with Anglicans, was presented in print as a guide to young clergy, and distanced himself from Unitarian dissenters. Social and educational commitments that were grounded in Christian principles were shared by men from different denominations and exerted a considerable influence on English culture in the period.

ii. Varieties of Religious Culture

As well as understanding eighteenth-century religion in denominational terms (which were primarily theologically and socially determined), it is important to consider the intellectual strands of religious culture which profoundly shaped people's thought and actions. This was, after all, the end to which a great deal of writing by ministers of all denominations was directed. The religious dimension to the rationalist, empirical culture of enlightenment in England has been amply demonstrated. 'The English Enlightenment was not an irreligious moment', Robert H. Ingram has declared: it was clerical and conservative (as J. G. A. Pocock and Brian Young have shown), and Jonathan Sheehan has delineated the collaborative character of its scholarly endeavours.[26] Such analysis of English intellectual life in the eighteenth century has largely concentrated on Anglicans working within establishment religious environments such as the universities and the Royal Society, Unitarians, and rational dissenters, who were a very small group within dissent.[27] Karen O'Brien finds the Pocockian clerical enlightenment 'helpful for what it excludes, specifically the high church and evangelical elements of eighteenth-century intellectual life' but as this book seeks to show, evangelical faith did not preclude rational scholarship, cross-denominational educational projects, or a commitment to liberal thought.[28] Evangelical (Gospel-centred) faith and

---

[26] Robert G. Ingram, 'William Warburton, Divine Action, and Enlightened Christianity', in *Religious Identities in Britain, 1660–1830*, ed. William Gibson and Robert G. Ingram (Farnham, 2005), 97–118 (97); J. G. A. Pocock, 'Post-Puritan England and the Problem of the Enlightenment', in *Culture and Politics from Puritanism to the Enlightenment*, ed. Perez Zagorin (Berkeley and Los Angeles, 1980), 91–112; B. W. Young, *Religion and Enlightenment in Eighteenth-Century England: Theological Debate from Locke to Burke* (Oxford, 1998); Jonathan Sheehan, *The Enlightenment Bible: Translation, Scholarship, Culture* (Princeton, 2005).

[27] Studies of rational dissenters include Isabel Rivers and David L. Wykes (eds), *Joseph Priestley: Scientist, Philosopher, and Theologian* (Oxford, 2008) and William McCarthy, *Anna Letitia Barbauld: Voice of the Enlightenment* (Baltimore, 2008).

[28] Karen O'Brien, *Women and Enlightenment in Eighteenth-Century Britain* (Cambridge, 2009), 6.

enlightenment learning were not mutually exclusive and historians of religion have found plenty of points of contact between the two.[29] In the case of dissenters, attributes of sociability and commitment to education associated with enlightenment can be found throughout the teaching and publishing activities of Watts, Jennings, Doddridge, Orton, Palmer, and Kippis. Reluctance to impose religious tests was a significant (though much-debated) tenet of some groups of dissenters, while the educational practice of all the men considered here encouraged students to read widely and question what they read ('free enquiry').

These factors, along with commitment to Lockean epistemology and political theory that aligned them with the rationalist mode of anglophone moderate enlightenment philosophy, led Caroline Robbins to characterize Watts and Doddridge as 'eighteenth-century Commonwealthmen'.[30] But considering the two men in those rather narrow political terms has a limiting effect, for it fails to consider the influence they had on their own community, or the crossings between religious and political commitments and practical action. These dissenters' enactments of learned friendship within and beyond their own community fed into British enlightenment-era culture both in terms of the information and ideas they shared, and the models they provided for future exchanges when their letters were printed.

Enlightenment culture was as much about action as thought: Larry Stewart and Maximilian Novak have both characterized it as 'an age of projects', and this designation can be applied as much to religious endeavours as scientific ones.[31] Studies of individuals such as John Wesley, George Whitefield, and Hannah More have drawn attention to the

[29] D. Bruce Hindmarsh, *The Evangelical Conversion Narrative: Spiritual Autobiography in Early Modern England* (Oxford, 2005); Jonathan Yeager, *Enlightened Evangelicalism: The Life and Thought* of John Erskine (Oxford, 2011).

[30] Caroline Robbins, *The Eighteenth-Century Commonwealthman: Studies in the Transmission, Development and Circumstance of English Liberal Thought from the Restoration of Charles II until the War with the Thirteen Colonies* (Cambridge, Mass., 1959), 9–13, 231. In *Letters Concerning the English Nation* (London, 1733)—particularly letter 13 on John Locke—Voltaire debates the extent to which philosophy can support religion, and throughout the work he praises English liberty of thought. For dissenters' commitment to freedom of conscience, see David L. Wykes, 'Subscribers and Non-subscribers at the Salters' Hall debate (act. 1719)', *Oxford Dictionary of National Biography*; Isabel Rivers, '*The Defence of Truth Through the Knowledge of Error: Philip Doddridge's Academy Lectures* (London, 2003); Mark Goldie (ed.), *John Locke: Letter on Toleration and Other Writings* (Indianapolis, 2010).

[31] Novak and Stewart echo Daniel Defoe, who referred to '*The Projecting Age*' in *An Essay Upon Projects* (London, 1697), 1. See Larry Stewart, *The Rise of Public Science: Rhetoric, Technology and Natural Philosophy in Newtonian Britain* (Cambridge, 1992), 184 and Maximilian E. Novak, *The Age of Projects* (Toronto, 2008), 1.

innovative ways in which they created social structures with corporate, collaborative, and activist characteristics.[32] The projects of dissenters can be accommodated within this picture of 'enlightened evangelicalism', in Jonathan Yeager's phrase. Watts published in support of charity schools, many of which were operated by dissenters; Doddridge was actively involved in the foundation of the subscription funded hospital at Northampton; a succession of dissenting tutors delivered Doddridge's theological lectures (whose method was based on sending students to look up references in works on either side of particular questions). These and many other instances of their participation in intellectual and educational culture will be found in the pages of this book. It is in this complex world of social activism, belief in saving faith, commitment to Lockean epistemology, experimentation with genres and printed forms, engagement with works of controversy, and energetic pastoral care that Watts, Doddridge, and their successors and associates can be situated, conducting what Donald Davie has called 'the enlightening and civilizing work for Dissent' but also, it is contended here, doing that work for widely imagined publics beyond dissent as well.[33] While the particularities of dissenters' experience are in need of careful explication (which is one of the tasks of this book), their situation in a world at once enlightened and evangelical was not unique, and charting those intersections will contribute to a fuller understanding of religious, intellectual, and social commitments in the eighteenth century.[34] This certainly confirms the conclusion that the period did not see a consistent, dominating drive towards a secular culture. But the purpose here is to analyse the productive tension between denominational loyalty and participation in wider cultural movements strongly influenced by Christianity in order to understand the reciprocal influences of coterie, national, and international interests.

[32] See Henry Rack, *John Wesley: Reasonable Enthusiast* (London, 1989); Anne Stott, *Hannah More: The First Victorian* (Oxford, 2003); Jeremy Gregory, 'Religion in the Age of Enlightenment: Putting John Wesley in Context', *Religion in the Age of Enlightenment*, 2 (2010), 19–53.

[33] Donald Davie, *A Gathered Church: The Literature of the Dissenting Interest, 1700–1930* (New York, 1978), 10. For a strong argument against equating enlightenment with unbelief see also his 'Enlightenment and Dissent' in *Dissentient Voice* (Notre Dame, Ind., 1982), 20–31.

[34] For Pietist support for enlightened reforms in Germany, see Hartmutt Lehmann, 'Continental Protestant Europe', in *The Cambridge History of Christianity, VII: Enlightenment, Reawakening and Revolution 1660–1815*, ed. Stewart J. Brown and Timothy Tackett (Cambridge, 2006), 33–55 (48–51).

3. EDUCATION AND PARTICIPATION

Many of the textual and social activities described in this book took place in dissenting academies or emerged out of them, and therefore a considerable amount of information about these sites appears at certain points, especially in Chapters 1–3. But first, an overview of their importance in the context of education provision in the eighteenth century is necessary. Dissenting academies were central to the self-understanding of the men in this book; they all spent at least three years in academies and made them part of their adult lives. Isaac Watts, for example, was not a tutor but kept himself informed about the conduct and curriculum of academies by corresponding with tutors and students such as Thomas Secker (later Archbishop of Canterbury) and Philip Doddridge. Indeed, it was Doddridge's written description of John Jennings's academy that brought him into personal contact with Watts for the first time. Academies were places where bonds were forged and where the commitment to dissenting education exhibited by all the men discussed here began.

In order to understand what dissenting academies were and how they were viewed requires some explanation of how they fitted into the educational landscape. They were, like the universities, intended to provide post-grammar school education for young men under the care of a tutor. Many of the first dissenting tutors had been fellows of Oxford and Cambridge colleges and as such were ordained clergy in the Church of England. In 1662, those who could not in conscience accept the terms of the Restoration religious settlement lost their fellowships. These nonconformists imagined the schism would be temporary, and that the English church would soon be reunited. When it became clear that this was not to be the case, nonconformists saw that they must train a new generation of ministers to carry on their religious tradition. Thus academies emerged, which tended at first to be operated by ministers who had previously been university teachers. These informal and furtive establishments often comprised only a couple of students living with or close to a tutor who might have to move or close his academy at short notice.[35] Academies, and the men who ran them, were the target of repressive legislation intended to stamp out nonconformity. Following the accession of William and Mary in 1688, legislation enacting religious toleration of 'certain other persons,

---

[35] See Mark Burden, 'Academical Learning in the Dissenters' Private Academies, 1660–1720' (unpublished doctoral dissertation, University of London, 2012), ch. 1 and Herbert McLachlan, *English Education Under the Test Acts* (Manchester, 1931), 2.

Dissenters from the Church of England' was passed.[36] However, additional punitive laws were enacted during Anne's reign, particularly the Act for Preventing Occasional Conformity (which required those holding public office to worship publicly) in 1711 and the 1714 Schism Act, which made teaching by those who attending dissenting meetings punishable with imprisonment. These were both repealed by George I in 1719.[37] Throughout the Hanoverian period, older penal legislation remained on the statute books and those trinitarian Christians to whom the Act of Toleration applied—and who referred to themselves as dissenters—were still subject to religious and political disabilities. However, they did now have freedom to worship and perform their ministry, and academies operated far less covertly. It has traditionally been argued that over the course of the eighteenth century, dissenting academies developed into larger, more formal institutions, offering a wider range of subjects, employing a range of specialist tutors, and educating an increasing number of lay students.[38] While this is true, the contention that Watts and Doddridge fitted within a tradition that believed '[e]ducation should be secularized and directed toward the training of citizens rather than of clergy' is not helpful.[39] Rather, it is important to remember that theological education and the training of the dissenting ministry were the core aim of academies, even those with a markedly liberal approach to education.[40]

In the eighteenth century, there were important similarities between the dissenting academies and the colleges of Oxford and Cambridge. Most required a certain level of competency in the classics for entry.[41] There was some overlap in the curriculum, particularly in the first couple of years, as can be seen by comparing study guides produced by university tutors

---

[36] 'Dissenter': *OED* definition 2.b. For a study of the legislation surrounding toleration which emphasizes the heterogeneous understanding of what toleration entailed, see Nicholas Tyacke, 'The "Rise of Puritanism" and the Legalizing of Dissent, 1571–1719', in *From Persecution to Toleration: The Glorious Revolution in England*, ed. Ole Peter Grell, Jonathan I. Israel, and Nicholas Tyacke (Oxford, 1991), 17–49.

[37] Watts, *The Dissenters*, I, 266–7; David L. Wykes 'Dissenting Academies Historical Information: Legislation'. URL: <http://www.english.qmul.ac.uk/drwilliams/academies/legislation.html>.

[38] Irene Parker, *Dissenting Academies in England* (Cambridge, 1914); Gregory Claeys, 'Virtuous Commerce and Free Theology: Political Economy and the Dissenting Academies 1750–1800', *History of Political Thought*, 20 (1999), 141–72.

[39] Robbins, *The Eighteenth-Century Commonwealthman*, 12.

[40] David L. Wykes, 'The Contribution of the Dissenting Academy to the Emergence of Rational Dissent', in *Enlightenment and Religion: Rational Dissent in Eighteenth-Century Britain*, ed. Knud Haakonssen (Cambridge, 1996), 99–139.

[41] Academies are often conflated with schools and this widespread misunderstanding has prevented them being analysed accurately. See, for example, Ian Green, *Humanism and Protestantism in Early Modern English Education* (Farnham, 2009), 124–5, which treats Warrington academy as a school.

such as Daniel Waterland with those of Doddridge and other dissenting educators. One key difference in course content between the academies and the universities was that theology was not a formal element of the central undergraduate curriculum at Oxford and Cambridge during the eighteenth century, whereas theological study was at the centre of the dissenting academies discussed in this book.[42]

As the example of the dissenting academies illustrates very clearly, religious commitments usually lay behind formal sites of education. Charity schools, grammar schools, universities, and dissenting academies all supported and sustained the central place of literacy in Protestantism.[43] The universities of Oxford and Cambridge still existed primarily to educate the future clergy of the Church of England and in this respect, as well as in aspects of their curriculum and the age of their students, dissenting academies are comparable.[44] But academies were not necessarily in competition with universities because they taught different kinds of students. For dissenters, the alternative to academies was more likely to be universities in Europe and Scotland if the student was wealthy enough or able to win financial support. These alternatives had been a particularly popular choice for dissenters in the Restoration era, when academies were persecuted particularly strongly. By the eighteenth century, Latin was less often the primary language of instruction and this made it more difficult for students to study overseas. The reputation of Dutch universities waned, and attendance at the English universities also fell in the period.[45] All these factors contributed to the growing importance of dissenting academies, but this influence has not been reflected in the historiography. For example, the chapter on 'Oxford and the Church' in *The History of the University of Oxford* reiterates the role of the universities in maintaining

[42]   R. Greaves, 'Religion in the University 1715–1800', in *The History of the University of Oxford Volume V: The Eighteenth Century*, ed. L. S. Sutherland and L. G. Mitchell (Oxford, 1986), 401–24 (403). The religious instruction offered at colleges varied, and could comprise little more than attendance at chapel and lectures on the Greek Testament, see V. H. H. Green, 'Religion in the Colleges 1715–1800', in *The History of the University of Oxford*, V, 425–67 (425). For contemporary guidelines on philosophical, theological, and classical studies, see Daniel Waterland, *Advice to a Young Student. With a Method of Study for the Four First Years* (London, 1730).

[43]   David Cressy, *Literacy and the Social Order: Reading and Writing in Tudor and Stuart England* (Cambridge, 1980), 3–8 and 175–90.

[44]   W. M. Jacob, *The Clerical Profession in the Long Eighteenth Century: 1680–1840* (Oxford, 2007), 43–52.

[45]   See Lawrence Stone, 'The Size and Composition of the Oxford Student Body, 1580–1910', in *The University in Society*, ed. Lawrence Stone, 2 vols (Princeton, 1974), I, 3–110 (esp. 37–57). An investigation of scientific learning at Cambridge which attends carefully to differences within Protestant Christianity can be found in John Gascoigne, *Cambridge in the Age of the Enlightenment: Science, Religion and Politics from the Restoration to the French Revolution* (Cambridge, 1989).

the state religion, declaring early on that 'Oxford and Cambridge were the key-institutions in the national religious establishment.'[46] It does not, however, consider the implications of the absence of those who did not belong to the national religious establishment.[47]

This oversight has serious implications for our historical understanding of eighteenth-century life and discourse. First of all, failing to consider the specific experience of dissenting ministers curtails a nuanced and context-ually informed analysis of participation in the public sphere. Lacking free access to the physical institutions of the national establishment, dissenters were highly motivated to construct print as an alternative institution which could grant them a public voice. For while the dissenting ministers investigated in this book were certainly not comfortably settled within the political and legal establishment, they did not see themselves in opposition to it or even necessarily as sidelined from it either. These men were active and well-known participants in the Republic of Letters. This confidence had two aspects: their strong sense of communal identity (sustained through friendship, educational sites, expressions of faith, and the exchange of letters) on one hand provided intellectual confidence and a sense of purpose within their own community, while their zealous use of print to participate in international debates about education, religion, and culture on the other demonstrates their urgent wish to reach beyond their own circle. Further-more, the two realms of community and the public are not mutually exclusive: it was in part the conditions of dissenting education that prepared the men studied here for their work of public participation.

Despite effort to produce an interpretation of the public sphere that is sensitive to gender, geography, and class and which questions some of the long-standing assumptions about the metropolitan, male complexion of that sphere, the role of religious identity in shaping public discourse is seldom directly addressed.[48] Even those accounts which do think seriously

[46] G. V. Bennett, 'University, Society and Church 1688–1714', in *The History of the University of Oxford*, V, 359–400 (360).

[47] See J. Yolton's discussion of Watts in 'Schoolmen, Logic and Philosophy', in *The History of the University of Oxford*, V, 568–77 (569, 575–6); the observation that the 'Anglican monopoly' and the social homogeneity of the university populations contributed to a decline in intellectual life is taken no further by V. H. H. Green in 'Religion in the Universities after the Restoration', in *Religion at Oxford and Cambridge* (London, 1964), 153–77 (175).

[48] For important essays refining Habermas's theory of the emergence of public sphere as delineated in *The Structural Transformation of the Public Sphere: An Inquiry into a Category of Bourgeois Society*, tr. Thomas Burger and Frederick Lawrence (Cambridge, Mass., 1989), and applying it to contexts within and beyond eighteenth-century London, see *Habermas and the Public Sphere*, ed. Craig Calhoun (Boston, 1992); Lawrence Klein, 'Gender, Conversation and the Public Sphere in Early Eighteenth-Century England', in *Textuality and Sexuality: Reading Theories and Practices*, ed. Judith Still and Michael Worton (Manchester, 1993),

about the place of religion in a broader political public sphere or which posit the existence of a religious public sphere focus primarily on North America and on international associations.[49] There is still some way to go before the ongoing role of religion (and specifically Protestant nonconformity) in shaping an imagined transnational community into an English participatory public sphere constructed through the circulation of printed materials is properly documented and understood.[50] By considering the international but also the provincial, the publication of religious works but also the activities of dissenting ministers in apparently secular publishing endeavours (such as Kippis's work on national publications such as the *Biographia Britannica* and *New Annual Register*), and by tracing the relationships within and across religious denominations, this book suggests some reasons for the importance of assessing these moments and models some methods of describing them.

Dissenting academies operated within a patchwork of educational provision, nationally and internationally. But what role did academies play in the textual culture of English Protestant dissent? And what place did dissenters occupy in a wider public sphere thanks to their textual culture? These are central questions of this book, which seeks to answer them through accounts of dissenters' textual engagements in their intellectual and social contexts. Chapter 1 describes the circumstances of dissenting ministers' friendships and educational networks in the early eighteenth century and considers the importance of letter writing for their community. On this basis, it argues that the epistolary engagements that acted as a prelude to the foundation of Philip Doddridge's dissenting academy in 1729 presented carefully wrought claims for and demonstrations of dissenting politeness and good learning which set the tenor of an intellectual culture for the century to come. Chapters 2 and 3 develop this argument by examining the particular courses of study, recommended texts, and methods of transmitting and adapting lectures within the dissenting community and, through print, to a wider intellectual public. Chapters 4 and 5 consider Isaac Watts as an educationalist, editor, and facilitator of international projects of improvement. The pedagogic principles he espoused

---

100–15; Elizabeth Eger, Charlotte Grant, Clíona Ó Gallchoir, and Penny Warburton (eds), *Women, Writing and the Public Sphere 1700–1830* (Cambridge, 2001).

[49] Mark A. Peterson, '*Theopolis Americana*: Boston and the Protestant International', in *Soundings in Atlantic History: Latent Structures and Intellectual Currents 1500–1830*, ed. Bernard Bailyn and Patricia L. Denault (Cambridge, Mass., 2009), 329–69; Jennifer Snead, 'Print, Predestination, and the Public Sphere: Transatlantic Evangelical Periodicals, 1740–1745', in *Early American Literature*, 45 (2010), 93–118.

[50] For the distinction between a community and a public, see Michael Warner, 'Publics and Counterpublics', repr. in *Publics and Counterpublics* (New York, 2005), 65–124 (120).

informed the conduct of dissenting academies and had far-reaching effects on domestic, educational, and intellectual culture in the anglophone Protestant world. These chapters therefore emphasize the movements Watts constantly effected across boundaries (of denomination, nation, and textual format). Chapter 6 considers Watts and Doddridge together, showing how posthumous editions of their significant works were constructed and what their successors hoped these would stand for in order to demonstrate that the high status both men had in the literary world was considerably bolstered by the efforts of their friends and associates. Throughout, the importance these dissenters attached to friendly communal endeavour in support of a broadly conceived project of improvement and education is noted and addressed: the conclusion points to ways in which these attitudes shaped texts and acts into the nineteenth century.

1

Instituting Dissent and the
Role of Friendship

'Whenever I have been so happy as to converse with you, my countenance must have discovered the inward pleasure which diffused itself over my mind on the occasion,' wrote Philip Doddridge to Isaac Watts in 1731. He continued, 'I hope, indeed, Sir, if God should continue my life, to find in you a counsellor and a friend!'[1] In this letter Doddridge is characteristically effusive in his emotional expression when he declares that friendship and conversation are transformative, God-given gifts. His hope for an ongoing relationship with Watts (for at this point their relationship was fairly new) is strongly expressed, and the tenor of that relationship will, he imagines, be both intimate and advisory. These components—friendship, guidance, feeling, conversation, and epistolarity—strongly marked the educational and textual culture of Protestant dissent in the eighteenth century. But dissenters did not live in isolation, and their behaviour was shaped by wider cultural patterns as well as by factors specific to their community. Polite sociability—which developed out of humanist and enlightenment concerns and was idealized and popularized in conduct literature and periodicals such as the *Spectator*—was a key paradigm for eighteenth-century thought and praxis, as Lawrence Klein has shown.[2] While this framework was very important for dissenters, their religious commitments and recent history gave the sociability of their textual culture a particular complexion. Christian antecedents and motivations were powerful influences on a distinctive 'Puritan Republic of Letters'

---

[1] Philip Doddridge to Isaac Watts, 5 April [or May] 1731. *Calendar* 357; Humphreys, III, 73–4. Another printed version of this letter gives May 1731 as the date. There are small differences between the two versions of the letter in wording, but the content and Doddridge's sentiments are the same in each: see *The Posthumous Works of the Late Learned and Reverend Isaac Watts...Adjusted and Published by a Gentleman of the University of Cambridge*, 2 vols (London, 1779), II, 25–8.
[2] Lawrence E. Klein, *Shaftesbury and the Culture of Politeness: Moral Discourse and Cultural Politics in Early Eighteenth Century England* (Cambridge, 1994); 'Politeness and the Interpretation of the British Eighteenth Century', *Historical Journal*, 45 (2002), 869–98.

which operated both on a local level and an international stage.[3] Registering the effect of the activities of faith communities within the public sphere is part of an important ongoing process of reconfiguring current understanding of that public in broader terms than have sometimes been allowed.[4] Just as dissenting culture was a complex blend of historical, contemporary, national, and sectarian factors, 'dissent' was not a single, easily identified movement. Therefore, while the rest of this book investigates the dissemination of dissenters' ideas and manners among themselves and to broadly imagined publics, the present chapter sets out the background to such activity and defines the mechanisms which made it possible. To do so it introduces the particular individuals meant here by the phrase 'Protestant dissenters' and identifies their characteristic intellectual and social practices. The letters written by these dissenting ministers show that the combination of these factors made for a distinctive form of sociability with education and friendship at its heart.

1. CONFIGURING THE 'WATTS–DODDRIDGE CIRCLE'

Figure 1 presents the names and life-dates of the main subjects of this study. Following the tradition of dissent's own historiography, there are biographical sketches of these men at the end of the book. Here, I would like simply to draw attention to the multiple connections that are evident between men of different generations, between friends and fellow-students, between tutors and pupils, among brothers, fathers, and sons. The lines show the numerous, overlapping relationships forged between them through education, personal association, and textual work. There are three broad categories of connection which were the principal means by which relationships among these dissenters were established and perpetuated. However, these categories do not fully encompass the complexities of those relationships in life, which will become clear over the course of this book.

Although the diagram differentiates between familial and academic connections, such a distinction was by no means a sharp one for these men. For Doddridge, orphaned at a young age and with only one

---

[3] Alison Searle, ' "Though I am a stranger to you by face, yet in neere bonds by faith": A Transatlantic Puritan Republic of Letters', *Early American Literature*, 43 (2008), 277–308.

[4] Ongoing work by Michael Warner, Mark A. Peterson, and Charles Taylor is important in this regard.

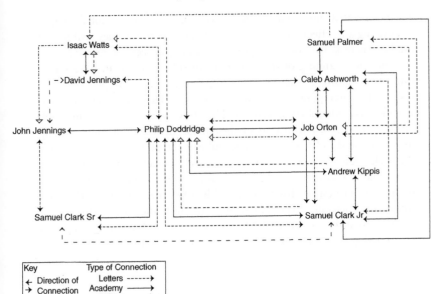

Figure 1. The Watts–Doddridge Circle

surviving immediate relative, relationships with fellow dissenters could substitute for the family he lacked until his marriage. Doddridge himself emphasized the affective dimension of these relationships. Throughout his letters, Samuel Clark senior and John Jennings (who both taught him) are addressed as avuncular, almost father-like figures. He thanked Clark for 'excellent advice & affectionate wishes & a thousand other instances of your goodness', and later compared the two men in terms of their personal qualities and his emotional attachment to them:

> my good tutor, whom I shall always respect as one of my best f[rie]nds, is alw[ays]. ready to give me such caution & admonition as he thinks necessary; & then he has that happy art, wch so few besides Mr J. & Mr Clark can pretend to, of giving ye plainest & sincerest advice wth all ye good nature & decency that one c^d desire or imagine.[5]

Doddridge's emphasis on sincerity and good nature is indicative of the tendency to attach positive ethical purpose to personal relationships. It was partly the domestic arrangements at dissenting academies that made

---

[5] Doddridge to Samuel Clark, 2 May 1722, *Calendar* 26, JRUL UCC MS B2, p. 71 and 26 January 1723. *Calendar* 48, JRUL UCC MS B2, p. 134.

such affective bonds so important. Dissenting academies were routinely called 'the family' by dissenting tutors and students, and Doddridge's position as a student lodging in the home of his tutor reminds us that in this period the family was not necessarily a private sphere defined exclusively by kinship.

Calling the academy a 'family' was consistent with the widespread seventeenth- and eighteenth-century use of the term to denote an entire household, as delineated by Naomi Tadmor.[6] However, the example of dissenting academies complicates Tadmor's model of the 'household-family' in some respects: it blurs the distinction Tadmor notes between the male householder and 'dependants' who were either blood relatives or 'mostly servants'.[7] Because of the presence of groups of students, the academy-family could be larger than most family-households and the interpersonal relationships within the household were complicated. The connective force of faith was an important aspect of academy-families, one which both sustained spiritual life and forged personal, practical, and business connections between current and former members of academy-families.

Narratives about how the family was understood in the eighteenth century tend to focus on political, economic, and sentimental aspects of its conceptualization.[8] The example of actual sites can remind us that religious belief could shape ideas of family and the social practices of family life. The dissenting academy, for instance, was an educational establishment that was consistently figured as a domestic one by Doddridge and his students and successors.[9] The title of Doddridge's key publication was *The Family Expositor*, indicating that the concept of the gathered household (with its roots in Congregationalist practice from the seventeenth century onwards) was foundational to the intertwined educational and social structures of this tradition within dissent throughout the eighteenth century. The extent to which the texts dissenters produced

[6] Naomi Tadmor, *Family and Friends in Eighteenth-Century England: Household, Kinship, and Patronage* (Cambridge, 2001), 19–24.

[7] Tadmor, *Family and Friends*, 23.

[8] Sarah M. S. Pearsall, *Atlantic Families: Lives and Letters in the Later Eighteenth Century* (Oxford, 2008), 7.

[9] Numerous instances of 'the Family' being used to include the academy will be found in the following pages. Two examples are Doddridge explaining how 'after we laid aside Hebrew in the Lecture Room continued throughout all the Second Year to read from it in the Family almost every Day', in 'An Account of Mr Jennings's Method', in *Dissenting Education and the Legacy of John Jennings c.1720–c.1729*, ed. Whitehouse, fol. 8, and Caleb Ashworth telling Mercy Doddridge: 'I have read his F.E. twice over in the family, & always speak in terms of the highest respect', 12 December 1759. DWL MS NCL L. 63/14.

could articulate and enact these social formations is investigated through-out this book.

Elements of these dissenters' textual culture associated with the passage of time are particularly difficult to diagrammatize. These are the moments, processes, and structures described and analysed in the chapters to come. Pairs and groups of men worked together to edit and publish the works of others: Isaac Watts and David Jennings for John Jennings; David Jennings and Doddridge for Watts; Job Orton and Samuel Clark junior for Doddridge; and Job Orton advised Samuel Palmer on his work. That this intensity of collaboration is both reflective of and helped to perpetuate dissenters' high regard for collective, cumulative intellectual endeavours (and that this influenced the wider literary world) is a central argument of this book. Another important point relating to the world of print is that it is not possible to represent the full range of printed books and their uses in this chart. Isaac Watts, although only directly connected to four of the other men, was a very strong intellectual influence on moderate, orthodox dissent in this period. His reputation was not a straightforward one, but in his own writings as well as his energetic work editing and promoting books written by others (in England, America, and internationally) he shaped what all these dissenters read and how they published. All the men figured here read and responded to his work, and so did large numbers of eighteenth-century readers, ministers, and educators.

Another central aspect of dissent's textual culture which the chart cannot depict was the geographical extent of personal and institutional relationships. Dissenters' networks were particularly closely knit around the Midlands and southern England, especially London. They also crossed between Germany, the Low Countries, Scotland, and New England. These networks extended sociologically as well as geographically: to the universities of Oxford, Cambridge, and Aberdeen, to men with high status in the national establishment including bishops and members of the royal household, to members of rural dissenting congregations and students at numerous academies, and to the professional world of London booksellers. All these connections both contributed to and benefited from the dynamic and effective textual culture generated by the men figured in the diagram.

Finally I would like to draw attention to the effect of removing Philip Doddridge from the chart.[10] At a stroke, the network collapses. The outer edges remain in contact, but the centre is reduced to fragments. The 'cogs in a finely tuned watch' (as G. F. Nuttall characterized Doddridge's

---

[10] This method is inspired by the (far more complex) diagrams produced by Franco Moretti to chart the relations between characters in *Hamlet*, first published as 'Network Theory, Plot Analysis', in *New Left Review*, 2nd ser., 68 (2011), 80–102, esp. fig. 7.

networks) are broken to pieces.[11] Removing Doddridge graphically confirms the view of scholars from Alexander Gordon to Isabel Rivers that his
influence on dissenting education in the eighteenth century is difficult to
overstate. As Gordon said, 'Doddridge initiated an important change in
the Nonconformist Academy, amounting to a revolution', and the textual
and social means by which this happened will be investigated below.[12]
But Doddridge aside, the diagram shows the rich and numerous connections both personal and textual that existed between these men from four
generations who had a strong sense of shared purpose through their work as
ministers and tutors. The way they understood these relationships and the
means they used to sustain them were strongly marked by their educational
and religious heritage. The social and literary manifestations of this were
friendship, conversation and letters, academies, and publishing.

2. CLASSICAL AND CHRISTIAN IDEALS OF FRIENDSHIP

Friendship, understood in terms of both classical amity and Christian
fellowship, was the privileged basis of relationships between these dissenters. Many of the aspects of friendship articulated by Doddridge in his
letter to Watts derived from the classical literature he had read at grammar
school and the start of his academy course, and both Senecan and
Ciceronian models influenced Doddridge's depictions of friendship as
well as his conduct towards friends. In Cicero's *De amicitia*, friendship
is defined as 'an accord in all things, human and divine, conjoined with
mutual goodwill and affection'. It is valued extremely highly: 'with the
exception of wisdom, no better thing has been given to man by the
immortal gods'.[13] Friendship is characterized by reciprocity and brings
its beneficiaries affection, loyalty, and pleasure. It is particularly esteemed
because virtue is both its basis and its result. All these aspects of friendship,
and the use of letters as appropriate vehicles for their expression, were
promoted as part of the great educational project of Renaissance humanism. Erasmus was the strongest proponent of this nexus of ethical and
social values which he set out in his handbook of model letters, *De
conscribendi epistolis* (1534), which became an important educational

---

[11] *Calendar*, xxxii.

[12] Alexander Gordon, *Essays and Addresses, Biographical and Historical* (London, 1922), 76.

[13] Cicero, *De amicitia*, tr. W. A. Falconer, Loeb Classical Library 154, Cicero vol. XXI (London and Cambridge, Mass., 1923), vi. 20.

resource throughout Europe.[14] English grammar schools continued to follow the style and content of education based on classical texts and humanist methods into the eighteenth century and beyond. All the men at the centre of this book were educated at grammar schools before attending dissenting academies. Like students at the universities and Inns of Court, they had encountered Stoic texts and humanist pedagogy from an early age and had imbibed the principles of friendship expressed therein.

But in the eighteenth century, classical ideas were not, of course, the only model. Protestant understanding of the principles of Christian fellowship strongly influenced dissenters' attitudes.[15] This had both a theoretical and practical dimension: the complications Christianity posed to the secular definition and conduct of virtuous friendship had been directly addressed by seventeenth-century puritan and nonconformist writers, and their writings exerted a profound influence on dissenting culture in the eighteenth century both in terms of how individuals behaved and the fact that their conceptualization of friendship recalled their connection to a historical tradition. Friendship was 'a spiritual as well as a social relationship', as Francis Bremer has said.[16] This meant that the conduct of friendship was governed by godly as well as social concerns. '*Is it contrary to the nature of true friendship, to keep any secret from such a bosom friend, or to retain any suspicion of him, or to suppose that he may possibly prove unfaithful to us and forsake us?*' wrote Richard Baxter in *The Christian Directory*. He continued:

> *Cicero* and the old Doctors of *Friendship* say, that all this is inconsistent with true friendship: and it is true, that it is contrary to *perfect friendship*. But it is as true, that perfect friendship cannot be, nor must not be among imperfect Men: And that the nature of Mankind is so much depraved, that the best are *unmeet for perfect Friendship*.[17]

This stern differentiation between an idealized principle and its compromised, imperfect reality is investigated later in the same section of *The Christian Directory*. In answer to the question '*Why should we restrain our Love to a bosom friend (contrary to* Cicero's *Doctrine) and what sin or danger is in loving him too much?*' Baxter highlights the points at which

[14] Erika Rummel, *Desiderius Erasmus* (London, 2004), esp. ch. 2; Charles G. Nauert, *Humanism and the Culture of Renaissance Europe* (rev. edn, Cambridge, 2008).

[15] The mapping of Protestant concepts of friendships here is rather different to the more generalized Christian account given in Tadmor, *Family and Friends*, 239–45 and the focus on church fathers in A. C. Grayling, *Friendship* (New Haven, 2013), ch. 4.

[16] Francis Bremer, *Congregational Communion: Clerical Friendship in the Anglo-American Community, 1610–1692* (Boston, 1994), 6.

[17] Richard Baxter, *The Christian Directory*, in *Practical Works*, 4 vols (London, 1707), I, 855.

adherence to a Ciceronian model of friendship will prevent someone fulfilling their Christian duties to God and to their wider community: 'It very often taketh up Mens Minds, so as to hinder their love to God . . . it diverteth them from higher and better things' and 'It oft maketh Men ill Members of the Church and Common-wealth. For it contracteth that love to one over-valued Person, which should be diffused abroad among many.'[18] Getting the form of friendship right was acutely necessary in the puritan tradition because salvation depended in part on how and with whom one contracted friendships: as Francis Bremer puts it, 'the godly were no mere group of drinking associates, but a communion of the elect'.[19]

The emotional force of friendship was intensified for godly communities by its anticipated eternal duration. Persistent questions about individual salvation and how to prepare for life after death motivated the puritan reconfiguration of friendship. In *The Saint's Everlasting Rest*, Baxter takes examples of enjoyable aspects of human life and reminds readers that their fulfilment in heaven is beyond present comprehension:

> [I]f the Delights of close and cordial Friendship be so great, what Delight we shall have in the friendship of the most high? and in our Amity with Jesus Christ? and in the dearest Love and Comfort with the Saints? Surely this will be a closer and stricter Friendship, than ever was betwixt any Friends on Earth: And these will be more lovely desirable Friends than any that ever the Sun beheld and both our Affections to our Father, and our Saviour, but especially his Affection to us, will be such as we never knew.[20]

The 'closer and stricter' demands placed on friendship by Christian eschatology is the crux at which the nonconformist understanding of friendship diverges from the version idealized in classical literature. But for eighteenth-century dissenting ministers, the positive force of the classical model retained its attraction despite Baxter's words of warning.

As a young man, Doddridge thanked his friend Obadiah Hughes for recommending the letters of Pliny the Younger, observing 'there is seldom a day in which I do not read two or three of his epistles'. He claimed to see Pliny's influence on Hughes's own letters:

> nothing gave me so lively an idea of his excellence as to observe the perfection to which you have arrived by studying him, for every letter of yours is a panegyric upon Pliny, though you do not mention his name.[21]

[18] Baxter, *The Christian Directory*, in *Practical Works*, I, 855. This section of *The Christian Directory* is 'Cases and Directions for intimate special Friends'.

[19] Bremer, *Congregational Communion*, 6.

[20] Richard Baxter, *The Saint's Everlasting Rest*, part IV, in *Practical Works*, III, 297.

[21] Philip Doddridge to Obadiah Hughes, 28 June 1726. *Calendar* 214; Humphreys, II, 133.

Doddridge's playful comparison of Hughes with Pliny (an example of his tendency to flattery) registers the efforts of these young ministers to write with dignity, polish, learning, and wit by following classical models. New impetus for this pattern came from the *Spectator* and other periodicals, which dissenting ministers read just as eagerly as other citizens learning to imagine themselves as participants in the public sphere. In the *Spectator*, Joseph Addison describes the advantages of withdrawing from 'numerous assemblies' to 'Clubs and Knots of Friendship' while invoking Cicero and Francis Bacon.[22] But he also takes what he presents as an unusual step, introducing biblical statements on friendship (principally from Ecclesiasticus and Proverbs), in which he appreciates the conjunction of ideas and expression using critical techniques more typically applied (as he says) to classical moral writers.[23] Such a context—in which the wisdom and expressive qualities of the Bible are compared favourably to the wit and fine examples of Cicero, Horace, and Epictetus—is important for understanding the meaning of friendship for religious communities who tempered their culture of godly exceptionalism by privileging candour. In the eighteenth century, to be candid (or 'free from malice, not desirous to find faults') meant that one was open to conversation with those whose ideas were not necessarily identical with one's own.[24]

This culture of openness, facilitated by the conventions of polite discourse modelled in the *Spectator*, was welcomed by dissenters who valued candour, such as Watts, Doddridge, and their circle. But their participation in the polite, public world of post-Toleration England was not straightforward. Powerful historical, doctrinal, scriptural, and emotional forces affected dissenters' friendships just as much as worldly conventions and the dictates of taste did. Addison's efforts to bring classical moral writing, biblical precepts, and modern 'wits' and essayists together certainly affected the writing and attitudes of Doddridge and his friends, who read the *Spectator* as ministerial students. The interplay of elements was complicated, though, and as the eighteenth century went on Doddridge's associates struggled to harmonize the requirements of Christian and worldly friendship with the dangers of heterodoxy that candour was later feared to pose.[25]

---

[22] Joseph Addison and Richard Steele, *The Spectator*, ed. Donald F. Bond, 5 vols (2nd edn, Oxford, 1985), I:289, No. 68, 18 May 1711.

[23] *The Spectator*, I:290–1, No. 68.

[24] *OED* 'candid', definition 4, attributed to Johnson.

[25] For the 'disrepute' into which candour had fallen by the century's end, and Doddridge's perceived role in it, see Davie, *A Gathered Church*, 138–40.

3. CONVERSATION AND LETTERS

In *Spectator* 93, Addison portrayed conversation with friends as a good and virtuous use of time:

> the Mind never unbends it self so agreeably as in the Conversation of a well chosen Friend. There is indeed no Blessing of Life that is any way comparable to the Enjoyment of a discreet and virtuous Friend. It eases and unloads the Mind, clears and improves the Understanding, engenders Thoughts and Knowledge, animates Virtue and good Resolutions, sooths and allays the Passions, and finds Employment for most of vacant Hours of Life.[26]

The effects of conversation among friends all lead to ethical, intellectual, and practical improvement. Indeed, conversation as the mechanism of friendship was highly privileged—by Cicero and his peers, and in early modern Europe—because of its mutually beneficial potential. Dissenting ministers who had grown up reading the *Spectator* welcomed Addison's vision of friendship which emphasized the points of contact between classical and Christian models by celebrating the capacity of friendly converse to sustain and improve moral behaviour, and understood the important place of conversation in this process.

Addison's characterization of conversation is heavily indebted to classical precedents. The dialogic form of *De amicitia* indicates the high value Cicero placed on conversation as a means of developing ethical principles through a collaborative process of articulating, testing out, and adapting ideas. While dialogue could also be combative, particularly in intellectual and political debate, the later seventeenth century saw a renewed commitment to reciprocal processes of social and intellectual exchange in situations as diverse as the reporting of experimental science, news exchange in coffee-houses, and printed debates in international journals that connected the learned men of Europe.[27] Conversation had also become the way to demonstrate one's civility in public as well as at home, and doing so was facilitated by prescriptions on speech that sought to ensure that conversation was characterized by harmonious exchange.

---

[26] *The Spectator*, I:397, No. 93, 16 June 1711.
[27] Walter J. Ong, *Orality and Literacy: The Technologizing of the Word* (1982, repr. London, 2002), 43–5; Steven Shapin and Simon Schaffer, *Leviathan and the Air-Pump: Hobbes, Boyle and the Experimental Life* (Princeton, 1985); Michael Hunter (ed.), *Archives of the Scientific Revolution: The Formation and Exchange of Ideas in Seventeenth-Century Europe* (Woodbridge, 1998); Anne Goldgar, *Impolite Learning: Conduct and Community in the Republic of Letters 1680–1850* (New Haven, 1995); Lawrence E. Klein, 'Coffeehouse Civility, 1660–1714: An Aspect of Post-Courtly Culture in England', *Huntingdon Library Quarterly*, 59 (1996), 30–51.

'What is striking about early modern accounts of good manners in speech', Anna Bryson observes in her study of elite civility in early modern England, 'is the interest in discourse and conversation as social activities which are important in themselves, not just incidental to the ritual of hospitality.'[28] As the example of Cicero shows, this was a return to classical principles rather than a new development.

The importance of conversation was not restricted to the private function of sustaining an individual's status or securing friendships. It had a significant role to play in the way society talked about itself. Describing the 'Republic of Letters' whose participants gathered in the salons of Paris in the second half of the eighteenth century, Dena Goodman has argued that conviviality and sociable exchange were seen to be essential to the advancement of philosophy:

> As a worldly activity, philosophy now had two major implications: first, it was not confined within the individual, disembodied (Cartesian) mind; and, second, its tasks could be completed only in a social setting, as a social practice.[29]

Because of this conceptual basis, the method of learning through conversation, dialogue, and exploration was fundamental to salon culture, where it was nurtured and displayed. The ideals of community, discourse, and intellectual development are mutually supportive and all enacted in conversation. Underpinning these practices was natural law theory and the principle that sociability lay at the basis of benevolence.[30] As well as these secular theories, the Gospel example of godly community was an important philosophical as well as practical antecedent, particularly for communities formed around shared religious faith such as dissenters. Whether they privileged the example of Christ's ministry, a historical narrative of human sociability as an achievement which had displaced more violent forms, or a belief in humans' fundamentally social nature, individuals gathered into groups formed on principles that valued a participatory community within a wider society, defined in its own terms, and constructed out of conversation, letters, and friendship.

Polite conversation was understood to have particular power as a means of stabilizing society, described by Jon Mee as 'a crucial paradigm for the early eighteenth-century national imaginary . . . as a comforting sign of a complex social machinery in action'.[31] The influence of moral periodicals

---

[28] Anne Bryson, *From Courtesy to Civility: Changing Codes of Conduct in Early Modern Europe* (Oxford, 1998), 153.

[29] Dena Goodman, *The Republic of Letters: A Cultural History of the French Enlightenment* (2nd edn, Ithaca, NY, 1996), 8.

[30] Goodman, *The Republic of Letters*, 4–7.

[31] Jon Mee, *Conversable Worlds: Literature, Contention and Community 1762–1830* (Oxford, 2011), 8.

such as the *Spectator* is credited with the widespread diffusion of this notion, and with the construction of a characteristic mode of urbane, Whig civility that became the paradigm for public discourse.[32] Although practitioners showed how rational, polite style sought to smooth out controversy and reform it into harmonious exchange—on the same philosophical principles as those Goodman identified for salon-goers in France—it did not erase differences or impose a single framework for social practice.[33]

Varieties of politeness were acknowledged within this generalized scheme: as Klein has shown, mercantile readers and apprentices could develop particular competencies within the wider category of polite behaviour.[34] Religious culture and political disposition were, like employment, factors which could affect an individual's social practice and complicate any attempt at formulating a single model for polite conduct. It is important to emphasize this because Protestant dissenters have traditionally been seen as outside this discourse, both because of their suspected enthusiasm and because their religious priorities set them at odds with a secular model of sociability.

Hannah Smith has claimed that polite conversation was seen by Tories as well as Whigs as an effective means of stabilizing society. While her argument is oriented towards recuperating polite values for a Tory culture strongly antithetical to the philosophies and practices of Protestant nonconformity, it usefully widens the conceptual scope of politeness so that it need not be seen only as a restrictive force, one which served the function of 'taming religion' (as John Brewer puts it) or of sidelining ideological opposition.[35] In Smith's argument, politeness was not the 'sole property' of the urban elite, and it is on this basis that the contribution dissenters made to patterns of polite conversation in public and among themselves can be considered.[36] Watts's *Improvement of the Mind*, for example, advocated 'social reading', as Mee has termed it, and the conversation and debate permitted by such models was presented in terms of positive

---

[32] Lawrence E. Klein, 'Sociability, Solitude, and Enlightenment', *Huntingdon Library Quarterly*, 60 (1997), 153–77 (164).

[33] Goodman, *The Republic of Letters*, 172–3 notes that the idea of the *Spectator* as a meeting ground influenced the French Republic of Letters.

[34] Lawrence E. Klein, 'Politeness for Plebes: Some Social Identities in Early Eighteenth-Century England', in Ann Bermingham and John Brewer (eds), *The Consumption of Culture: Word, Image, and Object in the Seventeenth and Eighteenth Centuries* (New York, 1995), 362–82.

[35] John Brewer, *The Pleasures of the Imagination: English Culture in the Eighteenth Century* (London, 1997), 99.

[36] Hannah Smith, 'English "Feminist" Writings and Judith Drake's *An Essay in Defence of the Female Sex* (1696)', *Historical Journal*, 44 (2001), 727–47 (744).

opportunities for 'collision and contention'.[37] While this might seem to echo Shaftesbury's liberal view of politeness emerging from 'amicable collision', for dissenters philosophy was not only worldly and exemplars of sociability were not only secular.[38] Their discursive practice was shaped by the dominant paradigm of politeness but also by a model of supportive communication among the godly which developed out of scriptural examples and the experience of seventeenth-century religious communities. Both factors contributed to the commitment to orderly but searching conversation as the best mode for intellectual and spiritual development that characterized the educational and pastoral work of this group of dissenting ministers.

Reciprocity, essential to friendship and a characteristic of conversation, was also considered to be 'the distinctive feature of correspondence as a mode of communication' in the eighteenth century.[39] These three social structures were associated in both conceptual terms and through practical connections. Friendship was articulated and demonstrated in letters, for example, which are one of our principal sources of information about how eighteenth-century friendships worked in practice.[40] In the eighteenth century, one of the most powerful topoi of epistolarity was the convention that letters made the absent interlocutor present: Isaac Watts expressed this by the term 'epistolary converse'. This trope had strong effects, such as enabling familiarity to be created through descriptions of physical informality.[41] 'I am now sitting myself down to converse wth one of ye dearest of my friends,' wrote Doddridge to a former classmate, beginning a letter with a present-tense description of his physical movements ('sitting myself down') taking place in real time ('I am now').[42]

Another way in which letters foreclosed distance was by enabling friendship between men who had not actually met in person. Isaac Watts grieved the loss of one such friend when he wrote of the Lutheran royal chaplain and Pietist leader William Boehm: 'I am sorry the World & ye Church has sustained so heavy a Stroke, & that I have lost such a

---

[37] Mee, *Conversable Worlds*, 71–2.

[38] Mee, *Conversable Worlds*, 71 n. 90. For Watts's resistance to Shaftesbury's model of politeness, see Isabel Rivers, *Reason, Grace, and Sentiment: A Study of the Language of Religion and Ethics in England 1660–1780*, 2 vols (Cambridge, 1991–2000), I, 175–6.

[39] Goodman, *The Republic of Letters*, 18.

[40] This was not confined to elite and classically educated groups. Susan Whyman has shown that 'epistolary literacy' could extended to those with only very limited functional literacy. See Susan Whyman, *The Pen and the People: English Letter Writers 1660–1800* (Oxford, 2009), 9–11, 76.

[41] Pearsall, *Atlantic Families*, 77–8.

[42] Doddridge to Obadiah Hughes, 8 May 1722, in UCC MS B2 p. 75; *Calendar* 28.

Friend, whom I had just begun to know by epistolary Converse.'[43] The immediacy and intimacy conveyed in these letters was a performative characteristic of the genre, and in the act of writing a letter correspondents adopted personae: in the case of intimate letters, the character appropriate to a friendly correspondent.[44] Familiar letters were suited to conversational prose (and therefore the impression of friendly exchange) because they had fewer formal constraints than other genres. Indeed, in their capacity for expressing intimacies, letters might even surpass face-to-face conversation.[45] Further, the surviving letters of a deceased relative, friend, or mentor could communicate guidance and fellow feeling across generations.

Letters were not only a literary genre, a vehicle for friendship, and a repository for traditions but a practical necessity. John Locke emphasized the consequent importance of mastering the art:

> The writing of Letters has so much to do in all the occurrences of Humane life, that no gentleman can avoid shewing himself in this kind of Writing. Occasions will daily force him to make this use of his Pen, which... always lays him open to a severer Examination of his Breeding, Sense, and Abilities than oral Discourses.[46]

Letters could be more desirable than face-to-face communication because writers could control the terms of a discussion and demonstrate their skills without running the risk of slipping up when challenged in the moment. Conducting a debate or negotiation via letter allowed each participant the time to consider, practise, and polish their responses. The professional and social benefits of possessing epistolary skill were not only to do with display, however: sharing 'the occurrences of human life' was widely understood to be one of the central purposes of epistolary converse. As Job Orton wrote:

> I am always glad to receive *chit-chat letters*, as they seem to come from the heart. Mr. POPE is I think right, who somewhere says, 'The letters of friends are not worse for being fit for none else to read. The effusion of a moment ought to be the characteristick of all familiar writing...'[47]

[43] Watts to J. C. Jacobi, 15 May 1722, in Archiv Franckesche Stiftungen, Halle, MS A 149:19.

[44] Clare Brant, *Eighteenth Century Letters and British Culture* (Houndmills, Basingstoke, 2006), 24.

[45] Gary Schneider, *The Culture of Epistolarity: Vernacular Letters and Letter Writing in Early Modern England, 1500–1700* (Newark, Del., 2005), 133.

[46] John Locke, *Some Thoughts Concerning Education*, eds. John W. and Jean S. Yolton (Oxford, 1989), §§189, 243.

[47] Orton to Stedman, January 1779, in Thomas Stedman, *Letters to a Young Clergyman*, 2 vols (2nd edn, 1805), I, 266.

The informal exchange of news in letters confirms and sustains the friendship upon which correspondence is founded, and Orton's invocation of the 'heart' is important in this respect. The correct expression of sentiment was one of the components of 'breeding, sense and abilities' which Locke said letters should demonstrate and which can be found throughout the letters exchanged among this group of dissenters, who held dear the emotional basis of personal relationships. 'News' was not always trivial '*chit-chat*', of course. It included new ideas, and the letters exchanged among dissenting ministers and students for the ministry are full this type of news. Comments on books they have read, ideas about religious doctrines and philosophical points they have been studying, and responses to sermons they have heard fill their letters, and the informal intellectual community created as a result is analogous to the 'Republic of Letters' centred in Paris described by Dena Goodman and the literary communities of Scottish authors and educators documented by Richard Sher, both of which are presented as centres of enlightenment.[48]

Letters first sent to convey news could, over time, change their function when circulated and published in fresh contexts. Because of their intellectual content and their informal polite style, dissenters' letters were considered to be invaluable to students as models of piety, learning, good conduct, and epistolary skill. The circulation of many letters shows them being used as models in these ways, continuing much older practices of what James Daybell has termed 'epistolary pedagogy' in which reading and writing letters developed penmanship and expression as well as 'inculcating codes of obedience'.[49] Letters allowed writers to act as teachers or advisers, and Job Orton imagined his own legacy in these terms when he wrote to Thomas Stedman that 'I have, I hope, have been of some little use and significancy in life by my correspondence.'[50] The publication of Orton's letters long after he wrote them served to continue his 'use and significancy' as a guide to young ministers long after his death.

As the foregoing examples show, letters written by dissenters conformed to classical, humanist, and enlightened principles of epistolary conduct and purpose. They also express the Christian commitments of their writers very strongly. Clare Brant argues that correspondents 'writing as a Christian'

---

[48] Goodman, *The Republic of Letters*, 27 and Richard B. Sher, *Church and University in the Scottish Enlightenment: The Moderate Literati of Edinburgh* (Edinburgh, 1985) and *The Enlightenment and the Book*, ch. 2 (esp. 131–47).

[49] James Daybell, *The Material Letter in Early Modern England: Manuscript Letters and the Culture and Practices of Letter-Writing, 1512–1635* (Houndmills, Basingstoke, 2012), 58.

[50] Orton to Stedman, 20 September 1777, in Stedman, *Letters to a Young Clergyman*, I, 265.

were perceived (and perceived themselves) to be a special category. Since 'it was understood that to write as Christian meant being impolite in so far as worldly people regarded religion as a duty rather than a passion, if they regarded it at all', those who did so were set apart from the wider world socially.[51] While Brant's statement might be qualified—for even the worldliest citizens were Christians and did not understand society in the secular terms many in the West do today—letters written by the dissenters studied here shared certain characteristics. The writers appealed to Christian fellowship, articulated their understanding of faith, and discussed sermons they had heard. As well as using letters as a site for doctrinal and practical conversation in a way that worldlier correspondents might not, there is also a conceptual particularity to 'writing as a Christian'. Brant notes that there is a three-way relationship in Christian letters of 'self–God–other rather than the usual self–other'.[52] This triangulation recalls Baxter's reconfiguring of friendship to incorporate a future state as well as the present, and duties to God as well as to one's friends. The condition of friendship and the site for expressing that friendship in writing are both shaped by evangelical commitment to the conduct endorsed by the New Testament Gospels and Epistles.

In practice, this reconfiguration of relations took several forms. Susan Whyman's case study of Congregationalist sisters finds that correspondents within the community of nonconformists recognized that their letters had special characteristics, as when one of the sisters is praised for 'writing as one in the School of Christ'.[53] Features of such writing might be built into epistolary conventions, as when Doddridge entreats Samuel Clark senior to 'remember me in your prayers'.[54] Expressing Christian sentiments at the end of letters was highly conventional and in this respect Baxter's subscription to the 'Address to the Christian Reader' at the start of *The Reasons of the Christian Religion*—'Your Brother in this Life of Faith'—is both typical and a model for incorporating real-life relations into the fictional spaces within printed texts. Thus the form of these subscriptions was no empty gesture: the act of writing out such appeals declared the faith in Jesus as redeemer that bound religious communities together. Another determining aspect of the pattern of triangulation was that particular actions and ways of expressing them were, for dissenters, governed by faith. Isaac Watts, sending the works of the 'Calvinisticall Writers' John Howe and William Bates to Elisha Williams of Yale

---

[51] Brant, *Eighteenth Century Letters*, 314.
[52] Brant, *Eighteenth Century Letters*, 314.
[53] Whyman, *The Pen and the People*, 114 and 144.
[54] Doddridge to Clark, 22 October 1724, in *Calendar* 149, JRUL UCC MS B2 p. 344.

College, asked that they be received 'as a token of my zeal'.[55] Writing as a Christian meant adapting epistolary conventions to accommodate particular modes of thought and using letters to facilitate the actions required of a Christian: spreading understanding and demonstrating 'zeal', in the case of Watts in the example above.

In this period, it was seldom assumed that a letter would only ever be read by its addressee. In Parisian salons, 'Letters were shared, read aloud, passed around, and generally inserted into the discourse' and this practice was just as common in godly communities as secular gatherings.[56] The circulation and public reading of letters was also understood by Christians of all confessions to fulfil the evangelical and pastoral aims of Christian ministry first modelled by St Paul. Quaker groups relied on letters to circulate news and strengthen their corporate identity even in their earliest days.[57] Letter writing was also an important vehicle of the religious revivals of the mid-eighteenth century. The Methodist leader and ceaseless letter-writer John Wesley was always conscious that his letters were not private documents, for he printed short runs of a single letter which he would send to different recipients, often wrote to more than one recipient within a single letter, encouraged recipients to circulate his letters, and printed letters he had written in his serially published *Journal*.[58] Letter writing was comparably important to the dissenters investigated here because, in addition to its pedagogic and scriptural capacities, the circulation of letters had been used to sustain religious purpose and pastoral authority in the seventeenth century by Baxter and other ministers, as Alison Searle has shown.[59] In the 1770s, Job Orton sent Samuel Palmer a bundle of Doddridge's letters written in the 1730s as a model, and told Thomas Stedman that a letter he had written to a trainee minister had provided deathbed comfort for a friend of that young man.[60] The act of sharing letters was given distinct social emphases depending on the contexts in which

[55] Isaac Watts to Elisha Williams, 7 June 1738, in MHS, *Proceedings*, 336.

[56] Goodman, *Republic of Letters*, 143; Anne Dunan-Page and Clotilde Prunier (eds), *Debating the Faith: Religion and Letter-Writing in Great Britain, 1550–1800* (Dordrecht, 2013), esp. chs 2, 4, and 8.

[57] Kate Peters, 'Patterns of Quaker Authorship, 1652–56', in *The Emergence of Quaker Writing: Dissenting Literature in Seventeenth-Century England*, ed. Thomas C. Corns and David Lowenstein (London, 1995), 6–24.

[58] John Wesley, *Works Volume 25: Letters I*, ed. Frank Baker (Oxford, 1980), 39–40, 64–8, 81. Baker gives Wesley's letters dated 15 October 1766 and 24 November 1767 as examples of duplicated and printed letters (40).

[59] Alison Searle, 'Writing Authority in the Interregnum: The Pastoral Letters of Richard Baxter', in *Debating the Faith* ed. Dunan-Page and Prunier, 49–68.

[60] Samuel Palmer, *Letters to Dissenting Ministers*, II, 201–2; Stedman, *Letters to a Young Clergyman*, I, 129.

it was done, but it always served to reinforce the bonds of common purpose among a community of readers.

The particular spur to action provided by evangelical commitments is documented throughout the letters of these dissenters. Thanking Samuel Clark junior for kind words about his latest publication, Orton piously declares, 'I have no greater joy than to hear that it is useful to souls.'[61] Attestations of this nature, that placed the hoped-for consequences of book reading above any expectations of money or reputation to be obtained from producing them, are characteristic of the letters of these dissenters. William Warburton (later Bishop of Gloucester) playfully mimicked this tendency when, praising Doddridge's *Life of Gardiner*, he concluded, 'On the whole, the book will do you honour, or what you like better, will be a blessing to you by its becoming an instrument of public good.'[62] Books to be distributed often accompanied letters, and in this respect correspondence networks were instrumental to the spread of religious knowledge. But the extent to which these features of Christian letters are the same for all Christians and what was particular to the epistolary practices of nonconformists is debatable. Certainly dissenters themselves considered their practice of faith to be distinctive within the English religious landscape. Watts, for instance, thought that the nonconformists' commitment to evangelical preaching and practical piety were strong characteristics of their tradition. In a letter to the American minister Benjamin Colman, Watts concludes that because of these strengths, George Whitefield's influence will be chiefly felt in the Church of England rather than in dissenting congregations.[63] Nor was it their evangelical and charitable practices alone that marked out nonconformists. In another letter to Colman, Watts discusses doctrinal differences about baptism and asserts strongly his disagreement with the Church of England on the subject, showing very clearly the importance he attached to his identity as a nonconformist Protestant.[64] Dissenters' sense of their identity as expressed in their correspondence was more specific than 'as a Christian' or even as a Protestant, and the practical actions of their Christianity were also viewed in this light.[65]

Letters did not have a single or finite life. As the written representation of conversation, letters were understood by different groups in the early

---

[61] Orton to Clark, 26 December 1762, in Palmer, *Letters to Dissenting Ministers*, I, 89.
[62] William Warburton to Philip Doddridge, 10 October 1747. *Calendar* 1282; *Letters to and from the Rev. Philip Doddridge, D.D.*, ed. Thomas Stedman (Shrewsbury, 1793), 205.
[63] Watts to Colman, 23 May 1740, in MHS, *Proceedings*, 374.
[64] Watts to Colman, 14 September 1742, in MHS, *Proceedings*, 401.
[65] Brant, *Eighteenth Century Letters*, 281–330.

modern period to have an important role to play in the real and imagined communities that formed the international Republic of Letters, be that republic philosophical or puritan. As well as their practical functions for communities in the present moment, letters' historical associations and future potential contributed to their emotional and intellectual power, particularly for religious nonconformists. For seventeenth-century ministers such as Richard Baxter, letter writing was a mechanism for creating and sustaining godly communities, and the correspondence of eighteenth-century dissenters should be seen in the context of the epistolary traditions of their forebears.[66] Letters enabled dissenters to articulate and practise their identities; and later, published collections of dissenters' letters broadcast their epistolary literacy in print. For the men discussed in this book, the tools for such self-fashioning were acquired at dissenting academies.

4. STRUCTURING THE DISSENTING COMMUNITY: FRIENDSHIP, LETTERS, AND ACADEMIES

In *De amicitia*, Laelius asks: 'And who is there from whom solitude would not snatch the enjoyment of every pleasure? . . . nature, loving nothing solitary, always strives for some sort of support, and man's best support is a very dear friend.'[67] The specific circumstances in which many dissenting ministers found themselves made them acutely aware of the need for the 'support' of 'very dear friends' that epistolary converse could provide. Similar in some ways to curates in the Church of England, they often expressed feelings of isolation as they fulfilled their ministry in rural communities where they were conscious of being classically educated and committed to further reading and study but of having no one with whom to discuss intellectual matters.[68] 'I have no other tutor, but a few honest farmers & good old women', Doddridge wrote to John Mason, careful not to disparage his 'honest' and 'good' companions but clear that they could not meet his need for sociable intellectual exchange as men like Mason, who had been his fellow-student at Jennings's academy, could.[69]

---

[66] See N. H. Keeble, *'Loving and Free Converse': Richard Baxter in his Letters* (London, 1991); Alison Searle, ' "Though I am a stranger to you by face, yet in neere bonds by faith": A Transatlantic Puritan Republic of Letters', *Early American Literature*, 43 (2008), 277–308.

[67] Cicero, *De amicitia*, xiv.88.

[68] Jacob, *The Clerical Profession*, 167–8; but as Jacob points out, the clergy of the established church 'were all-pervasive in English and Welsh society. Dissenting ministers, by comparison, were few and scattered' (9).

[69] Doddridge to Mason, 11 May 1724, *Calendar* 123, JRUL UCC MS B2 p. 300.

Doddridge used his wide correspondence with peers and mentors to talk through his reading and his early experiences as a minister. He was using letters to continue his education informally.

The value he and his associates attached to ongoing intellectual development was instilled at the academies they attended, the experience of which left a deep impression on the men in this book. Their letters and published works repeatedly state that they considered academies to be sites where inherited ideals were transmitted along with their basic task of training ministers in how to preach and ensuring they had a secure academic grounding. Academies were fundamental to the religious intellectual life of these dissenting ministers, who were trained to believe that learning and piety were the best means of ensuring that doctrinally correct and emotionally engaging religious principles were transmitted to congregations. Having an educated ministry had always been fundamental to the Presbyterian and Congregational confessions, and in this respect eighteenth-century dissenting ministers and educators were following their seventeenth-century forebears. By the eighteenth century, this principle was both axiomatic and pragmatic: dissenting academies were viewed as crucial to the continued life of dissenting congregations which, it was feared, were in decline. For, though legal restrictions on dissenters had been eased by William III and George I, and attacks on dissenting education became rarer, dissenters' separation from the establishment was still strongly felt, not least in the sphere of education.[70] For both Watts and Doddridge, the decision to attend a dissenting academy rather than enter one of the universities was a key moment when they renewed their commitment to the tradition of dissent.[71] Academies can be understood both as real institutions which contributed to the ongoing existence of dissent and as symbols of the historical principles and future hopes of the dissenting tradition.

What this actually meant in practice varied from academy to academy. Each was independent, which makes it difficult to generalize about curriculum, reading, and social arrangements. However, affiliations emerged among academies, often engendered by the use of the same educational materials or the movement of students from one academy to work as tutors at another. The focus of this book is the Jennings–Doddridge tradition of

---

[70] Doddridge faced prosecution for running his academy without an episcopal licence in 1733, though the case was eventually rejected at the intervention of the Earl of Halifax and Robert Walpole. See *Calendar* 375, 377–9, 392–7, and 399–400.

[71] A Southampton doctor called John Speed offered to fund Watts's education at one of the two English universities and the Duchess of Bedford did the same for Doddridge: see Rivers, 'Watts, Isaac (1674–1748)' and 'Doddridge, Philip (1702–1751)', *ODNB*.

moderate orthodox academies, where particularities of denomination were played down in favour of a broad consensus that freedom of conscience, intellectual enquiry, and wide reading were to be encouraged. The example of Doddridge's experience (which is well documented) can be used to establish some key elements of this type of dissenting academy in the Hanoverian period. His post-grammar school education began under the care of Samuel Clark senior, a dissenting minister in St Albans in around 1718, when Doddridge was sixteen.[72] In 1718 the Countess of Bedford, Lady Russell, offered to support Doddridge at either of the universities so that he could take orders in the Church of England. Doddridge chose instead to be educated among the dissenters. In October 1719, he arrived at John Jennings's academy in Kibworth, the primary purpose of which was to train candidates for the dissenting ministry.[73] He remained there for four years, which was about average.[74] The curriculum students followed varied between academies because the head tutor of each set his own course and decided whether to accept lay students alongside ministerial candidates.

A significant feature of Jennings's system was that students received a wide grounding in the subjects of polite learning. Theology was always the focus of the academy course (and this was different from the universities, where formal theology teaching was not given to BA students) but a range of other subjects were taught including languages, mathematics, and history, all of which had a particular part to play in the formation of learned and polite ministers. Instruction in classical architecture, the principles of heraldry, and public speaking were part of the curriculum and were presented as components of a gentleman's education.[75] These elements of Jennings's course suggests that contemporary characterizations of dissenters as rude, rustic, and interested only in dogmatic religion were exaggerated.[76] Lecture notes from the 1750s

[72] Clark received several payments for teaching Doddridge between 1718 and 1720. DWL MS OD68, Presbyterian Fund Board Minutes, 5 February 1694/5–4 June 1722 (337, 344, 352, 362). I am grateful to David Wykes for this reference.

[73] Several of Jennings's students later conformed to the Church of England: see Wykes, 'Jennings, John (1687/8–1722)', *ODNB*.

[74] His learning and fitness to work as a minister were examined in January, but he remained a student until the early summer. See *Calendar* 47 and 48 for his examination on 24 January 1722/3.

[75] John Jennings, *Miscellanea in usum juventutis academicae* (Northampton, 1721), items II, VII, XIV. For the reading recommended to university students, see Waterland, *Advice to a Young Student*, 12–17, 18, 22, 25, and 27.

[76] Eighteenth-century pamphlets reproduced these portrayals of dissenters. See, for example, the collection of tracts bound together in the BL, shelfmark T.814.

and 1760s also reveal that demonstrating politeness was considered part of the ministerial role.[77]

Politeness had social, spiritual, and pastoral purposes for dissenters. While many of the examples presented so far indicate that Doddridge and his associates had absorbed Addisonian norms of urbane, domestic politeness, it is nevertheless difficult to accommodate these men within generalized arguments about eighteenth-century masculinity, which tend (albeit implicitly) to follow a secularization narrative.[78] For scholars of eighteenth-century conduct and religion, a problematic aspect of these dissenters' identity was that their commitment to the religious principles of Richard Baxter and his seventeenth-century peers coexisted with a determination to move away from the stereotypes of nonconformist ministers based on the most bombastic Restoration-era preachers that were still current in the eighteenth century.[79] This apparent paradox cannot be resolved in a few sentences: after all, it troubled many of the men in this book throughout their professional lives. It should be noted, though, that eighteenth-century dissenters took seriously the need to reconcile older models of dogmatic piety with new paradigms that valued social ease, and many of their educational and publishing projects can be seen as reflections of and contributions to that effort.

In June 1723, in the early days of his Kibworth ministry, Doddridge described his rural community as 'one of the most unpolite congregations I ever knew . . . [there is] but one hoop-petticoat within the whole circuit'.[80] In this light-hearted conjunction of current fashions in dress and acceptable conventions for behaviour which identified his new social world as markedly lacking both, Doddridge articulated a difficulty faced by many dissenting ministers who had been educated in the academies. In their efforts to participate in polite and learned national culture (through publishing, by reading, discussing, and corresponding with journals, and in friendships with learned figures within the establishment) dissenting ministers risked separating themselves from their own congregations. The

---

[77] CHCN Blackmore MS 4 is a volume of student notes entitled 'Rules of Conduct' which delineate good conduct before God, in relation to one's work, among one's peers, and in the world.

[78] For example, Philip Carter, *Men and the Emergence of Polite Society* (Harlow, 2001). Two exceptions are Jeremy Gregory, '*Homo Religiosus*: Masculinity and Religion in the Long Eighteenth Century', in *English Masculinities 1660–1800*, ed. Tim Hitchcock and Michèle Cohen (Harlow, 2001), 85–110 and William van Reyk, 'Christian Ideals of Manliness in the Eighteenth and Early Nineteenth Centuries', *Historical Journal*, 52 (2009), 1053–73.

[79] For a caricature of a bombastic dissenting preacher, see *The Tatler*, ed. D. F. Bond, 3 vols (Oxford, 1987), I:453–7, No. 66, 10 September 1709.

[80] Doddridge to Mrs Farrington, 8 June 1723, *Calendar* 66.

competing demands of ministering to the needs and expectations of rural workers and comporting themselves in a gentlemanlike way in different public arenas created difficulties—such as how to prioritize their daily tasks—which Doddridge and his associates addressed in their guidance to ministers.[81] The problem of finding oneself in an uncongenial social setting was not unique to dissenting ministers.[82] I would like to suggest, however, that the questions of how to appear polite and why it mattered even when confined to a provincial and unlearned sphere of pastoral action were particularly heightened for classically educated dissenting ministers because exclusion was a condition of their legal identity and politeness the means by which they could overcome that enforced exclusion in their professional and social lives. By labelling his new congregation as 'unpolite'—a rather ungallant act, even in jest—Doddridge made a striking choice of adjective, as he applied the insult he most feared to those around him in order to mark the social distance between himself as a minister and his congregation.

The focus of the present study is a single (albeit catholic) tradition within dissent, and while there are divergences within this tradition and overlaps with other models of dissenting education, it is important to emphasize that this book is not about *all* dissenting academies.[83] The diversity and distinctiveness of dissenting academies contributed to their unique intellectual, religious, and social environment, which in turn shaped the ministerial activities and published works of men who had attended them. Some key traits of academies in the Jennings–Doddridge tradition are that they were familial, that the ministerial training they provided combined detailed theoretical and practical education, and that tutors and students took pride in the academic rigour and breadth of their curriculum. Delineating the place in the wider currents of intellectual and literary life that the acts and books marked by these tenets occupied reveals the considerable influence of older patterns of religious knowledge on the modern, enlightened developments of the eighteenth century. The wealth of evidence for this claim is presented and analysed over the course of this book. Some preliminary examples can indicate the range of engagements

---

[81] See Philip Doddridge, 'Life of Steffe', in Thomas Steffe, *Sermons on Several Subjects* (London, 1742), xxvii–xviii, *Lectures on Preaching* (London, 1805), lectures XVII–XXIV.

[82] The frequent complaints about inadequate company across a range of surviving eighteenth-century correspondence attests to this, and bishops advised clergy against 'too familiar involvement in local society', see Jacob, *The Clerical Profession*, 2.

[83] The nature of dissenting academy education (including the curriculum, locations, discipline, and intellectual connections of particular academies) will be thoroughly investigated in *A History of the Dissenting Academies in the British Isles, 1660–1860*, ed. Isabel Rivers, Mark Burden, assistant ed. (Cambridge, forthcoming).

that these community endeavours encompassed in print and manuscript, within their own network, and to an international learned community. Job Orton, Samuel Clark junior, and Caleb Ashworth were all Doddridge's former students and between them oversaw the posthumous publication of his works. Caleb Ashworth also led the academy at Daventry which succeeded Doddridge's own, ensuring his educational legacy. Job Orton corresponded with students at academies, advising them on reading and conduct, and reflecting on the social realities of life as a dissenter. Many of these letters were collected and edited by Samuel Palmer (a former student of Ashworth's at Daventry) who published them under the title *Letters to Dissenting Ministers* (1806) so that they might provide informal guidance in personal, intellectual, and epistolary conduct to dissenting ministers half a century after they were written.

The fact that in the nineteenth century Samuel Palmer could address his publications to dissenting ministers attests to the longevity of their educational tradition. This was a significant (if bittersweet) achievement; though many dissenting ministers in the eighteenth century would have preferred not to bear the negative label 'dissenter', the fact that their tradition had endured despite its situation outside the mainstream was a matter of pride. After all, its survival was by no means assured, particularly not in the 1720s when educational provision for potential ministers was at a low ebb.

5. 'AN ACCOUNT OF MR JENNINGS'S METHOD': LETTERS AS ACTION

The associations among dissenting ministers that this book investigates developed around the figure of Philip Doddridge. It is my contention that they did so primarily because of his academy, which opened in 1729. I will explore how and why his academy became the centre of a tradition characterized by sociable learning in the coming chapters, but here I want to concentrate on its pre-history in order to highlight the ways in which these characteristics shaped the way the academy came into being. Before becoming a tutor himself, Doddridge initiated discussion about the ideal form for dissenting education and the conduct of students and tutors. He did this by circulating materials which described Jennings's academy and suggested improvements, and he invited comments from ministers on those materials. Doddridge ensured that the information spread by textual means as well as by conversation, and that the form and content of those documents signalled that this academy had absorbed influences from mainstream culture as well as the world of dissenting academies. Therefore I will close this chapter by considering how the traditions, ideals, priorities, and practices that have been outlined above shaped the discourse surrounding the formation of a new academy in 1728–1729.

John Jennings died in 1723 and no new academy opened in the East Midlands to replace his. By the end of the decade the issue of reviving an academy in the region was becoming one of increasing concern to Isaac Watts (himself based in London) and other dissenters. They feared that reduced numbers of academies would mean fewer dissenting ministers were trained, with a consequent decline in the number of active dissenting congregations in the country. Doddridge, a young minister to a rural community, with plenty of time for reading and letter writing but few opportunities to use his classical learning or develop his social polish, participated in conversations about a new academy. He produced a detailed 'Account of Mr Jennings's Method' which Isaac Watts read and commented on. This document, though purportedly addressed to an unnamed 'friend' (who was, Doddridge claimed, an associate planning to set up a new academy) actually led to Doddridge himself becoming a tutor. The 'Account' was the foundation stone of his own academy.

The 'Account of Mr Jennings's Method' describes the course, proposes developments to the structure of the curriculum, suggests new subjects to be taught, and recommends new authors to be added to the syllabus. It suggests preparatory reading a prospective tutor should undertake as well as the qualities he ought to cultivate. It also offers a personal view of academy life, describing day-to-day routines and extra-curricular activities, and sketches a vivid picture of an ideal tutor, based on Jennings. Doddridge emphasized that he took his information from papers belonging to Jennings as well as his own notes and memories. The textual basis of this information is asserted to give the 'Account' factual authority. Meanwhile the descriptions that evoke Doddridge's relationship with Jennings remind the reader of the personal association that granted Doddridge the authority to comment.

Doddridge begins his 'Account of Mr Jennings' Method' with a memory that triggers present action:

My dear friend,
You seem'd to enter so deeply into the Subject of our Discourse, the last Time I had the pleasure of your Company, that I cannot imagine you have ^yet^ forgot it, or think it necessary that it should be repeated, in order to introduce the Letter, which at your desire, I am now setting myself to write.[84]

---

[84] Doddridge, 'An Account of Mr Jennings's Method', fol. 3.

The direct address and imagined scene depicted at the opening of this letter explicitly evoke a situation of friendly discourse. A project begun in the pleasurable circumstances of conversation among friends is now, appropriately, being continued in its written equivalent. Janet Gurkin Altman has defined epistolarity as 'the use of the letter's formal properties to create meaning'.[85] Casting his 'Account' as a letter enabled Doddridge to embed into his 'Account' of dissenting education two of the most significant features of the intellectual culture from which it emerged and which it sought to depict: collaboration and friendly exchange. Epistolary form also enabled Doddridge to preserve a particular decorum. A letter must have an addressee, and in this case Doddridge gives that person—his 'friend'—a particular role by specifying that he 'had some Thoughts of reviving' the academy. By addressing his 'Account' to a clearly characterized recipient, Doddridge separates the person describing the academy (himself) from the proposed tutor of that academy even though ultimately they were one and the same.[86] This was an important distinction for Doddridge, who was anxious it should not appear as though he was pushing himself forward and begging for a job. Further, writing as a representative of Jennings's educational method, it was important that he should demonstrate the politeness, learning, and piety he claimed the method inculcated. For a man who noted with regret (however light-hearted) that few of the accoutrements of polite society could be found in his rural community, demonstrating mastery of epistolary conventions was both a social and professional skill.

Creating the character of a warmly invoked friend as the recipient for the letter yet leaving that recipient unnamed encourages readers of the 'Account' to identify themselves as 'My dear Friend', and thereby invites them into a world of personal exchanges. The letter form foregrounds participation from readers, suggests Gary Schneider: 'One of the most salient early modern characteristics of letters was that they embodied a sense of "dialogic" discourse, predicated as letters were on the assumption of exchange, response, and reciprocity.'[87] In the case of Doddridge's 'Account', the communicative purpose of the letter has a goal beyond that of speaking to a single absent friend. As Schneider asserts, 'The traditional dyadic model of letter exchange... is insufficient to comprehend the

---

[85] Janet Gurkin Altman, *Epistolarity: Approaches to a Form* (Columbus, Oh., 1993), 4.
[86] It is not clear when precisely Doddridge decided to become a tutor. In February 1728 he told Samuel Clark he had only 'Slight Thoughts' of renewing Jennings's course (*Calendar* 291), and by March 1729 he was considering taking Joseph Saunders through Jennings's course (*Calendar* 315).
[87] Schneider, *The Culture of Epistolarity*, 189.

collective nature of letter writing, transmission, and reception.'[88] Behind Doddridge's 'Account' lies the assumption that the letter would circulate beyond a single recipient, and this belief was fundamental to the construction of communal effort to build an academy out of the expertise and ideas of numerous readers. The rhetoric of response is also crucial: Doddridge was not generating demands for a new academy, but responding to the suggestions of others, such as his friend Thomas Saunders.[89]

Doddridge wanted his 'Account of Mr Jennings's Method' to be affective as well as informative. He explicitly combines these strands when he writes:

> it wou'd be easy for me to break out into something very passionate, if I wou'd indulge to the Show of my affections; nay it is very difficult to refrain from doing it. But I will not give way to the Fulness of my Heart, nor to those Tears which have often forc'd themselves into my Eyes since I begun this Letter. I wou'd rather chuse to express my regards to the Memory of so great a Friend, in a more manly and rational Way. And I can recollect none more proper than this Attempt, to continue the Remembrance of this useful scheme he had form'd, and if possible to revive the prosecution of it.[90]

This striking display of passion moderated by reason has significant implications. As Klein has argued, 'reason was a public, social, and even sociable process' in post-Restoration discourse.[91] Articulating his sense that there is a 'more manly and rational Way' to commemorate a lost friend than through tears, Doddridge simultaneously demonstrates that his education (that is, the education he has just described) has instilled in him the beneficial habit of good use of natural reason, and insists on the place of emotion as a spur to human good works. This letter is an appropriate site for his statement of esteem for 'so great a Friend' as John Jennings because it is an intimate and sociable space. The decorum of a letter to invite response is used here to call for collective participation in the foundation of a new academy and it thereby becomes a mechanism for creating an institution which builds on the foundations of Jennings's educational system. This is the most fitting memorial to his tutor Doddridge can devise. His presentation of the scheme in these closing lines conforms to the discursive rules of a polite and sociable intellectual world while calling on his fellow dissenters to act in the interest and manner of their particular tradition by using the power of past examples to secure the future.

---

[88] Schneider, *The Culture of Epistolarity*, 33.   [89] *Calendar* 287, 290.
[90] Doddridge, 'An Account of Mr Jennings's Method', fol. 47.
[91] Klein, 'Sociability, Solitude, and Enthusiasm', 173.

Doddridge's 'Account of Mr Jennings's Method' is an artfully constructed demonstration of dissenting learning, an appeal to the reader to support the proposal for a new academy, and a physical document that circulated among groups of readers. It welcomed inclusive, thoughtful debate and promoted warm personal relationships: the very features which were to characterize the conduct of the tradition in which he participated. Its resemblance to an epistolary treatise rather than a familiar letter notwithstanding, the 'Account' did fulfil the dialogic function of letters. Once it began to circulate, what Daybell might call its 'social materiality' was activated and the 'Account' became the site around which responses to and modifications of Jennings's system clustered.[92] Chief among these was the written response from Isaac Watts, the first direct communication between him and Doddridge. Watts's intervention was important for the success of the nascent scheme because Doddridge (an unknown, relatively inexperienced minister) needed the support of the wider ministerial community if he was to be nominated as the best candidate as tutor and was to attract students to his provincial academy. Receiving the approval and advice of Watts (who was famous as a hymnodist and commentator on congregational practice and whose sermons, treatises, and educational works had won him widespread respect) was a significant endorsement for the intellectual and pastoral training scheme of the curriculum Doddridge proposed.

Watts's response to Doddridge's 'Account' participates in the collective process of adaptation and consolidation by which Jennings's method—as presented by Doddridge—became the blueprint for a real academy. Watts begins his response with warm expressions of approval, both for the 'beauties & Congruities' of the course and for the way in which Doddridge has 'so admirably' described it.[93] Having created a frame of positive engagement, he proceeds to pose searching questions on the syllabus and practicalities of the course: why are Latin poets not taught until the second semester? Why is oratory training not continued throughout the course? Is adopting a mathematical method for some subjects really appropriate?[94] Watts also gives additional suggestions based on his own education—such as reading 'plain Easy books of Divinity' on Saturdays—and expresses reservations about some of the practices Doddridge described. In particular, acting out dramas and visiting the local church are singled out as

---

[92] Daybell, *The Material Letter*, 230.
[93] Watts's 'Reply to Doddridge's "Account"', in 'An Account of Mr Jennings's Method', in *Dissenting Education and the Legacy of John Jennings c.1720–c.1729*, ed. Whitehouse.
[94] Watts's 'Reply to Doddridge's "Account"', fol. 2–2v.

dangerous activities.[95] Watts's suggestions are presented in the form of a list, and the tone of his questions is abrupt. This is in contrast to the polished language and syntax of Doddridge's 'Account'.

Watts's comments have been annotated with numbers in Doddridge's hand which correspond to a numbered list of responses on the final leaf. Here, Doddridge answers some of Watts's questions: he says whose maps he prefers, suggests that Watts might like to draw up a system of ontology which could become the academy's textbook, and accepts almost all of Watts's suggested changes with the unequivocal 'Allow'd in its full force. I propose to alter that Circumstance.'[96] Did the paper, having been sent to Doddridge, return to Watts so that he could see Doddridge's responses? Then what happened to it? There are some clues in the final remark from Doddridge:

> N°. 15. I should be very glad of the Concurrence of a person capable of taking a part in the Course if I publickly under<*take th*>e Work as a Tutor...I trust that if God favour me with anything of yᵉ success wᶜʰ my Friends encourage me to expect, the Attempt will be for my own Improvement & that of my pupils:...I earnestly desire the Advice & prayers of all my pious & learned Friends, & peculiarly of Dʳ Watts to whom I acknowledge my self exceedingly indebted for these Remarks & his other Favours.[97]

This is the first time Doddridge acknowledges that he himself (not his 'Friend') will undertake the work of a tutor: this announcement in some respects seems oddly placed, in an annotation to an informal note to a manuscript epistolary treatise. Doddridge's invocation of 'all my pious and learned friends', his acknowledgement of Watts's assistance, and his use of third-person rather than second-person address all suggest that he anticipated readers beyond himself and Watts. Such readers could examine this document in conjunction with 'An Account of Mr Jennings's Method' in order to be conversant with the process by which Doddridge's proposals were being adapted and the latest developments in the scheme. Here they would also find themselves and their friends thanked for their encouragement and asked for their prayers: even in this closing note, Doddridge was opening the project up so that readers could become participants.[98]

---

[95] 'Watts's Reply to Doddridge's "Account"', fol. 2, fol. 3.

[96] Watts's 'Reply to Doddridge's "Account"', fol. 4.

[97] Watts's 'Reply to Doddridge's "Account"', fol. 4v. Words within angle brackets offer a conjectural reading of words lost where the manuscript is damaged.

[98] The two documents may have circulated together: see *Calendar* 315, where Doddridge seeks information about the present location of some 'MSS of education' that he had sent around.

Despite their shared purpose, these complementary documents are quite different in their appearance and manner of composition. Watts writes:

> At ye End of this Course I do not find ˆthisˆ one thing mentioned in the whole of it which must be granted to be very necessary & ought not to be omitted. (Viz) that ye whole Scripture should be read over in ye 4 years time ~~with ye Tu~~ perhaps at Morning & evening prayer with ye Tutors remarks on ye difficult texts, both Criticall & Controversiall. Whatsoever is omitted this ought not. NB. Page 100 answers this.[99]

Crossings out and self-correction in this extract are consistent with Watts's document as a whole, and indicate this was a rough paper, in contrast to the carefully presented and neatly transcribed 'Account', to which it responds. Watts added 'NB Page 100 answers this' later, which indicates that he was drafting these comments as he read, and did not send Doddridge a fair copy. Meanwhile Doddridge's 'Account' is not quite (or only) the letter it purports to be. It is sturdily bound, anticipating sustained use. It has a title page which echoes that of a printed book and which anticipates the affectionate yet anonymous formulation of the letter to 'My dear friend' in the subtitle it gives the 'Account': 'a Letter to M^r xxxx'.[100] The series of crosses that replace the name evoke personal intimacy which is withdrawn by the anonymity of the addressee and the presentation of this letter, stitched into a tooled calfskin binding and introduced by a neatly laid out title page. The carefully staged intimacy of tone and formality of physical presentation direct the reception of the document. Readers would be drawn to participate in the collaborative process being worked out and would see the seriousness with which Doddridge was approaching his task. The physical document declares its completeness (at 123 pages, it extended far beyond the usual bounds of a letter) and its intended permanence.

Evidence suggests that there were several copies of this account, for Watts's page references do not correspond to the pages of the surviving 'Account' on which that information appears. 'An Account of Mr Jennings's Method' is undoubtedly in Doddridge's hand, so there must have been more than one copy in existence in the eighteenth century. Considered together, all these factors—the neat presentation, sturdy binding, and title page of the 'Account', its existence in more than one copy, and the evidence that 'individual control over the social use of the text has been replaced by the control of a community'—all meet Harold Love's criteria

---

[99] Watts's 'Reply to Doddridge's "Account"', fol. 2v.
[100] Doddridge, 'An Account of Mr Jennings's Method', fol. 1.

for scribal publication.[101] As Love, McKenzie, and other scholars have demonstrated, manuscript publication remained widespread into the late seventeenth century.[102] The survival of Doddridge's 'Account' is evidence that manuscript continued to be an attractive form of publication into the eighteenth century. It was also apparently an effective one, given the fact that the academy successfully recruited students and received financial support, gifts of books, and goodwill from the wider dissenting community. In choosing not to print the 'Account', it is unlikely that economic or other practical factors were primary for Doddridge. The social and psychological attractions of manuscript publication identified by McKenzie appear to be more applicable in this case. If 'printing was too impersonal, too public, too fixed' for certain situations, then scribal publication permitted a degree of formality and registered that a public declaration had been made but at the same time retained the writer's 'presence' and the personal scope of the address.[103] By appealing to a coterie readership it conformed to moderate dissenters' tendency to show restraint in public discourse and made a virtue of that attitude. The material form of Doddridge's 'Account' reiterated and amplified the appeals to personal association, friendly discourse, and collective action that its literary form articulated in words.

Doddridge's manuscript publication continued to be used by dissenting tutors and ministers throughout the eighteenth century. In a letter written to Doddridge's widow by Job Orton more than twenty years after Doddridge's death, he told her:

A Bookseller of Bewdley, with whom I have no Dealings, lately sent me a Catalogue of Books to be sold at Leeds. My Curiosity led me to look into it, & there to my great Surprize I found 'Dr D's MS Account of Mr Jennings's Method of academical Education' charged 3s . . . I lately rec'd it safe & in good Order. I remember the Author lent me the Book in the Year 1736 & I safely returned it. But I never saw it, or could hear of it, since . . . As the Catalogue, in which I saw it, contained the Library of Dr Legh, I conclude Dr D. lent it him . . . I have sent it to Daventry for the use of ye Tutors & academy there, & put it under the particular Care of Mr Robins. There

---

[101] Love, *Scribal Publication*, 42–9 (44).

[102] Arthur Marotti, *Manuscript, Print, and the English Renaissance Lyric* (Ithaca, NY, 1995); Margaret Ezell, 'The Social Author' in *Social Authorship and the Advent of Print* (Baltimore, Md., 1999), 21–44; Love, 'Restoration Scriptorial Satire', in *Scribal Publication*, 231–83; George Justice and Nathan Tinker (eds), *Women's Writing and the Circulation of Ideas: Manuscript Publication in England, 1550–1800* (Cambridge, 2002); D. F. McKenzie, 'Script—Manuscript—Print', in *Making Meaning: 'Printers of the Mind' and Other Essays*, ed. Peter McDonald and Michael F. Suarez, SJ (Cambridge, 2002), 237–58.

[103] McKenzie, 'Script—Manuscript—Print', 247.

I hope it will be safe & useful. And I am thankful to God that after so many Years Fruitless Inquiry for it & Despair of finding it, it is recovered, in a place of Safety, & where it will be doing good.[104]

Orton's description forty years later of how Doddridge circulated the document in the 1730s as a shared resource for tutors attests to the ongoing importance of the manuscript 'Account' as a complete picture of the ideal educational for dissenting ministers and as a document through which the community of dissenting ministers could define its intellectual projects. This evidence also strongly indicates that Doddridge kept a personal copy of 'An Account of Mr Jennings's Method', perhaps to consult in his own work as a tutor. The dual aims of the 'Account' are contained in its genre and physical form: its immediate aim was to develop a new academy in a communal, friendly way. Its long-term use was as a document to which a tutor could turn for guidance in matters of curriculum and conduct. Doddridge's successors took pride in restoring the 'Account' to its original purpose of facilitating improvement and collective action among dissenting tutors and ministers.

Through a series of discursive and textual strategies, Doddridge had created a certain reputation for this academy even before it opened. It would be learned, it would inculcate piety, and it would serve its communities, understood to be both the affiliative network of dissenting ministers with an interest in the continued education of future ministers (and with the authority to grant funds to chosen students through the charitable Boards of which they were trustees) and the local congregations which would be supplied with ministers. Ministers would form the connections between the learned world and the local community, and bonds of piety and scriptural knowledge would unite their different intellectual and social needs.

Doddridge's account of his own tutor's system generated an episode of intellectual friendly exchange in which written documents demonstrated and encouraged the qualities of polite, participative learning and improvement as the basis of an educational project which would further those very principles. Dissenting academies were sites where the values of polite culture were assimilated in the context of rigorous educational practices. The forms of textual production in and around academies provide significant evidence for this, as the following chapters will show.

---

[104] DWL NCL MS L.1/8/76, 22 April 1776. It has not been possible to identify 'Mr Legh'. Thomas Robins (1732–1810) was minister and tutor at Daventry academy from 1775 until 1781. Daventry academy was named by Doddridge as the successor to his own academy at Northampton.

This chapter began by introducing those features of dissenting conduct—friendship, guidance, feeling, conversation, and epistolarity—that characterized the clerical culture of moderate nonconformity in the eighteenth century. Having shown how these positive, affective, and communal qualities were presented by dissenters as belonging to the pedagogy and culture of dissenting academies, Chapters 2 and 3 will look at the specific content of lectures and processes of their dissemination within and beyond dissent. By considering the conjunction of intellectual activities with social, educational, and publishing conditions, the ways in which dissenting educational practices were shaped by apparently competing cultural demands can be understood. The construction of dissenting identity has elements of a 'counterpublic' on one hand (in that it identifies itself as subordinate to the dominant culture in some ways, for example) but dissenters were eager to put their educational work in conversation with the concerns of the public sphere on the other. This simultaneously inward- and outward-facing project forged a long-lasting and self-reflexive textual community.

2

Dissenting Academy Traditions

This chapter outlines the educational tradition of orthodox, moderate dissent by presenting subjects taught and approaches taken, principally in dissenting academies supported by Congregationalist charities, but also in other educational settings. It asks how and why certain educational models were disseminated and adapted, and considers the connections between academies and other sites where Protestant ministers were educated in the eighteenth century. Such relationships were personal and institutional, characterized by varying degrees of formality and public responsibility, and sustained by textual circulation in manuscript and print. The chapter concentrates on academies associated with Doddridge's own Congregationalist denomination in order to rebalance the weight of scholarly attention, which has tended to investigate Doddridge's legacy as found in heterodox traditions and Unitarian institutions associated with Warrington, Manchester, and Hackney academies. While it is undeniably the case that Doddridge was important to that particular tradition, connections across the spectrum of dissent in terms of both theology and pedagogy are just as significant for understanding the role Doddridge played in his own lifetime and afterwards in sustaining cross-denominational patterns for ministerial education.

In his first weeks as a tutor, Doddridge began to record 'An Account of the Exercises assign'd to my Pupils through out their whole Course' in a notebook. Beginning on 30 June 1729, he listed beside each student's name the task he had been set. In the first week, one of his students was to translate Pliny's letter to Erucius into English. In it, Pliny praises his friend Saturninus for his oratorical, epistolary, and poetic style in terms that would provide useful hints to the eighteenth-century student making the translation. In the second week, each pupil was assigned a different English essay to translate into Latin. One was set Francis Bacon's essay on death, another his essay on adversity, and a third was to translate Addison's *Spectator* essay on the immortality of the soul (*Spectator* 111). Though these students were candidates for the dissenting ministry, theology was by no means all their course covered. Proficiency in the classical languages and familiarity with contemporary polite writers (in Addisonian terms) was a feature of their education. The students were given classical and modern models of good morals and good expression to emulate from the start of their training, a practice which is consistent with the principles outlined in the preceding chapter.

Evidence of the teaching that took place at Doddridge's academy is richly documented in extant sources that include lecture notes (both his own and those made by students), remarks in letters, and printed texts of theological and preaching lectures. This chapter, which is about pedagogy and conduct, uses these sources to build a picture of intellectual work in and around Doddridge's academy and connected sites, in terms of ideas and practices. The processes of adaptation that shaped educational materials are considered in terms of denominational differences, methods of dissemination, and changes over time in order to draw out the particularities of the moderate orthodox dissenting tradition in England and its connections with Scotland, Europe, and North America. Doddridge and his activities provide the focus and starting point, but the chapter reaches beyond the example of particular academies to offer observations about the nature of dissenting international educational connections. Documents surviving from the academies and used here require careful explanation, as there is considerable variation in presentation and purpose across manuscript materials of different kinds. This chapter therefore attends to academy curricula, evidence of student activities, the use of printed books for presenting educational ideas, academic traditions of note-taking, and the circulation of lectures in social and material terms to draw out the distinctive properties of different documents that have been labelled 'academy manuscripts'.

Doddridge only recorded the exercises he had set for the first month in his 'Account of the Exercises'. But though the record of his teaching in this particular notebook is short-lived, his choice to use it at this time is significant. The volume had previously belonged to his own tutor, John Jennings, who had used it for a class-by-class timetable, various lists of books for students, dramatic scenes for students to improvise, and scripts of prologues and epilogues to dramatic stories. Doddridge had a practical resource to help him in his teaching. By using an item owned by his tutor to document his own first steps as a tutor he made a material connection between the two academies. He later used it to record books given to the academy, a list which shows that works Jennings had recommended to his pupils were donated to the academy started by his student, many of them by acquaintances who would have known Jennings. The contents of this notebook register the continuation of Jennings's intellectual tradition at Doddridge's academy, and in the 1770s and 1780s it was owned by a third dissenting tutor, Thomas Belsham at Daventry (the successor academy to

Doddridge's). The notebook became a site for informally storing the efforts and ideas of successive tutors. This use emblematizes the shared pedagogic culture at three dissenting academies over half a century.[1]

In his 'Account of Mr Jennings's Method', Doddridge described the course he had followed at the academy run by John Jennings. 'Academical exercises' very similar to those described above were part of the course:

> Our Academical Exercises were continued Weekly through the first and second Half Years; nor were they wholly laid aside in the third, tho' much more frequently omitted in that than in either of the former. We began with translating some select Passages from Latin into English, and from English into Latin. And I particularly remember that some pages in the Spectators, and Tatlers both serious and humourous were assign'd us on this Occasion. We used also to translate from one Style to another, v.g. to turn part of a Sermon of D[r] Tillotson into Sprats style, and vice versa; which oblig'd us to enter more critically into the Characteristicks in the Style of our most celebrated Writers than it is probable we shou'd otherwise have done.[2]

Doddridge states that one purpose of these exercises was to make students understand how those Anglican clergymen most highly regarded for their homiletic style achieved the effects for which their preaching was famed. Students were introduced to models of good style in secular and homiletic writings so that they might absorb these 'Characteristicks' into their own compositions from the beginning of their training. In the manuscript, 'Characteristicks' is written larger than the words around it and italicized, invoking the title of Lord Shaftesbury's 1711 compendium of philosophy, ethics, and wit. The conjunction of this word with the use of Addison by both Jennings and Doddridge indicates that these tutors intended to give fledgling ministers training in the verbal arts of politeness that followed Whiggish, urbane standards of conduct and discourse.

Doddridge's academy was modelled closely on that of his own tutor, and as Rivers has explained Doddridge had made an effort to understand the pedagogical and intellectual purpose of each aspect of Jennings's course before he began work as a tutor, from at least 1725.[3] By examining materials relating to the course that Jennings originated, and describing how it was presented and taught by Doddridge and his successors, this chapter traces one intellectual tradition within dissenting education that came to have a wide influence. It delineates academy life through facts,

---

[1] DWL NCL MS L185. A transcription of the timetables and booklists in this volume are available in *Dissenting Education and the Legacy of John Jennings, c.1720–c.1729*, ed. Whitehouse.

[2] Doddridge, 'An Account of Mr Jennings's Method', fol. 8.

[3] Rivers, *The Defence of Truth*, 12–13.

materials, representations, and in relation to comparable institutions in order to argue that the semi-formal circulation and use of certain materials contributed to a dispersed dissenting educational culture that had wide geographical coverage. This culture had some cross-institutional aspects, though individual freedoms of academies were preserved. In this respect, academies resembled the gathered churches they existed to support.

This chapter and the next are both about academy practices and publishing procedures over the best part of a century. The varied, complex uses of manuscript and printed materials in different academies at particular times are delineated in order to establish the practical characteristics of this educational tradition and to approach the question of how certain dissenting principles diffused into other educational traditions. To facilitate the analysis of these divergent factors, the chronology of the chapter is not strictly linear: scribal practices for the dissemination of teaching materials are pursued from the 1720s up to the 1800s before looping back to the 1730s in order to consider the representation of academies in print. The liberal character of the content and conduct of Doddridge's course presented here is the educational context to the publishing projects investigated in later chapters, for both the development of the lectures and the methods taken to circulate and adapt them over time marked out this particular dissenting way of education and intellectual life. The forms in which Doddridge circulated his own ideas about education and presented the example of his academy to other educators meant that his model of education became influential beyond his own tradition. But he insisted, at least initially, that he was following the example of his own tutor, John Jennings.

1. THE JENNINGS–DODDRIDGE TRADITION: CONCEPTS—CONTENTS—CONTEXTS

Students at Jennings's academy followed a four-year course, divided into eight semesters (known as 'half-years') which ran from September to January and February to June. The introductory phase of the course, occupying the first year and a half, consisted of lectures in mathematics and natural philosophy, classical languages and French, civil history, Jewish antiquities, and logic. In the fourth semester students completed their introductory studies and began pneumatology, the first part of the theological course and defined by Doddridge as the study of 'the doctrine of *Spirits*'.[4] For the

---

[4] *A Course of Lectures* (1763) Definition VII. For another definition, see Samuel Johnson, *An Introduction to the Elements of Philosophy* (London, 1744), 16–17.

third and fourth years, students concentrated on pneumatology, ethics, and divinity (the three components of the interconnected theological course devised by Jennings) while studying ecclesiastical history and the history of controversies, and preparing theological disputations and homilies. The final part of the course introduced lectures on preaching and pastoral care, which offered practical guidance on undertaking ministerial duties. Outside the lecture room, students practised public speaking and acted in dramatic interludes on Wednesday evenings and often began to preach publicly in their seventh half-year.[5] Throughout a student's four years at the academy, Bible reading in Hebrew, Greek, and French was a constant practice. Students were also encouraged to undertake additional reading on topics not covered in their lectures for a particular semester.[6] While the tripartite theological training formed the spine of the academic course, a significant feature of Jennings's system was that students received a wide grounding in the subjects of polite learning.

According to Isabel Rivers, 'four essential aspects of Jennings's course, which were of great importance to Doddridge' were the ordering of subjects, the use of references, pursuing a mathematical method and encouraging free enquiry.[7] Jennings himself emphasized that his pedagogy was unusual. In a draft letter to a prospective parent, he explained 'That I take None from other Academys . . . because my Scheme is So particular, I can build upon no Mans Foundation.'[8] In his accounts of Jennings's course, Doddridge stated that it was Jennings's arrangement of subjects across the course and presentation of information within each lecture which constituted that particularity. Structuring the course to facilitate liberal thought was evidently remarkable too, for Doddridge told Samuel Clark in a letter, 'M^r J encourages ye greatest freedom of Enquiry' before explaining that in teaching the central doctrines of Christianity, 'M^r J has not follow'd ye doctrines or phrases of any particular party; but is

---

[5] Doddridge started preaching in September 1722 at the beginning of his seventh half-year, to Jennings's congregation: see *Calendar* 31. He was examined in January 1723 by 'a committee of the neighbouring ministers . . . chosen for that purpose at a general county meeting': see Humphreys, I, 171. For Doddridge's account of the examination, see JRUL UCC MS B2, p. 134 (dated 26 January 1722); *Calendar* 48; Humphreys, I, 189–90 (dated 28 January 1723).

[6] Doddridge gave accounts of his reading in letters to Clark and Nettleton, from which it is clear that he maintained his classical reading even after he had completed the first half of the academy course: see JRUL UCC MS B2, p. 4. Jennings guided his students in their extra-curricular reading: 'it was by my tutor's advice, that I defer'd reading [Locke] entirely over till this half year.' Philip Doddridge to Samuel Clark, 13 December 1721. JRUL UCC MS B2, p. 1; *Calendar* 3; Humphreys, I, 41.

[7] Rivers, *The Defence of Truth*, 7.

[8] 'John Jennings's description of his academy, c.1720', in *Dissenting Education and the Legacy of John Jennings c.1700–1729*, ed. Whitehouse.

sometimes a calvinist, sometimes an arminian, & sometimes a Baxterian, as truth & evidence determine him.'[9] Doddridge was later to present this method as being as motivated by Jennings's conviction that free enquiry was essential to understanding Christianity, and that by following it, Jennings 'was animating us to the most laborious Enquiry after Truth'.[10]

The symbolic significance of free enquiry for dissenters should not be underestimated. It was fundamental both to an individual's understanding of religion and to the pedagogic principles of Jennings's academy, Doddridge's own, and those later academies of various denominations that made use of teaching materials from the Jennings–Doddridge tradition. Joseph Priestley, for instance, recalled that at Daventry academy, students 'were permitted to ask whatever questions, and to make whatever remarks, [they] pleased' and that the two tutors, Caleb Ashworth and Samuel Clark (both former students of Doddridge's), would argue respectively for the orthodox and heterodox side of theological questions.[11] By privileging and practising open debate, these educators believed they were sustaining their 'commitments to . . . openness', shown by Sharon Aichinstein to be one of the central intellectual modes of dissenting intellectual life.[12]

The openness Jennings and Doddridge prized was facilitated by the structure of the pneumatology, ethics, and divinity course, founded on what they called a mathematical method (i.e. a demonstrative approach) of 'Definitions, Propositions, Demonstrations, Corollaries, and Scholia'.[13] In 'An Account of Mr Jennings's Method' Doddridge observed that to Jennings, the value of mathematics was that it 'might render them [the students] capable of thinking with greater steadiness and Accuracy on other Subjects of Enquiry'.[14] Doddridge embeds this instrumental view within a broader idea about pedagogy, recommending that the course of education be considered holistically:

> this Thought shou'd be carried along with us in judging of all the Branches of a Scheme for Academical Education. Each Part is to be regarded in its

---

[9] Philip Doddridge to Samuel Clark, 22 September 1722. JRUL UCC MS B2, p. 94; *Calendar* 35; Humphreys, I, 156.

[10] Doddridge, 'An Account of Mr Jennings's Method', fol. 39.

[11] J. T. Rutt, *The Theological and Miscellaneous Works of Joseph Priestley*, 25 vols (London, 1817–32), I, i, 23–4. Quoted in Simon Mills, 'Joseph Priestley and the Intellectual Culture of Rational Dissent, 1752–1796' (unpublished doctoral dissertation, University of London, 2009), 31–2.

[12] Sharon Achinstein, *Literature and Dissent in Milton's England* (Cambridge, 2003), 19.

[13] Doddridge, 'An Account of Mr Jennings's Method', fols 11–12. As Rivers notes, this was the method of Newton's *Philosophia naturalis principia mathematica* (1687) and Spinoza's *Ethica more gemetrico demonstrata* (1677), but its use in ethics and divinity teaching was unusual. Rivers, *The Defence of Truth*, 8.

[14] Doddridge, 'An Account of Mr Jennings's Method', fol. 13.

Proportion & Relation to the rest, and the great Question is concerning the whole how far it is calculated to promote the usefulness of those that go thro it and not concerning the Provision which is made for Improvement in any single part of knowledge consider'd in an abstracted view.[15]

As well as highlighting usefulness as the goal of education, Doddridge here connects Jennings's idea that the skills developed in one sphere of education will form the basis of later patterns of learning with his own project of developing Jennings's course. He does so by extending the metaphor of learning as an organic whole. A body, constructed of interconnected parts, grows. Jennings's course, conceived as an organic body, not only *can* absorb additions but *requires* them.

Having created a framework within which the reader might assess his suggestions for the improvement of the course, Doddridge addresses each subject in turn. He emphasizes that the practice of mathematical enquiry should be continued for as long as possible, for 'This wou'd prevent that forgetfulness of these kinds of Operations' which are essential to maintain an active and interrogative mind.[16] Doddridge's account of the mathematical section of the course specifies the crucial role it was considered to play in preparation for the pneumatology, ethics, and divinity lectures which began later. To Doddridge, the connection between mathematical thinking and philosophical understanding articulated by John Locke was an essential component of Jennings's course:

would you have a Man reason well, you must use him to it betimes, exercise his Mind in observing the Connection of Ideas and following them in train. Nothing does this better than Mathematicks, which therefore I think should be taught all those who have the time and opportunity, not so much to make them Mathematicians, as to make them reasonable Creatures.[17]

Because Doddridge promoted and pursued a Lockean foundation for the academy curriculum from the outset and advocated it in person, in letters as well as the teaching he describes in his manuscript 'Account' and later in print, the principle that originated with Jennings became associated most strongly with Doddridge himself from 1730 onwards. The focus on mathematics and free enquiry, and the use of Locke's authority to justify such an approach, locates this educational tradition within rationalist epistemology. Practices of learning through investigation of nature were encouraged and the 'light of nature' was a popular concept in academy

---

[15] Doddridge, 'An Account of Mr Jennings's Method', fols 13–14.

[16] Doddridge, 'An Account of Mr Jennings's Method', fol. 15.

[17] John Locke, 'Of the Conduct of the Understanding', in *Posthumous Works of Mr John Locke* (London, 1706), 26.

teaching, indicating that metaphors of enlightenment as well as rational models of learning were not seen as antithetical to religious training.[18] Dissenting tutors participated in a culture of knowledge nourished by many traditions, neither exclusively scientific nor narrowly pious.

This contention is supported by the particular texts Doddridge identified as valuable in his proposals for improving Jennings's course. In order to secure this rational foundation for the course with the latest mathematical advances, he advocated that Jennings's treatment of physics be updated. His suggestions for the introduction of recent works on natural philosophy—such as Henry Pemberton's digest of Isaac Newton's *Principia* published in 1728—indicate that in this area Doddridge kept his reading up to date. Doddridge did adapt the course he taught in the way he suggests in 'An Account of Mr Jennings's Method'. Various notebooks of lecture notes survive which previously belonged to Jennings and have been added to by Doddridge or which contain Doddridge's version of Jennings's notes with further additions of Doddridge's own.[19] Doddridge's key suggestion for the development of the course was to enhance the element of practical experimentation. He anticipated the objection that purchasing scientific apparatus such as an air pump, a microscope, and a telescope would be too expensive and suggested that students give a partially refundable donation on entering the academy.[20] Notebooks owned by Doddridge contain additional diagrams of mathematical apparatus drawn by the tutor Caleb Ashworth, indicating that practical aspects of natural philosophy were promoted at Doddridge's academy and continued by Doddridge's successor.[21]

One purpose of Doddridge's proposed improvements was to reinforce the interconnected nature of the course of study. Proficiency in oriental

[18] DWL NCL MS L.185, Jennings's timetable for class VI.

[19] See, for example, the following DWL NCL MSS: L.227/1 is John Jennings's 'Arithmetica' with Doddridge's additions; L.113/1 is an 'Appendix to John Jennings's Algebra' in Doddridge's hand; L.114 is Doddridge's shorthand notes on John Eames's lectures on Anatomy. L.113/2, L.171, and L.559/1–12 are all notebooks of lecture notes in Doddridge's hand which bear marks of use by a later hand. Doddridge's use of notes by Eames, along with the presence of 'Phaenomena Hydrostatica *Per J.E.*' (i.e. 'John Eames') in John Jennings's volume for academy students, *Miscellanea in usum juventutis academicae* (Northampton, 1721), indicate the circulation of resources among dissenting tutors in the 1720s. Eames was tutor of the dissenting academy at Moorfields, London.

[20] In a letter Doddridge noted that Lady Russell had donated a pair of globes to the academy, and said he would welcome a microscope. Doddridge to Ebenezer Hankins, 10 May 1731. *Calendar* 358. The academy did receive a microscope from a Dr Beard: see Malcolm Deacon, *Philip Doddridge of Northampton, 1702–51* (Northampton, 1980), 98.

[21] In October 1753, the Coward Trust purchased the Northampton Academy apparatus from Doddridge's widow and transferred it to Daventry, and funds were allocated for the repair and improvement of the apparatus in 1759 and again in 1767. DWL NCL MS CT1 pp. 141, 172, and 203.

languages was important because of their connection to ecclesiastical history and biblical criticism, and all these subjects also supported the ethics and theology course. Doddridge devoted considerable space to presenting a connected and expanded way of teaching ancient, ecclesiastical, and civil history, and Jewish antiquities, and lecturing on scholarly accounts of the history of the Bible. The extant manuscript notebook in Doddridge's hand on Jewish antiquities suggests that Doddridge developed these parts of the course independently, perhaps drawing on his personal associations with scholars such as William Warburton and Nathaniel Lardner.[22]

Comparing Doddridge's suggested changes with what was taught at his own academy confirms that while there were some additions to Jennings's course, students at Northampton academy followed a curriculum relatively close to that instituted by Jennings in the 1710s. The range of studies in the non-theological part of the course—and the attention they received—is striking. As well as being important components of a general education, many of the preparatory subjects were thought to contribute to the theology course. Doddridge's careful explanation of the beneficial habits of mind formed by mathematical study, for example, or the framing of his discussion of historical study in terms of biblical understanding, demonstrate that in the educational programme instituted by Jennings, the entire system contributed practically and intellectually to ministerial training.

Doddridge's emphasis on the intellectual rigour demanded by Jennings and the way in which he foregrounds the traditional elements of a polite education in his account of Jennings's course show that the nature and purpose of the education provided by a dissenting academy was conceived by these tutors in terms of a wide world of learning and on the view that theological training could not be separated from endeavours that nourished scholarship across disciplines. That this was a key principle of Doddridge's own pedagogy is noted in both Job Orton's and Andrew Kippis's accounts of Doddridge's academy in their biographies of him. They each write that 'He was more and more convinced, the longer he lived, of the great Importance of a *learned* as well as a *pious* Education for the Ministry.'[23] Doddridge himself emphasizes that one of the central aspects of Jennings's educational philosophy was that expertise in classical, mathematical, philosophical, and theological subjects was not ancillary,

---

[22] A copy of Doddridge's lectures on Jewish antiquities in his own hand survives, DWL MS NCL L.102. These are in shorthand.

[23] Orton, *Memoirs*, 90. Kippis is borrowing from Orton at this point of his article in *Biographia Britannica*, V, 279.

but crucial to ministerial training. This tenet was absorbed and developed by Doddridge and transmitted to his own students. Some of those students became tutors in their turn, and these men continued Doddridge's practice of sustaining a curriculum that valued scholarship and supplementing it with fresh insights to such an extent that this enquiring, innovative, and collaborative method of developing teaching resources remained a characteristic of dissenting education in the Jennings–Doddridge tradition.

Though Doddridge modelled his own academy very closely on the one he had attended, his work as a tutor was also shaped by the wider structures of dissent. The way orthodox academies were funded and organized encouraged interaction with ministers and educators outside any single institution. Trusts organized on denominational lines such as the Congregational Fund Board and the Presbyterian Fund Board (both of which funded students at Doddridge's academy) played an important role. In the mid-eighteenth century a new educational Trust was formed to distribute the legacy of the wealthy merchant William Coward according to the terms of his will. The Coward Trustees had financial and doctrinal responsibilities for academies at Northampton, Daventry, Wellclose Square, and Hoxton.[24] Their power to appoint tutors, examine students, and purchase books and equipment contributed to the intellectual culture of moderate orthodoxy in these places and to the movement of tutors and teaching materials across academies.

Isaac Watts was a Coward Trustee from the foundation of the Trust until his death in 1748 and as such played a practical role in the lives of tutors and students. He was also an important presence in academy teaching. The informal advice he gave Doddridge in 1728 contributed to the intellectual tenor of Doddridge's academy and his printed works had a place in the curriculum of academies. There are references to sixteen of his published works in Doddridge's *Course of Lectures*, and copies of no fewer than twenty-five different titles were held in the libraries of academies of different denominations and intellectual tempers over the eighteenth century: at Homerton academy, Coward academy, and New College, Hackney; at Warrington and Manchester College (in Manchester and later York); and at Bristol Baptist College.

---

[24] This was in accordance with the terms of the will of William Coward, the wealthy dissenting layman who left money for the furtherance of ministerial training but insisted that Calvinist orthodoxy be maintained in the institutions he supported. See John Handby Thompson, *A History of the Coward Trust: The First Two Hundred and Fifty Years 1738–1988* (London, 1998). For the minutes of the trustees' meetings in the eighteenth century, see DWL NCL MSS CT.1–2.

Watts's work as a trustee led him to write books specifically for academy students. He told Benjamin Colman:

> there has been a considerable legacy left by one Mr Coward towards the education of Dissenting ministers, and he has sett Dr Guyse, Mr Neal, and myself at the head of it. we do what we can . . . to promote ye work of the plan which he fixed in London under Mr Eames, and in Northampton under Dr Doddridge. This put me upon drawing up a few questions this winter for the service of young students and young Christians, which I here take the freedom to transmitt to you. You will please to bestow them as directed.[25]

Questions Proper for Students in Divinity (1741) follows a catechetical method to prompt students to examine their knowledge and to articulate their doctrinal and biblical understanding. There is evidence that Doddridge used this in the final stages of ministerial training, for in the copy now in the John Rylands Library he wrote the names of eight particular students beside certain questions in section III, 'Practical and Casuistical Questions for Candidates of the Ministry, and young Preachers'. For instance, 'Mr Fawcett' (Benjamin Fawcett) is written beside the question 'What Encouragements would you give to one who is overwhelmed with a Sense of the Greatness, the Multitude and Aggravation of his Sins, in order to keep him from Despair?', while 'Mr Brabant' (Thomas Brabant, later Doddridge's assistant tutor) appears on page fourteen alongside 'What would you say to encourage those who are diligent in the Practice of Religion, but complain they feel no Pleasure in it?'. Both these students completed the academy course in 1741, indicating that Doddridge used this work of Watts's as soon as it was printed. The tutor developed the curriculum of his academy in conjunction with senior figures within his community and had recourse to their expertise in the lecture room.

2. THE CIRCULATION OF DODDRIDGE'S LECTURES: ADAPTATION

Complex patterns of borrowing and adaptation of teaching materials that took place at dissenting academies are richly documented. But reconstructing the Jennings–Doddridge educational culture from primary sources (rather than from published memoirs, for example) presents challenges. Numerous manuscript copies of lectures have survived and these provide a long spanning record of subjects taught and printed texts consulted, enabling 'the study of . . . widely shared practices', as Ann Blair

[25] Watts to Colman, 18 March 1740/1. MHS, *Proceedings*, 381.

puts it. As she also observes, there are interpretative difficulties associated with the use of notes, which are a source providing 'partial and scattered evidence'.[26] Many academy manuscripts are not named or dated, so it cannot be known who made them or when. They do not allow a complete chronological survey of the use of Doddridge's lectures, but instead provide snapshots of teaching in different academies at different times. Lectures in manuscript are not all alike: they range from rough notes taken in class to fair copies made retrospectively, from tutors' *aides-mémoires* through complete sets of student notes to professional transcriptions. Writing about student notes in early modern Europe and America, Blair notes that very few *Mitschriften* (drafts) survive in comparison to *Nachschriften* (fair copies), and though this is largely true for academy materials there are nevertheless some very rough notes still in existence.[27] Their survival highlights the considerable difference in appearance between full transcriptions of lecture propositions with attendant references, and informal collections of references or points.

Each written snapshot of academic endeavour is incomplete because the vast majority of the lectures are written in shorthand, which was integral to Doddridge's system, and was one of the first things students learned on arrival at the academy.[28] Other tutors also promoted the use of shorthand. In an introductory lecture, Caleb Ashworth explained to his students its two advantages: it allowed for swift copying of large quantities of material, and would 'prevent some Inconvenience from its being subject to every eye'.[29] What was to Ashworth a benefit of shorthand is an inconvenience to researchers unable to read the materials. Though the lecture notes cannot be read in their entirety, references to authors and page numbers are often given in longhand, and sometimes running heads are too. In these cases, different manuscripts can be compared to each other, and to printed editions of Doddridge's lectures. The conclusions that can be drawn from the comparison of manuscripts are specific to particular copies but the insights they offer, though partial, do reveal the ways in which different tutors used Doddridge's methods and materials. They not only confirm Blair's view that notes are an important source of information

[26] Ann Blair, 'An Early Modernist's Perspective', *Isis*, 95 (2004), 420–30 (421).

[27] Ann Blair, 'Student Manuscripts and the Textbook', in *Scholarly Knowledge: Textbooks in Early Modern Europe*, ed. Emidio Campi, Simone De Angelis, Anja-Silvia Goeing, and Anthony Grafton (Geneva, 2008), 39–74 (40).

[28] Doddridge, 'Life of Thomas Steffe' in Thomas Steffe, *Sermons on Several Subjects* (London, 1742), xiv. A variety of shorthand systems were in use during the eighteenth century. Doddridge developed a simplified version of Jeremiah Rich's method: see Françoise Deconinck-Brossard, 'La Sténographie de Philip Doddridge (1702–1751)', *Bulletin de la Société d'Études Anglo-Américaines des XVIIe et XVIIIe Siècles*, 12 (1981), 29–43.

[29] CHCN Blackmore MS 1, fol. 4.

about collective reading but also bear witness to these dissenters' collective culture of learning that names and celebrates honoured teachers, perpetuates valued methods, but adapts specific references in order to preserve a tradition while absorbing contemporary influences.[30]

The physical appearance of surviving educational manuscripts offers clues about academy pedagogy and practice. For example, paratextual features such as title pages to volumes (often with ink-ruled borders), division of a course into parts bound into volumes (each with its own title pages), and the inclusion of indexes recur in numerous volumes, constituting regular patterns in the production of lecture notes consonant with the practices of scribal publication. The presence of dates (usually marking the commencement and completion of the lectures or certain sections within a longer course) and the names of transcribers indicate efforts were made to record the details of time and place in documents anticipated to have ongoing and future use. That said, the fact that names are not always recorded suggests that the individual transcriber was less important than the originator in this process of scribal publication, for even in copies where the student transcriber is identified, his name is invariably smaller in size and less centrally placed than Doddridge's. The careful treatment and preservation of a relatively high number of sets of lecture notes indicates that academy tutors impressed on their students the importance of keeping durable records of their education. Making copies of lectures according to certain templates was not an ad hoc activity but a formal aspect of academy training. The process of composition was characterized by long duration over a number of decades and concurrent production: both elements served sociological as well as intellectual purposes by binding dissenting students into a 'scribal community' which shared and practised a particular body of knowledge which it produced and distributed for itself.[31] The manuscripts that enshrined that tradition were treated with care.

Charting the use of Doddridge's materials over time and in different academies is important because, though historians of dissent have tended to agree that his course was influential, the encouragement to read works from a variety of doctrinal and denominational perspectives meant that his system was contentious in some circles.[32] Doddridge's influence on

[30] Blair, 'An Early Modernist's Perspective', 426. An incomplete set of Caleb Ashworth's lectures on pneumatology, ethics, and civil government based on Doddridge's and made by Thomas Blackmore in the 1760s is in longhand (CHCN Blackmore MSS 1–3 and 6–9). Several sets of Doddridge's 'Lectures on Preaching' are also in longhand, see section 3.

[31] Harold Love, 'Oral and Scribal Texts in Early Modern England', in *CHBB*, IV, 97–121, 106–7.

[32] Evangelical dissenters such as the historians David Bogue and James Bennett, the Baptist Robert Hall, and Thomas Turton (the Regius Professor of Divinity at the University

dissenting education was certainly not straightforward, but it was remarkably long lasting. The ways in which teaching materials which originated with Jennings and Doddridge were used in later academies offer insights into the difficulties that different denominational circumstances or social pressures (within and beyond the academy) posed to tutors wishing to use these intellectually valuable teaching resources.

John Jennings's course was the basis for Doddridge's academy, and Doddridge acknowledged his intellectual debt to Jennings throughout his 'Account of Mr Jennings's Method' and in letters to friends. Once Doddridge was established as a tutor, though, the course became uniquely identified with him. Manuscript copies of lecture notes by him and his students are never attributed to Jennings, unlike teaching materials from later academies which often identify that they derive from Doddridge's.[33] Title pages of manuscripts attest to Doddridge's influence: 'Divinity Lectures Drawn up by P. Doddridge, D.D.', 'Lectures on Divinity chiefly extracted from the Books principally referred to upon that subject by Dr Doddridge Mr Belsham &c', 'A System of Theological Lectures drawn up by P. Doddridge DD.', and so on.[34] One possible reason for Doddridge's name outlasting Jennings's as an ongoing influence is temporality. Jennings was a tutor for less than a decade whereas Doddridge ran an academy for more than twenty years. Over that time, his academy became a far bigger operation than Jennings's, with a larger annual intake and more than one tutor. As Jennings had influenced Doddridge, so Doddridge's academy was an important precursor to later eighteenth-century institutions. His name is especially prominent in materials from Daventry academy, which was the immediate successor to Doddridge's own, and which was led for many years by his former student Caleb Ashworth. The web of friends, mentors, and former students that Doddridge wove may well have contributed to his enduring reputation, and his commitment to widening those circles—for example, by publishing—was in contrast to the more intimate stage preferred by Jennings, who published little, was not personally known to his contemporary Isaac Watts, and preferred students not to transfer to his academy from elsewhere.

Several full sets of student lecture notes for the pneumatology, ethics, and divinity course survive from Daventry academy, and indicate the close

---

of Cambridge in 1835) all objected to the freedom of enquiry promoted by Doddridge's course. See Rivers, *The Defence of Truth*, 27–8.

[33] The reasons for this are not clear. It is not possible to discover how extensively Doddridge altered Jennings's pneumatology course, because only the second part of the theology course survives: see DWL MS 28.117. One notable change Doddridge made was to teach in English rather than Latin.

[34] DWL MS 28.39, HMCO Heineken MS 6, DWL MS NCL L.29/12.

resemblance of the education there to the course taught by Doddridge at Northampton.[35] The evidence of the materials from Daventry indicates that over time, however, adherence to Doddridge's content and methods diminished. The survival of carefully written longhand volumes with elegant hand drawn title pages, and uniformly bound sequences of note-books written in shorthand, suggests that students valued the materials they were introduced to, and attempted to preserve them. While the considerable number of neatly copied and bound sets of notes strongly suggests that students were encouraged to preserve their notes for future reference, disparities in the appearance of surviving lecture notes makes it impossible to make any strong claims about student responses to the course. Ashworth retained almost all of Doddridge's materials, and refor-mulated the course within the categories and structure for theological study created by Jennings and developed by Doddridge, and it was probably due to this way of presenting the course that its association with Doddridge remained strong.

Ashworth and his successors used the printed text of Doddridge's *Course of Lectures* (1763) within their own lectures based on that course. The mingling of manuscript and printed sources for Doddridge's method and references characterized the course at Daventry, which remained rooted in the ideas of its originator while incorporating references to additional texts. The recurring use of materials attributed to Doddridge is comparable to the sustained European circulation of different copies of two particular sets of annotations on Copernicus. Blair suggests that these manuscript notes substituted for oral commentary from an acknowledged expert, 'and made possible a reading experience shared across distances of space and time'.[36] Such durational practices were not limited to sustained private reading of a single text but encompassed hearing lectures in a classroom setting and rereading notes and pursuing references. Connect-ing these deep reading practices with a named individual worked also to secure cultural authority for methods or texts which might otherwise, as Jonathan Topham has argued, become sites of contestation.[37] Given the potential for heterodoxy that the Jennings–Doddridge method of free enquiry opened up, keeping the method closely associated with the figure of Doddridge (who had a respectable public profile as an orthodox pub-lished author) regulated the disruptive potential of the method as well as

[35] DWL MS 28.35–44, CHCN Blackmore MSS, HMCO Heineken MS 6.

[36] Blair, 'An Early Modernist's Perspective', 425. The study of Copernicus commentaries is in Owen Gingerich, *An Annotated Census of Copernicus' De revolutionibus (Nürnberg, 1543 and Basel, 1566)* (Leiden, 2002).

[37] Jonathan Topham, 'A View from the Industrial Age', *Isis*, 95 (2004), 431–42 (432).

enabling dissenting educators to protect themselves from accusations of radicalism by invoking Doddridge's authority for their pedagogy.

An outline of how debates about the soul were taught in the later 1780s illustrates continuities with Doddridge's teaching and elements that changed over time in relation to growing unease about the spread of heterodox opinion in dissenting academies. The notes owned by the tutor Thomas Belsham from his time as a student do not follow Doddridge's course structure exactly but they are arranged according to the mathematical method. A further surviving set of notes which belonged to Nicholas Thomas Heineken (a student at Daventry between 1780 and 1785) are probably based on lectures delivered by Belsham, who was divinity tutor there from 1782 to 1789. The title page of this volume claims that the lectures draw on Doddridge's, but they have been further adapted. In particular the arrangement of the notes is rather different from Doddridge's mathematical method. There are occasional scholia, but no definitions or propositions. Doddridge's emphasis on presenting arguments from different sides is retained, but in the form of sequences of 'arguments' which are followed by numbered 'objections', which in turn receive 'answers'.[38] The structure, then, is reminiscent of but different from Doddridge's.

In respect of the other important aspect of the lectures—directing students to works on both sides of a question—Belsham, like his predecessors, follows Doddridge's example. The lecture on 'the materiality of the Soul' lists four references: 'Baxter on the Soul V. I', Priestley's *Disquisitions*, and 'Correspondence between Price & Priestley'.[39] Furthermore, Doddridge's own posthumously published volume of academy lectures in pneumatology, ethics, and divinity is used as a source. Students are referred to 'Doddridge's Lect^s. p. 204. 211', which is the section exploring the immateriality and immortality of the soul beginning at the definition 'The mind may be said to be corporeal, if thought arise from and be inseparably connected with a certain system of matter.'[40] Belsham presumably selected this passage because it could be used to show that Doddridge supported investigation into the question of the soul's mortality (a highly controversial topic) though the words 'may' and 'if' are heavily equivocal and certainly do not establish Doddridge's own views as heterodox. Belsham took advantage of the method of free enquiry endorsed by Doddridge to expose students to intellectually risky current debates. The example shows that pedagogic structures inherited by Belsham did not

---

[38] HMCO MS Heineken 6, fols 1–6; Mills, 'Joseph Priestley', 221–5.
[39] HMCO MS Heineken 6, fol. 49v.
[40] Doddridge, *A Course of Lectures* (1763), 204.

confine the tutor or his students to orthodox reading or require conformity to references selected forty years earlier.

The section of *A Course of Lectures* given as a reference here includes several references to the same work by Andrew Baxter as that given in the manuscript, as well as to Locke, Samuel Clarke, and Isaac Watts's *Philosophical Essays*.[41] The printed volume of Doddridge's lectures provided a body of materials which later tutors reinforced, supplemented, and modified in the lecture room and by guiding student reading and writing. In this case, the orthodox views on the immortality and immateriality of the soul presented by Doddridge are recommended to students and supplemented with reference to contemporary debates within dissent on the freighted subjects of materialism and philosophical necessity as represented by the exchange between Joseph Priestley and Richard Price.[42] The use of Doddridge in this way proves that though their own course was not in exactly the same form as Doddridge's, students at Daventry academy in the 1780s were familiar with the structure and content of those earlier lectures. Citing the printed volume of Doddridge's lectures affirmed to students (and any other interested parties such as Trustees) the consonance of the current theology tutor's teaching with the topics and texts approved by Doddridge. Belsham resigned from his post at Daventry in 1789 on account of his heterodox views on the Trinity and Simon Mills suggests that he actively endorsed mechanistic theories of the soul (such as those of Priestley and Hartley) in his teaching.[43] He may therefore have been using Doddridge's printed text to make clear the distinction between his personal opinions and the views demanded by those funding the academy.

Doddridge's teaching was also familiar to tutors pursuing highly orthodox and evangelical ministerial education at other Congregationalist-funded academies. John Conder, tutor at Mile End academy and later at Homerton, possessed a copy of the section of Doddridge's course on the evidences for Christianity.[44] The volume labelled 'Dr John Conder's copy of Doddridge's Lectures' is written in longhand, and the propositions and definitions have been matched to those of Doddridge's printed *Course of*

---

[41] Doddridge, *A Course of Lectures* (1763), 205–6.

[42] The doctrine was not particular to dissenters, however. See B. W. Young, '"The Soul-Sleeping System": Politics and Heresy in Eighteenth-Century England', *Journal of Ecclesiastical History*, 45 (1994), 64–81.

[43] Mills, 'Joseph Priestley', 224.

[44] Conder was committed to promoting orthodox doctrines and scholarly evangelicalism in the dissenting ministry. He insisted that ministerial students' academic and vocational commitment should be thoroughly tested before they could become ministers. Homerton academy in the 1780s was a very different academic environment from Daventry.

Lectures.[45] Conder may have used Doddridge's lectures as a source for his own, and elements of Doddridge's course certainly influenced the teaching at Homerton academy in the 1770s. Conder's theology course followed a mathematical method of definitions, propositions, and scholia, though the content is different from Doddridge's *Course of Lectures*: Doddridge's inclusion of metaphysics and moral philosophy in theology is not followed as there is no interweaving of different aspects of ministerial learning.[46] Though the mathematical method is retained, the way Doddridge used it to encourage free enquiry is not: orthodoxy (particularly relating to the Trinity) is emphatically reinforced throughout, and those with other ideas are referred to as 'our adversaries'.[47]

Dissenting educational institutions within Doddridge's own Congregationalist denomination shared pedagogic resources and methods in the service of quite distinct ideals of ministerial conduct and education. Furthermore, such heterogeneity of practice was welcomed by the pedagogical principles espoused by Jennings and championed by Doddridge. The ways in which Doddridge's pneumatology, ethics, and divinity lectures were preserved and reused indicates that later tutors saw the value of his system as a resource and took the opportunity afforded by its structure to add elements or rearrange them. This loose adoption of certain features of a given course was not the only possible means of using his teaching materials after his death, however, as the survival and circulation of Doddridge's 'Lectures on Preaching' shows.

3. THE CIRCULATION OF DODDRIDGE'S LECTURES: CONTINUITY

In 'An Account of Mr Jennings's Method', Doddridge opined, 'The Lectures on the art of Preaching are admirable, but might be improv'd by new References, and by adding a Chapter concerning the Character of our most celebrated practical Writers.'[48] Doddridge's own 'Lectures on

---

[45] DWL MS NCL L.29/11.
[46] DWL MSS NCL L.28/1–2. Volume one begins with an introductory lecture which outlines liberal education at Oxford, Cambridge, and Scottish universities (fols 1–9). The theology course of thirty-nine lectures covers dogmatic theology and scripture doctrines in detail. Volume one also includes lectures on preaching and pastoral care. Volume two contains lectures on Jewish antiquities, secular and ecclesiastical history, chronology, scriptural chronology, and notes on English preachers derived from Doddridge's 'Lectures on Preaching'.
[47] DWL MS NCL L.28/1, fols 16–19.
[48] Doddridge, 'An Account of Mr Jennings's Method', fol. 27.

Preaching' did precisely this, as manuscript copies of his lectures on preaching in Dr Williams's Library, Harris Manchester College Oxford, the University of Wales, and the Bristol Baptist College archive show.[49] The early lectures give summaries of the greatest nonconformist and Church of England preachers and orators of the seventeenth and eighteenth centuries, before moving on to practical advice for composing sermons and then offering detailed comments about the appropriate comportment for a minister while executing his pastoral responsibilities.[50] The one surviving manuscript copy of lecture notes that can be positively identified as coming from Doddridge's own academy contains twenty-two lectures which are in shorthand.[51] They appear to cover the same material and follow the same structure as later copies. There is great consistency in content and layout of the manuscript copies, indicating that these lectures were not adapted as freely as Doddridge's theology course.

As with the theology lectures, the majority of surviving lecture notes come from Daventry academy, affirming the particular strength and longevity of Doddridge's influence over the academy that succeeded his own. One shorthand copy was owned by Thomas Belsham, and the notes were completed in July 1768, when he was a student at the academy. A second set belonging to Heineken may well be of lectures delivered by Belsham a generation later. Names of the preachers recommended, and even the order in which they were listed, are identical in each copy, and there are virtually no differences to the order of lectures or the topics covered between these two shorthand copies made by Daventry students.[52] Doddridge's lectures provided the formal guidelines for ministerial practice for three generations of dissenting ministers. Tutors used lectures that they had heard as students, and this helped define an enduring homiletic tradition among ministers trained in orthodox Congregationalist

---

[49] The manuscripts are: DWL MSS 24.179.11, 28.44, 69.21, NCL MSS L.28/3, L.29/22, L.29/23, L.29/24, HMCO MSS Heineken 10 and Belsham 7, The Roderic Bowen Library and Archives, University of Wales, Trinity Saint David MS UA/TP/8, and BBC MS G 93. No full survey of all these manuscripts has been made before.

[50] For the range of published guides to pulpit oratory in the period, see Françoise Deconinck-Brossard, 'The Art of Preaching', in *Preaching, Sermon and Cultural Change in the Long Eighteenth Century*, ed. Joris van Eijnatten (Leiden, 2009), 95–130.

[51] DWL MS NCL L.29/22. The title page reads: 'Lectures on the Composition & Delivery of Sermons Prayer ye Administration of ye Sacraments & other Branches of the Ministerial & Pastoral office By P Doddridge DD Northampton 1744'.

[52] Samuel Henley's set contains shorthand notes on twenty-two lectures (DWL MS 28.44), and the volume ends 'Finis. Sept. 17th. 1761'. DWL MS 24.179.11 is a longhand copy made by Samuel Palmer. It is not dated, but as he joined Daventry academy in 1759 and took up his first ministerial post in 1762 it is likely that he made this transcription in 1761 or early 1762. The copy, containing nineteen lectures, is not complete. Blackmore's notes do not include the preaching lectures.

academies which combined features of what Nigel Aston has called the age's 'predominant homiletic style . . . of the *simplicitas evangelica*' associated with the Restoration Church of England clergymen Robert South and John Tillotson with a specifically nonconformist style characterized by the best aspects of preachers selected from seventeenth-century puritans and nonconformists, and eighteenth-century dissenting ministers.[53] Doddridge's lectures influenced ministerial attitudes towards their pastoral duties as well as their manner of preaching through the guidance about behaviour they provided.

The 'Lectures on Preaching' were considered to be important by educators of other nonconformist denominations. In 1779, the Bristol Education Society, which administered the Bristol Baptist College, paid one guinea for a professional transcription of Doddridge's preaching lectures.[54] This copy is the best-preserved manuscript of the 'Lectures on Preaching', being sturdily bound in leather. It is dated 1778 and is transcribed in longhand, with the verso pages left blank. The volume, which also contains lectures by David Jennings (tutor of Wellclose Square academy in London and John Jennings's brother) entitled 'The Christian Preacher' and extracts and summaries of lectures on preaching delivered by John Lavington, is paginated continuously throughout.[55] The copy contains cross-references: against Jennings's advice to use the voice to register emotion, it is noted that Doddridge 'cautions against overdoing in this matter see p. 107'.[56] A longhand copy now held at the University of Wales very closely resembles the Bristol copy (though it is in a different hand), to the extent that in each manuscript the same words or phrases are often underlined for emphasis. The number and arrangement of lectures is identical in the two copies, and both include navigation aids in the form of lists of contents and indexes of authors.

---

[53] Nigel Aston, 'Rationalism, The Enlightenment, and Sermons', in *The Oxford Handbook of the British Sermon 1689–1901*, ed. Keith A. Francis and William Gibson (Oxford, 2012), 390–405 (390).

[54] 'Cash Accounts of the Bristol Education Society, 1770' (no call number, collection of the Bristol Baptist College), Academic Year: 1778–1779: 'A transcript of Dr. Doddridges MS Lectures on preaching &c 1/1/0' (p. 9r). I am grateful to Kyle Roberts for this information.

[55] John Lavington (*c.*1715–1761) was a Presbyterian minister and tutor educated at Moorfields academy by John Eames, before settling in the West Country. His academy appears to have been established in Ottery St Mary, Devon in 1751. See David L. Wykes, 'Lavington, John (*c.*1690–1759)', *ODNB*. The section covering his lectures in BBC MS G 93 is nineteen pages long. The material is presented as supplementary to the rest of the volume, for the transcriber alerts the reader to points of overlap between Lavington and Doddridge.

[56] BBC MS G 93, p. 352.

Another longhand copy of the lectures survives in the New College Collection.[57] It is similar to the Bristol and University of Wales copies in nearly all particulars, being 'very neatly written, and containing twenty-four lectures. It also has an index of topics and authors and it notes, by way of a system of symbols, the denominational affiliation of the names listed and whether they are preachers or commentators. The close correspondence between these three copies indicates systematic efforts to make the lectures available to students in the last part of the eighteenth century. The influence of Doddridge's 'Lectures on Preaching' had extended beyond his students and contemporaries and scribally produced longhand copies rather than student-made shorthand ones were required for academy libraries.[58] As well as the personal mode of transmission by tutors who had been Doddridge's students, more formal scribal publications—that supplemented lecture texts supplemented with graphic explanatory tools—transformed Doddridge's lectures into a reference resource.

Tutors could also incorporate elements of Doddridge's lectures into their own lectures on preaching. John Conder added Doddridge's remarks on practical writers to the end of his own course. The list of authors, arranged chronologically into puritans, nonconformists, and dissenters 'of the present age', and followed by a section covering writers of the established church, is identical in names and order to the copies from Daventry and Bristol. The most significant addition to Doddridge's list of practical writers appears in two copies where there is a sketch of the character and preaching of Doddridge himself.[59] In the Bristol copy, this is attributed to Job Orton and is introduced with the confident assertion that 'To the Authors mention'd in the preceding Lectures may very properly be added Dr Doddridge.' Doddridge is characterized as embodying 'justness and sprightliness of Thought, clearness of Method, Propriety and Beauty of Stile . . . equal if not superior to any of the foregoing' and a summary of his devotional works and sermons is given.[60] Updating these lectures by incorporating their compiler pays tribute to Doddridge as an educator, indicates a pedagogic decision to bring the compendium up to date, and serves to write selected eighteenth-century dissenters into the canon of English preachers in terms that emphasize oratorical polish and rational methods of sermon composition.

---

[57] DWL MS NCL L.29/24. 'J. Stoddon 1779' is written on the flyleaf.
[58] The Bristol copy was held in the college library: see *An Alphabetical Catalogue of all the Books in the Library, belonging to the Bristol Education Society* (Bristol, 1795), 12.
[59] DWL MS NCL L.29/24, fols 314–16 and BBC MS G 93, pp. 261–3.
[60] BBC MS G 93, p. 261.

The fact that Doddridge and other recent writers are not routinely added to these lectures indicates that they were not usually considered by successor tutors to be open to additions and modifications. Indeed, John Conder's decision to keep Doddridge's remarks on practical writers together, rather than incorporate them into his own lectures, suggests that he considered this block of remarks a unit. The fact that they could unequivocally be said to register Doddridge's views only may also have been important. Perhaps later tutors presented Doddridge's remarks on writers as indicative of the views of an earlier age. It might also have been of benefit to tutors to present criticisms of preachers (some of which are quite sharp) as coming from Doddridge rather than themselves. Conder introduced the remarks by stressing Doddridge's high reputation:

> I have usually annexed yᵉ learned & ingenious Dʳ. Doddridges Characters of our most celebratᵈ English Writers you have yᵉ Dʳˢ: Sentiments of them & as you read yᵉ Authors you are to judge for yourself.[61]

Conder leaves open the question of whether Doddridge's assessments are accurate. His framing invites the students to do just what all Doddridge's own lectures encouraged—to judge for themselves—and thus the methods as well as the content represented by the name 'Doddridge' endowed later teaching activity with his cultural authority, legitimized the pedagogy of particular tutors, and contributed to a shared project of ministerial education across academies, decades, and denominations.

Lectures based on Doddridge's were in use in academies in different places up to fifty years after his death, though not in a fixed form. Even the 'Lectures on Preaching', which retained the most consistent form and content, were subject to change. While lectures associated with Doddridge's course are numerous, this pattern is not unique to him: Samuel Jones's lectures on Jewish antiquities circulated early in the century, David Jennings's lectures on preaching were also held at Bristol, and John Eames's mathematics lectures were used in several academies many decades after he had delivered them. One significant feature of dissenting education across denominations was that materials of one tutor were borrowed by other tutors, who adapted them. This process of adaptation is an important characteristic of Doddridge's pedagogy in particular though, for Doddridge himself had been suggesting how to improve and update teaching materials since before he became a tutor and he presented liberality (including freedom to offer one's own opinion) as necessary to

---

[61] DWL MS NCL L. 28/3, fol. 142. DWL MS NCL L.28/5 is another manuscript of the same lectures in shorthand which presents the material from Doddridge in the same way. It is dated 25 February 1780.

education. Doddridge applied the epistemological position of his tutor—
that the opinions of others should not be passively accepted—to his own
activities. His example apparently encouraged others to do the same and
authorized an adaptive, cumulative model of lecture use across dissenting
academies.

4. POLITE MINISTERS

The use of Doddridge's lectures to create and sustain cultural authority
for liberal models of orthodox education within dissenting educational
institutions was effected through numerous tutors affirming the status
of one figure. Doing so unified independent academies according to
central tenets. The mutually reinforcing positive capacities of piety and
learning were emphasized at all stages of the curriculum and in every
component of the course, which served to secure the conjunction of
politeness and religious purpose by identifying a recent history for
educational practices and renewing them for present and future generations of trainee ministers. The material and educational procedures
used to inculcate those virtues have been delineated in sections 1 to 3
of this chapter. In order to reflect on the complementary nature of the
secular and theological studies at moderate orthodox dissenting academies, I return now to the elements of academy life comprised in the
examples that opened this chapter: the blend of classical and modern,
literary and homiletic writers and the attention to practical skills as well
as theoretical knowledge.

Jennings and Doddridge both insisted that a dissenting education
provided students with a range of skills. By doing so they positioned
their academies as comparable, or even preferable, to the universities of
Oxford and Cambridge and suggested that the education they provided
developed the taste as well as learning of a gentleman. For reasons
elaborated in Chapter 1, establishing the intellectual and social status of
academy-trained ministers was a vital but troublesome matter for orthodox moderate dissenters. Take the 'Lectures on Preaching', which devote
as much attention to manners as to doctrine. It is the oratorical qualities of
various preachers as much as their piety that qualifies them for inclusion,
and the guidelines regarding behaviour that complete the lectures are
detailed. The young minister is, for example, recommended particular
catechisms to teach to children (including Isaac Watts's), and told how
a baptism ceremony should be conducted. This includes tips on how a
minister should behave at the post-ceremony party: 'Allow yourself inter-
vals of moderate cheerfulness, but rather err on the grave extreme; and

always retire as early as you conveniently and decently can.'[62] Advice is given on the most practical and sensitive way of visiting sick congregation members, and how to behave towards other ministers. The 'Lectures on Preaching' also contain sketches of the content and strengths of various Protestant commentators on the Bible including Erasmus, Calvin, Saurin, Locke, Witsius, William Whiston, Nathaniel Lardner, and others. The good minister conducts himself in an open but seemly way and preaches effectively. He can do so because he is a skilled orator with deep knowledge of scripture, adept in the use of scholarly resources, all of which is thanks to his academy training.

Soon after commencing his tutorial activities, Doddridge chose to demonstrate publicly the place of learned politeness in the piety of the educated moderate dissenting ministry as part of a pamphlet controversy. In *An Enquiry Concerning the Causes of the Decay of the Dissenting Interest*, Strickland Gough, a young Presbyterian minister who later conformed to the Church of England, made various suggestions for enhancing the status of dissent. He wished to have congregations run by more refined ministers with the intention of encouraging a better class of citizen to attend dissenting meeting houses. To Gough, it was very important that dissenting ministers cut an elegant figure in the world. One way of effecting this, he suggested, was for dissenting academies to provide a politer education. Gough's ideas included incorporating belles lettres, public speaking, and even dancing into the curriculum of a dissenting academy.[63] These might appear to mirror some of Doddridge's priorities in 'An Account of Mr Jennings's Method', in which he explained at length the structure of Wednesday afternoon drama and music performances and emphasized the importance of oratorical training.[64] Doddridge, however, used his (anonymous) response to stress the importance of applying Christ's example of humility to the work of a minister, rather than prizing worldly attainments. The public nature of this debate about politeness is as significant as the particular examples adduced in the arguments made by each side. Indeed, the print circumstance of the incident not only determined Doddridge's stance (including the choice to remain anonymous and thus put dissent and not himself at the centre of the debate) and his proposals, but also enacted a strong demonstration of the effective guidance to appropriate conduct in public debate inculcated by a dissenting

---

[62]   Doddridge, *Works*, V, 484.
[63]   Strickland Gough, *An Enquiry Concerning the Causes of the Decay of the Dissenting Interest* (1730), 43.
[64]   Doddridge, 'An Account of Mr Jennings's Method', fol. 10.

education and testified to Doddridge's confidence in speaking for his tradition, for this was his first publication.

The title of his pamphlet—*Free Thoughts on the Most Probable Means of Reviving the Dissenting Interest*—emphasizes its aim to be undogmatic and claims a certain degree of informality for the responses to Gough it contains by evoking, perhaps, the essayistic and conversational discursive models advocated by Shaftesbury.[65] Doddridge explains that he chose this title rather than '*a farther Enquiry into the causes of the decay of the Dissenting Interest*' because 'it seem'd most respectful to you' and so that 'I may not appear to advance any direct charge against any of my brethren in the process of this discourse.'[66] Maintaining harmony while attempting to express differences of opinion is thus foregrounded by Doddridge as an important dimension of candid, polite conduct that was recognizably influenced by early eighteenth-century Whig culture but oriented particularly to dissenters in this context of a debate about balancing the requirements of piety and politeness. In part this is effected by using his pamphlet's title to evoke the social benefits of dissenting education in the Jennings–Doddridge tradition that valued free enquiry. In this respect Doddridge is in accord with Gough, who begins his pamphlet by remarking that liberality of thought had characterized puritanism and should be retained by dissenters:

> The fundamental principle of the dissenters is, as I apprehend, a *liberty* for every man to form his own sentiments, and to pursue them by all lawful and regular methods; to disclaim the *impositions* of men, and to worship God according to the dictates of his conscience.[67]

Gough celebrates this principle, but regrets the recent tendency of dissent to fall into factionalism. He finds that internal disputes have damaged dissent's reputation in the world, and the poor manners and strange preaching style of its ministers have discouraged the laity from attending dissenting meetings. These are the two principal reasons for the decline in dissenting congregations. Since 'the credit of the interest can only arise from the learning and piety of those engag'd in it', dissenting education must be improved if dissenters wished their congregations to grow.[68]

---

[65] Klein, *Shaftesbury and the Culture of Politeness*, 114. For the influence of Shaftesbury on Doddridge's views about the regulation of the senses and the argument that Shaftesbury's encouragement of raillery 'is the corollary of the toleration of religious Dissent in the Whig state', see Jon Mee, *Romanticism, Enthusiasm and Regulation: Poetics and the Policing of Culture in the Romantic Period* (Oxford, 2003), 40–3 (41).

[66] Philip Doddridge, *Free Thoughts on the Most Probable Means of Reviving the Dissenting Interest* (London, 1730), 5.

[67] Gough, *An Enquiry*, 6.   [68] Gough, *An Enquiry*, 35.

While Gough and Doddridge agreed that promoting a polite and learned ministry ought to be a priority, their reasons for doing so were very different. Though it is clear from his 'Account of Mr Jennings's Method' that Doddridge prized thorough and wide-ranging learning, in print he warned against the 'mistaken haughty way of thinking' certain modes of polite education could engender. In *Free Thoughts*, he defines learned accomplishment differently to Gough:

> I cannot imagine that a man of tolerable sense, who is every day conversing with some of the finest writers of antiquity, and who is (as most of our students are) a little exercised in the mathematical sciences, (to teach him attention of thought, and strength, and perspicuity of reasoning) will be in great danger of saying any thing remarkably impertinent, or contemptibly low.[69]

Doddridge used his pamphlet to promote the idea that trainee ministers ought to concentrate on developing their warmth, honesty, and piety. Learning was important from a personal point of view, but the pastoral care of 'an honest mechanick, or day-labourer, who attends the Meeting from a religious principle' should be a minister's priority and ministerial education should emphasize these duties.[70] Doddridge thus contributed to articulating a distinctively dissenting model of professional comportment characterized as candid and polite.

Doddridge continued this process publicly a decade later in his next published work to address the topic of education for the dissenting ministry. In 1742, an octavo volume was published entitled *Sermons on Several Subjects* by Thomas Steffe, a young dissenting minister who had died in 1740 at the age of twenty-four. As well as containing ten of Steffe's sermons, there was a biographical sketch of their author written by Doddridge. The first part of this memorial is an account of the course of learning at the academy Steffe attended, which was Doddridge's own. The summary of the course of education lists the subjects covered: classical languages, logic, rhetoric, and metaphysics, mathematics and natural philosophy, Jewish antiquities, ecclesiastical history and pneumatology, ethics and divinity. The account also emphasizes the participation of students at the academy in the life of the congregation. Steffe joined 'a *Society of private Christians*, who met at stated Times for religious Discourse and Prayer' which 'consisted ... of Persons in lower Ranks of Life', and Doddridge highlights Steffe's humility and pleasure at being accepted into this society.[71]

---

[69] Doddridge, *Free Thoughts*, 37.   [70] Doddridge, *Free Thoughts*, 14.
[71] Doddridge, 'Life of Thomas Steffe', xxvii. This was the first time a detailed account of the curriculum of a dissenting academy had been set out in print since the 1703 pamphlet

As well as demonstrating the local, practical component of the ministerial training Steffe undertook, Doddridge emphasizes the learned scope of the academy in a summary of his 'Account of Mr Jennings's Method'. Doddridge's public description of his course repeats the claim for the intellectual benefits of mathematical studies as providing 'steady Command of Thought, and Attention of Mind' and 'the Tendency they have, to teach us to distinguish our Ideas with Accuracy, and to dispose our Arguments in a clear, concise, and convincing Manner'.[72] Doddridge extends the scope of this description by weaving advice to readers into an account of the practices of the academy. He introduces readers of the 'Life' to new books he considers remarkable. After noting the study of ecclesiastical history, he pauses to promote '*Lampe*'s admirable *Epitome* . . . which I mention because I wonder it is not more generally known, though so very far superior to any thing else of the like kind, for the vast Variety of judicious Hints which it contains' and recommends Buddaeus's *Compendium historiae philosophicae*.[73] Neither of these works was printed in England. By making these comments and introducing these texts, Doddridge is offering his views on the intellectual climate of the times and inviting readers to participate in a learned world of debate about new books throughout Europe within the frame of a biographical sketch that describes a dissenting academy.

By describing his academy in print in this way, Doddridge asserts his conviction of the necessity of a rigorous and effective education. He promotes his own academy's focus on a continually evolving curriculum which entails the introduction of new reading as new books are published, and experimentation with new teaching methods without overtly challenging other versions of higher education. He is presenting the practices, principles, and results of a dissenting academy education founded on lectures, reading, and practical activities to an open audience. The polite yet familiar tone of the work—in which he uses the passive voice and does not identify himself as Steffe's tutor—is a tool for presenting a memorial that also functions as an advertisement and does so without contravening decorum. This is both an innovative use of the memorial form and an

---

dispute between Samuel Wesley and Samuel Palmer. Samuel Wesley, *A Letter from a Country Divine to his Friend in London. Concerning the Education of the Dissenters* (London, 1703); Samuel Palmer, *A Defence of the Dissenters Education in their Private Academies* (London, 1703).

[72] Doddridge, 'Life of Thomas Steffe', xv.

[73] Doddridge, 'Life of Thomas Steffe', xvi. The works he refers to are Johannes Buddaeus, *Compendium historiae philosophicae* (Halle, 1731) and Friedrich Adolphus Lampe, *Synopsis historiæ sacræ ecclesiasticæ ab origine mundi ad præsentia tempora* (Utrecht, 1721).

example of the literary characteristics of Doddridge's writing. The form of the volume (a narrative biography and a series of sermons) combines a description of Doddridge's academic and pastoral course with a demonstration of the results of his educational programme. The sermons serve as a recommendation for the educational method; the biography as a template by which to form pious and learned young ministers.

5. INTERNATIONAL ANGLOPHONE EDUCATION FOR THE PROTESTANT MINISTRY

So far this chapter has focused on dissenting academies, but the existence of printed accounts of dissenting education raises the matter of moderate dissenters' presence on a bigger educational stage. Though Doddridge produced no other account of his academy during his lifetime, the 'Life of Steffe' and Doddridge's own reputation as a preacher, writer, and educator were sufficient to spread knowledge of his academy beyond his immediate circle. When Richard Newton—engaged in the process of refounding Hertford College, Oxford in the 1740s—wrote to Doddridge requesting an account of his academy, Doddridge sent him a copy of *Sermons on Several Subjects*, which included the 'Life of Steffe'.[74] The statutes for Hertford College drawn up by Newton emphasize the religious and social discipline expected of students. The example of the more closely supervised activities of students at dissenting academies may have informed efforts to combat the perceived intellectual and disciplinary laxity at the university, for Doddridge received a draft of the statutes (which were printed in 1747) some time before 1744. Newton may have been prepared to incorporate Doddridge's views and suggestions into the regulations for Hertford College, for he explains in the preface that the primary reason for printing the statutes is so that 'he may the better collect the Thoughts of serious Men concerning them, and have Opportunity to make such Alterations therein, as he shall be well Advised are Proper to be made'.[75] Doddridge thus participated in the exchange of ideas about the structures of education in the universities as well as in dissenting academies.[76]

---

[74] *Calendar* 947, 961. Newton's response—that 'there is no harm in making a perfect model'—indicates that he considered the portrayal of Steffe to have been an idealization, and that he feared his own students would not meet Steffe's standards of piety and diligence.

[75] Richard Newton, *Rules and Statutes for the Government of Hertford College* (London, 1747), iii–iv.

[76] Doddridge maintained correspondence with several Fellows of Oxford and Cambridge colleges, including Thomas Hunt of Hertford College, Professor of Hebrew.

There were also ties between Doddridge's academy and some Scottish universities. Several of his students (including Benjamin Fawcett) began or completed their education there; James Robertson, for example, was first Doddridge's student, then his assistant and later Professor of Hebrew at Edinburgh. Doddridge had a particularly strong intellectual and social affinity with Marischal College, Aberdeen, which bestowed his first honorary DD degree (in 1736), and was the alma mater of his correspondent David Fordyce (a lecturer at Marischal College between 1742 and 1751).[77] Wood has concluded that their correspondence 'strengthened the ties between Marischal College and leading dissenters in England'.[78] These personal connections notwithstanding, the influence of Doddridge's teaching, writing, or correspondence on the teaching in Scottish universities or vice versa is difficult to plot fully. The most significant connection appears to have been that Doddridge read carefully in the new works of moral philosophy emerging out of the Scottish universities by lecturer-authors such as Hutcheson, Turnbull, and Fordyce, all of whom appear as references in the section of his course of lectures that covers ethics.[79]

There is undoubtedly more to be said about the connections between English dissenting academies and the Scottish universities.[80] Given the need to wait until more data is available before reaching further conclusions, however, it is currently more fruitful to pursue the links forged by Doddridge and Watts with tutors and institutions across the Atlantic. Decades ago, Bernard Bailyn insisted on 'the importance of the English dissenting academies for American history', declaring:

> Examination should be made of the direct transfer of people, books, and ideas from nonconformist institutions to America... the general story of the flow of ideas between the English academies and the American schools and colleges—part of an intimate world of Anglo-American dissent—remains to be told.[81]

---

[77] Paul B. Wood, *The Aberdeen Enlightenment: The Arts Curriculum in the Eighteenth Century* (Aberdeen, 1993), 50–5; Mills, 'Joseph Priestley', 26; Thomas P. Miller, *The Formation of College English: Rhetoric and the Belles Lettres in the British Cultural Provinces* (Pittsburgh, 1997), 95, 162–3.

[78] Wood, *The Aberdeen Enlightenment*, 55. The direct influence of Fordyce on Doddridge's teaching was minimal, according to Mills, 'Joseph Priestley', 27 and Rivers, *Reason, Grace, and Sentiment*, II, 181–3.

[79] Mills, 'Joseph Priestley', 25–8.

[80] For Scottish connections with Warrington academy, see Mills, 'Joseph Priestley', 41–52. Further information will be provided in *The History of the Dissenting Academies in the British Isles*.

[81] Bernard Bailyn, *Education in the Forming of American Society* (New York, 1960), 64–5.

Since then, the relationship between American education and English dissenters in this period has often been described from an American perspective, but it was significant on both sides of the Atlantic.[82] For English dissenters, communicating with American educators continued a tradition of transatlantic religious friendships ongoing since the seventeenth century. Isaac Watts was particularly important in this respect. From the 1720s he corresponded with the Boston minister Benjamin Colman. As well as exchanging personal and religious news, Watts frequently sent gifts of books for the colleges of Harvard and Yale. In March 1730 he wrote:

> I have packt up all my writings at your request in a square box & directed every book to Yale College in New-England. Tis better it should be ye author's present than from any other hand. You are desired to convey it to them, with my hearty service to ye Rev Mr Williams, their Rector, whose character is very bright as I am informed.[83]

This example is characteristic of Watts's interactions with Colman. The traffic of knowledge is not in one direction only: Watts does not just donate books but informs himself of the people involved in ministerial education. Eight years later, he wrote directly to the bright-charactered Williams in response to a request:

> As for your want of Calvinisticall writers in your library, or moderate men on y^t side, I have herewith sent you in a box directed to Dr Colman of Boston for Yale College Mr Howe's Works, 2 vol., Dr Bates's Works in 1 volume, & Dr Ridgely's Body of Divinity in 2 volumes. I hope you will receive them safe as a token for my zeal for truth & respect to you. Dr Ridgely died quickly after his 2 vol^s were printed. You will find therein too large a discourse (in proportion) on the doctrine of ye Trinity, in the explication of which he was so singular that I know of no followers he has.[84]

Thomas Ridgely had been tutor at Moorfields academy in London. By sending the *Body of Divinity* (1731–1733), which expounded the Westminster Assembly's catechism and was based on Ridgely's lectures, Watts provided teaching materials that communicated orthodox Calvinist doctrines to

---

[82] James Axtell, *The School Upon a Hill: Education and Society in Colonial New England* (New Haven, 1974); Lawrence A. Cremin, *Traditions of American Education* (New York, 1977); Mark A. Noll, *Princeton and the Republic, 1768–1822: The Search for a Christian Enlightenment in the Era of Samuel Stanhope Smith* (Princeton, 1989). Some of Bailyn's questions are anticipated in Francis L. Broderick, 'Pulpit, Physics and Politics: The Curriculum of the College of New Jersey, 1746–1794', *William and Mary Quarterly*, 3rd ser., 6 (1949), 42–68.

[83] Isaac Watts to Benjamin Colman, 4–5 March 1729/30. MHS, *Proceedings*, 332.

[84] Watts to Elisha Williams, 7 June 1738. MHS, *Proceedings*, 336. Doddridge became acquainted with Williams in 1750, after the latter had resigned his position at Yale and become an army chaplain. He married the daughter of a friend of Doddridge's.

ministerial students across the Atlantic but took care to articulate his own reservations about the piece for the Yale tutor to bear in mind. Sending the works of Howe and Bates provided American colleges with the key works of seventeenth-century nonconformists. Watts was responding to Williams's request for orthodox books by promoting an English intellectual tradition in America.

Like Richard Newton in Oxford, Aaron Burr—the second principal of the College of New Jersey (which later became Princeton)—also sent Doddridge documents relating to the foundation of his college.[85] Doddridge evidently responded with a copy of Steffe's sermons, for Burr responded enthusiastically to the portrayal of Doddridge's diligent students, 'a delightful specimen of which I had in Mr Steffe' and requested that Doddridge compose 'A Letter of Advice to the students under my care, which is so much needed'.[86] Burr described the growth and conduct of his college, expressed his own ambitions for the education he offered, asked Doddridge's advice on potential teachers of oriental languages, sought information about Doddridge's method of teaching ecclesiastical history, and suggested that ministers trained by Doddridge travel to New England to work as tutors.[87] Doddridge supported the intellectual and pedagogical development of the college in America by offering Burr advice and by sending books to the college library. These exchanges partly account for what Broderick identified as a 'striking resemblance between the English dissenting academies and the college of New Jersey in its early period'.[88] Evidently the college's early tutors actively sought to model their college on successful English academies.

Books and letters were important intellectual and material tools in the cultivation of friendly transatlantic religious and educational relations. They served performative, symbolic, and practical functions. Though a less untiring benefactor than Watts, Doddridge also sent books to Yale and the College of New Jersey and provided interested Americans with epistolary and printed accounts of his academy.[89] Those on the American

---

[85] Burr refers to an enclosed 'Copy of our Charter for erecting a College', no longer extant: see Aaron Burr to Philip Doddridge, 24 November 1748, *Calendar* 1420.

[86] Aaron Burr to Philip Doddridge, 8 October 1749, *Calendar* 1544. There is no evidence that Doddridge sent any such letter of advice.

[87] Aaron Burr to Philip Doddridge, 8 October 1749 (*Calendar* 1544); 31 May 1750 (*Calendar* 1616); 26 September 1750 (*Calendar* 1661). Burr notes that he hopes to teach Hebrew to a higher level than he was taught it at Yale College.

[88] Broderick, 'Pulpit, Physics and Politics', 45.

[89] DWL NCL MS L.1/8/104. Burr also received donations of books from Scottish divines, including John Erskine. See L.1/4/157 and Yeager, *Enlightened Evangelicalism*, 189; Thomas Clap, *The Annals or History of Yale-College, 1700 to 1766* (Boston, 1766), 98; Philip Doddridge letters to Daniel Wadsworth, *Calendar* 663 and 705.

side lacked a developed scholarly and theological publishing industry, so for them donations were essential and advice was gratefully received. By sending books, English dissenters were directly intervening in the learned world of the American colleges by stocking the libraries. They saw this as an important duty. But the practice also strengthened sympathetic ties between English dissenters and American educators.[90]

Watts and Doddridge's own works were well represented in the libraries of colonial-era American colleges.[91] This was partly because of the gifts of books they themselves donated, of course, but their writings found their way into the colleges by other means. In 1755, the College of New Jersey accepted a large donation of books from Jonathan Belcher, the governor of New Jersey who had granted the charter for the founding of the college. Titles included Watts's *Improvement of the Mind, A Short View of the Whole of Scripture History*, and several sermons, Doddridge's substantial work *The Family Expositor*, and the works of English nonconformist writers including Elizabeth Rowe, Daniel Defoe, and the ministers John Howe and William Bates. Belcher was also acquainted with Watts, who sent thanks to him for distributing the contents of a packet of books in Massachusetts in 1736.[92] Watts and Doddridge were strong presences in Harvard College library both before and after the fire that devastated it in 1764. In the case of Doddridge, the printed catalogue of 1773 records 'all his works', which must have been acquired as single titles (since his collected works were not published until the nineteenth century) and from sources other than the author, who had died in 1751.[93] The more detailed 1790 catalogue lists individual books and pamphlets by category and contains a similar number of sermons by each man, as well as several editions of *The Family Expositor*, most of Watts's educational works, and his six-volume collected *Works*.[94] The evidence of the Harvard catalogues tells us that Watts and Doddridge kept their place in America's largest

[90]   David D. Hall, 'Learned Culture in the Eighteenth Century', in *A History of the Book in America: The Colonial Book in the Atlantic World*, ed. Hugh Amory and David D. Hall (Cambridge, 2000), 411–33 (413–15).
[91]   Mark Olsen and Louis-Georges Harvey, 'Reading in Revolutionary Times: Book Borrowing from the Harvard College Library, 1773–1782', *Harvard Library Bulletin*, new ser., 4 (1993), 57–72, esp. table five and table six.
[92]   Watts to Colman, 13 September 1736. MHS, *Proceedings*, 350; *A Catalogue of Books in the Library of the College of New-Jersey, January 29th 1760* (Woodbridge, Mass., 1760), 12–13, 34–5; Clap, *The Annals or History*, 97.
[93]   *Continuatio Supplementi catalogi librorum bibliothecae Collegii Harvardini* (Boston, 1735) and *Catalogus Librorum in Bibliotheca Cantabrigiensis selectus* (Boston, 1773), both repr. in *The Printed Catalogues of the Harvard College Library 1723–1790*, ed. W. H. Bond and Hugh Amory (Boston, 1996), 112, 142, 158.
[94]   *Catalogus Bibliothecae Harvardinae*, in *The Printed Catalogues of the Harvard College Library*, ed. Bond and Amory, 311, 336, 369, 451, 518.

academic library throughout the century. Furthermore, Americans who did not know Watts or Doddridge personally recommended their books to students. Samuel Johnson (the first principal of the Anglican King's College, which later became Columbia) wrote several introductory textbooks while a junior tutor at Yale in which he listed Watts as a source for the study of logic, metaphysics, astronomy, and pneumatology, for understanding recent debates about the divinity of Jesus, and recommended his sermons as a model for preaching.[95]

Across the middle decades of the eighteenth century there was ongoing communication about education between American minsters and Watts, Doddridge, and other dissenters which was pursued by ministers of different denominations on both sides of the Atlantic. One significant practical outcome of this was that books by Watts and Doddridge were in American college libraries and were used in the lectures there.[96] These donations were part of a supportive transatlantic culture committed to sharing educational practices and resources. Books by Watts and Doddridge are considerably less in evidence in the libraries of Oxford and Cambridge colleges for this period, indicating that these dissenters had the strongest direct influence within English dissent and on American educational culture.[97] As with their influence in the British Isles, it is striking that institutions with different denominational identities and various pedagogical approaches all used Watts and Doddridge.

6. CONDUCTING EDUCATION

The widespread and long lasting use of Doddridge's educational materials at dissenting academies confirms the importance of his educational system, as does his correspondence with educators at universities and colleges elsewhere. The chapter has followed a pattern of attending to Doddridge's words, then extending outwards, and has used many kinds of material evidence to show that dissenting educational practices were not denominationally or temporally specific.

[95] Johnson, *Introduction*, 24–6.
[96] Watts's works appear in all three eighteenth-century catalogues of the library of Harvard College, and titles by Doddridge are strongly in evidence in the 1773 and 1790 catalogues. As virtually the entire Harvard library was destroyed by fire on 14–15 January 1764, the Watts and Doddridge titles in the latter two catalogues were probably not donated by the authors.
[97] Though Doddridge was in correspondence with several fellows of Oxford colleges, including Thomas Hunt and Richard Newton, few of his works appear to have been held by libraries there.

Some significant points about the materials in use at academies emerge. The consistency of scribal practices in the production of manuscript copies of the core lectures on theology and preaching suggest that the process of copying and transmitting these materials should be understood as manuscript publication continued over a long duration. That scribal community certainly supported intimate and informal methods of dissemination (such as letters) and preservation (in shared notebooks) but, taken as a whole, the body of academy materials attests to an educational culture that was as professional as it was personal and which served both social and intellectual purposes.

The presentation of dissenting academy curriculum and practice in a restricted range of printed texts in the same period indicates that there was more freedom in manuscript than print and that the different media lent themselves to different functions, which in the case of print might include public claims for the utility and politeness of dissenting education. Importantly, scribal publication was not replaced by print until very late: manuscript circulation continued after lectures had been printed, and manuscript and print copies functioned alongside each other.

While Philip Doddridge has not been the sole object of study in this chapter, almost all the materials presented have some association with him and his academy. The extent to which his lectures were the basis for day-to-day teaching is not always clear, however (especially towards the end of the century). Nevertheless, the association of Doddridge's name with the materials described here strongly suggests that his example was respected by dissenting, Scottish, and American educators. The ambitious and lengthy project of putting his teaching material into print was both a mark of this respect and an attempt to present a positive model of dissenting education to a learned public in a confident and expansive way. But this process was not a smooth one, and Chapter 3 will describe the pressures (intellectual, commercial, doctrinal, and social) that Doddridge's editors faced when transforming informal, private, and shorthand materials into elegant printed books of substance.

3

Lectures in Print

On 25 April 1763, the forthcoming publication of Doddridge's *A Course of Lectures on the Principal Subjects in Pneumatology, Ethics and Divinity* was advertised in the London press. On Thursday 28 April, the public was told, the lectures 'Neatly printed in One Volume Quarto' would go on sale priced at sixteen shillings.[1] Since this represented the first published appearance of Doddridge's method of teaching, it is worth outlining the publishing landscape for works deriving from institutional lectures in the period. The lectures made their debut on rather an empty stage. Very few editions of theological or philosophical lecture courses from academic institutions were being published at this time or for several decades to come. When materials were printed it tended to be in the form of 'heads' (a summary of topics) rather than complete texts and the purpose of these was primarily to attract current university students to current courses.[2] *A Course of Lectures*—published twelve years after Doddridge's academy had closed—was far more substantial. It detailed all the information, arguments, and references for the complete, ten-part interwoven series of lectures on pneumatology, ethics, and divinity delivered at Northampton. In this respect it was closer to materials associated with Scottish universities (such as Francis Hutcheson's lectures) and to publications emerging from other dissenting academies (such as Henry Grove's *System of Moral Philosophy*) which were also posthumously published, though in smaller formats than Doddridge's.[3] While Hutcheson's and Grove's publications antedated Doddridge's lectures, there is nothing to suggest that his editors

---

[1] *London Chronicle*, 28 April 1763.

[2] For example Edward Bentham, *Reflexions upon the Study of Divinity. To which are Subjoined Heads of a Course of Lectures* (Oxford, 1771) and John Hey, *Heads of a Course of Lectures in Divinity* (Cambridge, 1783). Hey was Norrisian Professor of Divinity at the University of Cambridge. His lectures were published in full over a decade after he delivered them as *Lectures in Divinity*, 4 vols (Cambridge, 1796–1798).

[3] Hutcheson was Professor of Moral Philosophy at Glasgow University. He had Latin textbooks such as *Philosophiae moralis institutio compendiaria* (Glasgow, 1742) printed in his lifetime, though he insisted these were intended for student use only. The posthumous English translation was published as *A Short Introduction to Moral Philosophy* (Glasgow, 1747). Doddridge is listed as a subscriber in the first volume.

consciously followed the example of their editors in the presentation of lecture room materials in print.

Printed texts based on academy lectures in subjects other than philosophy and theology were available, usually (though not always) also in the form of 'heads'. These latter were printed locally and were probably, like the Oxford and Cambridge texts, for the use of current students.[4] The diverse appearance of all these books of lectures from universities and academies in England and Scotland suggests that, unlike manuscript production and circulation, there was no settled tradition for presenting higher-level educational material in print in the middle decades of the century. Further, the overlapping presence of manuscript and printed copies of lectures in classrooms and libraries as described in Chapter 2 suggests that the two forms coexisted in complementary ways right through the eighteenth century. Even though the increasing number of tutors committing their lectures to print does indicate a slow culture shift, print did not completely replace manuscript as the preferred mode of lecture dissemination in dissenting academies.

Doddridge's *Course of Lectures* was an unusual publishing project. Its elaborate structure, complicated *mise-en-page* to represent the mathematical method, large format and extent (600 pages), and expense placed the book beyond the means of most students and set it apart from more modest publications based on academic lectures. The nature and extent of the work's life following its first publication is also unusual. It had three editors (Samuel Clark, Andrew Kippis, and Edward Williams) over a forty-year period. In this chapter, the reasons for and consequences of the lectures' periodic republication are considered through readings of the prefatory rhetoric and textual interventions of each editor. Both Kippis and later Williams modified the work of their predecessors and made claims for a uniquely faithful relationship between their version of the lectures and Doddridge's own course, which the texts themselves belie. Each editor expresses his view of what the publication did to Doddridge as an author, to the lectures as a resource, and to their own dissenting community. The distinct appearances of printed publications under different editors and in different languages is unlike the gradually changing shape of his lecture course as represented in manuscript copies of student lecture notes. This chapter sets out the practical and intellectual dimensions of editing educational works as a form of stewardship by which a pedagogy and philosophy

---

[4] Examples include Joseph Priestley, *A Course of Lectures on the Theory of Language* (Warrington, 1762); *A Syllabus of a Course of Lectures on the Study of History* (Warrington, 1765); *A Course of Lectures on Oratory and Criticism* (London, 1777)—all 'heads' for present study. David Jennings, *Jewish Antiquities, or a Course of Lectures on the First Three Books of Godwin's Moses and Aaron*, 2 vols (London, 1766) is an example of a body of lectures transposed into a work of reference.

are preserved and transmitted. As such, it is concerned with the intellectual, editorial, and financial aspects of educational publishing in the second half of the eighteenth century and proposes that investigating the practice of publishing lectures reveals the interrelations of learned, educational, and religious endeavours in this period.

Editors were extremely important agents in the transformation and dissemination of teaching materials. But there was considerable variation in the duties and attitudes of editors depending on time, their own status, and the nature of the materials being edited. The role of particular editors in the provisional, partial, and cumulative publication of materials whose suitability for print was repeatedly questioned is therefore also explored in this chapter with reference to Doddridge's 'Lectures on Preaching'. The divergence of opinion among dissenters about what was fit to be published had a denominational dimension, as readers and editors sought to reaffirm the significance of Doddridge the writer, preacher, and educator as a figurehead for particular orthodox or heterodox branches of dissent. The different formats and print locations in which the 'Lectures on Preaching' were published gave it different meanings, and that story of publication can be told in terms of collaboration and the transition from manuscript to print, the movement from the private lecture room to the public world of letters. The publishing histories of *A Course of Lectures* and the 'Lectures on Preaching' together illustrate the different forms educational texts might take in print and the anxieties that attended the publication of dissenters' teaching materials. But the histories also clearly show that notwithstanding the difficulties they faced, Doddridge's former students and his widow were united by a strong sense of intellectual and evangelical purpose in carrying out Doddridge's wishes.

1. PUBLISHING *A COURSE OF LECTURES*

A Course of Lectures had three distinct printed appearances in England as well as editions in Dutch and French in the 1760s and 1770s, in addition to the various manuscript copies in longhand and shorthand that continued to be transcribed and circulated in the century after Doddridge's death. The first edition of 1763 was reprinted in 1776 in the same single quarto volume format. In 1794, Andrew Kippis's edition was published in two octavo volumes priced fifteen shillings in 'common paper' and one guinea in 'fine paper'.[5] This edition was reprinted in 1799. In the

---

[5] The price is given in the review of the work in the *Critical Review*, 12 (1794), 303–12. In the list of Kippis's works appended to Abraham Rees's funeral sermon, the price is given

nineteenth century, the lectures—edited by Edward Williams—appeared in Doddridge's complete works published in 1804–1805. They were published separately for the last time in 1822.[6]

Manuscript copies of the lectures formed part of Doddridge's literary property bequeathed to his widow Mercy at his death in 1751. His will specified that 'if the Theological Lectures be printed as I am very willing they should it may be done in a handsome manner and for the benefit of my ffamily'.[7] It therefore fell to a woman with no prior experience of publishing and no professional knowledge of the content of academy teaching to manage the publication process. Mercy Doddridge took the task of completing the publication of Doddridge's educational writings very seriously. '[M]y chief concern', she told a bookseller when negotiating the publication of *A Course of Lectures*, 'is to second to ye utmost of my power ye pious intentions of my ever Dear m^r D—by spreading [h]is writing as much as possible in the world.'[8] Her business acumen and understanding of the booktrade developed rapidly but were severely tested during the decade or so she spent guiding Doddridge's works into print. Doddridge arranged for assistance by requesting in his will that Job Orton oversee the preparation of the manuscript. He named James Waugh as the publisher, and asked that the work be issued in two quarto volumes. In the event, it was not until twelve years after his death that *A Course of Lectures* was published in one volume, edited not by Orton but by Doddridge's former student and assistant tutor Samuel Clark. Mercy Doddridge's correspondence sheds light on the reasons for the delays to the publication of what Job Orton characterized as Doddridge's 'capital posthumous work' and also reveals how Doddridge's friends and former students conceived his academy lectures as fitting into the project of publishing his works in order to consolidate his posthumous reputation.[9]

It also provides substantial information about the legal and financial aspects of publishing academic works. In 1759, during her negotiations with a new bookseller (the colourful and untrustworthy James Rivington), Mercy Doddridge presented the lectures as a tempting commercial proposition by reporting current interest in the lectures from 'the principle persons of the ye colldge of new Jersey' and 'a gentleman of considerable

as thirteen shillings. Abraham Rees, *A Sermon Preached… Upon Occasion of the Much Lamented Death of the Rev. Andrew Kippis* (London, 1795), 'List of works', item XXV.

[6] For a detailed chronology of the editions and a close study of the differences between the various editions of *A Course of Lectures*, see Rivers, *The Defence of Truth*, 18–26.

[7] TNA: PRO PROB 11/791, sig. 332.

[8] Mercy Doddridge to James Stonhouse, 11 March 1759. DWL MS NCL L.63/5.

[9] Job Orton to Mercy Doddridge, 18 August 1762. DWL MS NCL L.1/8/45.

rank in Swisstzertzer[land]'.[10] In laying out her terms for the sale of the manuscript, she declared a preference to sell the manuscript and rights to publish to the bookseller. Before reaching this decision she had sought advice from several of her husband's associates. William Warburton advised:

> I much suspect (considering the didactic and severe nature of such kind of compositions) that if you published them at your own expense you would hardly be a saver; if a Bookseller would undertake it at his, you would scarce be a gainer. I should therefore propose (if you think you lye under obligations to give them to the public), that they be printed by subscription.[11]

But rather than retaining the rights to the edition and funding the publication through subscriptions as he suggested, she offered the copyright of the edition for sale.[12]

The main advantage of selling the copyright was the greater likelihood of swift publication: once a bookseller had paid for a work it was in his financial interest to publish it as soon as possible so that he could begin to recoup his investment. It appears that by 1759 Mercy Doddridge wanted the lectures on sale. She wrote to Job Orton suggesting that he and 'M^r C' (presumably Samuel Clark) should work together 'to fit them for ye Publick', in accordance with Doddridge's will. In December 1759, Clark had taken charge of the process and he told Mercy Doddridge:

> ye Lect[ures] have been for some time at a stand. He [the bookseller] has several Sheets of ye Copy in his hands: but I have as yet rec^d but one from ye Press, tho' that indeed has been printed off 2 or 3 times in order to correct some errors I observ'd in ye 1st Impress—However I sh^d be glad to receive ye Remainder of ye Copy in y^r hands, as soon as you can conveniently send it.[13]

---

[10] Mercy Doddridge to James Rivington, 6 April 1759. DWL MS NCL L.63/8. A nineteenth-century biographer of Doddridge claimed, 'In the correspondence of Mrs. Doddridge with Mr. Orton there are references to a project by a Swiss gentleman, for translating her husband's hymns into French', but these letters cannot now be found: see John Stoughton, *Philip Doddridge: His Life and Labours* (London, 1851), 208. The identity of the Swiss gentleman has not been traced.

[11] William Warburton to Mercy Doddridge, 8 March 1759. Donald W. Nichol, *Pope's Literary Legacy: The Book-Trade Correspondence of William Warburton and John Knapton, with Other Letters and Documents, 1744–1780* (Oxford, 1992), 130.

[12] Ashworth calculated that the value of Doddridge's literary property excluding the lectures was £1,106 3d. The terms Mercy Doddridge proposed, and which Rivington accepted, were first set out by Caleb Ashworth in DWL MS NCL L.63/7. She asked for £1,200 for the complete property, suggesting that the copyright of *A Course of Lectures* was valued at £94.

[13] Samuel Clark to Mercy Doddridge, 10 December 1759. DWL MS NCL L.1/5/25. The MS reads 'at as stand', which has been adjusted to 'at a stand' in the transcription.

Preparing *A Course of Lectures* for the press involved not only checking the proofs of this structurally and visually complex work (itself a time-consuming task), but also seeking information on the publication schedule and conveying it to Mercy Doddridge. On her side, acting as executrix required her to supervise the editing, printing, and distribution of the work even once she had sold the copyright.

Some preliminary points emerge from this sketch of the publishing history of the first edition of *A Course of Lectures*. The publication of the lectures happens quite separately to the concurrent ongoing delivery of the lectures in academies and the production of manuscript copies. Notably, the theology tutor delivering lectures based on Doddridge's— Caleb Ashworth—is not the editor. This corresponds to a wider pattern for lecture publication in the period: theology tutors do not publish their own lectures, or editions of other theological lectures. The reason may be the practical one that they are too busy teaching to undertake the work of editing. In the case of Doddridge's lectures, the force driving their publication is not a colleague or tutor but his widow. The impetus comes from Doddridge's family rather than his academy associates: the motivation is (in Mercy Doddridge's terms) to honour the author's memory and (in Doddridge's own) to secure financial provision for the author's family, rather than any educational ambition to further diffuse the intellectual and pedagogic practices of dissent. What this set of circumstances says about the status of dissenting education as an intellectual enterprise in the world at large is a question that will be pursued over the duration of this chapter.

2. EDITING *A COURSE OF LECTURES*

None of Doddridge's teaching materials had appeared in print in the form of lectures before, and the matter of whom they were for and what publication was intended to achieve was to preoccupy successive editors. In the case of *A Course of Lectures*, how to define Doddridge as the author of a printed edition of lectures, which were still the basis of theological education at various academies after his death, was at issue. Doddridge insisted that the structure of the lectures encouraged their adaptation, and their flexibility was integral to their ongoing use. Printing the lectures, however, fixed their form and content for a given edition. It also introduced them to an audience beyond dissenting academies, unfamiliar with and possibly hostile towards Doddridge's methods. Different editors took different positions on the extent to which Doddridge's method of adaptation constituted an integral part of his work, and how the printed lectures should be used. Successive editorial prefaces are therefore important statements of purpose and interpretation.

Samuel Clark's 'Advertisement' opens each of the eighteenth-century English printed editions of *A Course of Lectures* and commences with the explanation that:

> This work was originally drawn up for the use of the students under the Author's care; but it appears by a clause in his will, that it was his intention it should be published after his decease.[14]

The original setting of the lecture room at Northampton academy and Doddridge's own directions that the work should be published are the frame through which the publication of these lectures is to be viewed. Clark's two preoccupations in the 'Advertisement' are with defending the propriety of the enterprise and establishing its purpose. He balances conventional assurances of fidelity to the source materials ('I have carefully compared [the transcript] with the original short-hand copy') with declarations that the work is new and important. He does this by emphasizing that, while the mathematical method came originally from Jennings, Doddridge extended and refined the content of the course to such a degree that 'the whole may properly be considered as a new work'.[15]

Clark's assertion that Doddridge used Jennings's lectures as his source but modified them as he saw fit underlines that the key feature of the scheme (on Clark's view) was that its structure permitted additions and alterations. By including this information, Clark provides an implicit justification for his own procedure of adapting existing materials: his approach has been in keeping with the origins of the course and he is following Doddridge's own practice.[16] In this way the published *Course of Lectures* becomes a location for Doddridge's ideas and, as importantly, a positive representation of his method. And while Clark acknowledges the originality of Doddridge's scheme, he carefully reassures the reader that his version of Doddridge's course is a faithful one: 'The public may be assured, that the Author's sentiments have been everywhere scrupulously preserved' and only 'a few references have been added'.[17] He does not, however, say what these additions are. Nor does he explain that successive tutors have adapted Doddridge's course, or that a modified version of the course is currently in use at Daventry and elsewhere. While the

---

[14] *A Course of Lectures* (1763), sig. A2. [15] *A Course of Lectures* (1763), sig. A2v.
[16] It also indicates Clark anticipated that the majority of readers of this printed edition would have no idea about the development of Doddridge's method.
[17] *A Course of Lectures* (1763), sig. A2. Rivers thinks it possible that Clark added the reference to David Hume: see Rivers, *The Defence of Truth*, 19.

publication of this work might be imagined to have been primarily of interest to men within the sphere of dissenting education, the fact that many of them had access to manuscript copies suggests that just as important a purpose was to portray the extent of dissenting learning to a world beyond the academies. In that case, the presentation of Doddridge's educational method to the public is rather uneasily poised between celebration and defence.

The title page of the 1794 two-volume edition generates the sense that the work is a refreshed version of the course by specifying that it contains additional references 'from writers who have appeared since the doctor's decease'. This expression of improvement is heightened by the use of terms of abundance: 'added', 'a great number of references', with 'many' notes on 'various' writers. The editor of this edition was Andrew Kippis, another former student of Doddridge's academy, who had experienced the system as a student, though Kippis downplayed his own familiarity with the lectures and the circumstances of his encounter with them, saying that he had 'only been occasionally a reader on a few detached parts Dr. Doddridge's Lectures'.[18] Kippis uses the flexible form of the lectures to add to the references and insert new ideas, and uses this as a way of promoting a new, expanded edition of the lectures. He explains that adding references follows Doddridge's own practice, thereby drawing on Doddridge's authority and reputation to legitimize the project. The form of the lectures means that supplementing them enacts fidelity to the author's ideas and, in Kippis's representation of it, the editor's responsibility includes updating the text according to the author's principles.

Recurring themes in the prefaces to the 1763 and 1794 editions are the richness and variety of the references the work contains and the fact that the present edition conforms to Doddridge's intentions. In several respects Clark and later Kippis follow the pattern Doddridge instituted when describing Jennings's academy and thus perpetuate a tradition in the dissemination of dissenting educational materials. They both make claims for the originality of their tutor's course which echo those made by Doddridge in relation to John Jennings's method, and their position as former students presenting a version of their tutor's educational system to the wider world is reminiscent of Doddridge's own in 1729 as he wrote and circulated 'An Account of Mr Jennings's Method'. However, neither editor specifically identifies himself as a former student in the way Doddridge does. The intimacy that Doddridge sought to create through his use of epistolary form, the affective representations of tear-inducing

---

[18] *A Course of Lectures* (1794), I, sig. a3.

memories, and repeated expressions of esteem are absent from these two printed prefatory statements which, though they record respect, do so in formulaic terms. This is partly a consequence of the different expectations surrounding the dissemination of a manuscript epistolary treatise on one hand and printed volumes of lectures on the other. After all, conventions determine the style and content of any written document and formal, rhetorical, paratextual, and memorial traditions all shape the presentation of these lectures.

Though it is far from unusual for a new editor to use a preface to claim that he has updated, refreshed, and improved a work, and though title page wording and layout might be a blunt way of conveying the essence of a text, these were the principal means available for shaping the presentation of a work 'in the strongest sense', as Gerard Genette puts it: 'to ensure the text's presence in the world' and to guide its reception.[19] Attending to how editors and authors use these conventional elements of a printed book—'a zone of transition but also of *transaction*'—to address their reading public can, as Genette demonstrates very thoroughly, offer insights into what those books are made to mean. Genette offers a taxonomy of prefatory functions—to declare novelty or adherence to a tradition; to claim unity and truthfulness for the work; to promote and guide reading—but though he states that 'the functions of the allographic preface overlap with, but at the same add some specificity to the functions of the original authorial preface', this is not borne out in his focus on authorial self-presentation and how it determines much prefatory rhetoric. The association of an individual author and a single creative work seems, on Genette's account, to animate almost all prefaces.[20] By contrast, Clark's defensive specificity ('my regard to the Author's memory, and my apprehension of the usefulness of the work itself' prompt him to explain 'what has been done in relation to them') and Kippis's more celebratory tone ('I have happily succeeded' in obtaining the assistance of various tutors in supplementing the references, he proclaims) show two distinct approaches to the conventional matter of explaining editorial rationale. The choices these editors made from within a restricted prefatory vocabulary when framing their versions of Doddridge's lectures indicate how the lectures have changed since the first semi-public account of them in Doddridge's 'Account of Mr Jennings's Method'. But despite the differences in tone, there is consistency across the two prefaces in the articulation of the key features of those lectures. Both editors highlight the

---

[19] Gerard Genette, *Paratexts: Thresholds of Interpretation*, tr. Jane E. Lewin (Cambridge, 1997), 1.

[20] Genette, *Paratexts*, 264–5, and ch. 9.

abundance of references, the lectures' usefulness to students, and the desirable intellectual habits of moderation and enquiry that their perusal would form.

In some respects neither Clark nor Kippis was particularly well suited to the editorship of these lectures. Both were former students of Doddridge and had studied the course they now edited, but neither advertised this fact in their prefatory remarks, unlike Doddridge's 'Account'. Neither man was a theological tutor and neither worked in an academy at the time his edition of Doddridge's lectures was published. Clark had been Doddridge's assistant tutor (meaning he taught classics and mathematics) and led Northampton academy for around a year during Doddridge's final illness and before the removal of the academy to Daventry in 1752. His final experience of academy teaching of any kind ended almost a decade before the publication of *A Course of Lectures*. Kippis had been tutor of rhetoric and belles lettres at Hoxton academy from 1764 to 1784, and following the closure of that institution he became a founding tutor at New College Hackney where he lectured on history and chronology between 1786 and 1791 but never ethics or theology. Thus Clark and Kippis, though both educated at Northampton under Doddridge, came to be associated with distinct traditions within dissent over time.

Neither editor made especially confident claims for their own fitness for the role. Clark's prefatory statements create the impression that he took on the editorship rather unwillingly. Kippis summarizes the requisite qualities for an editor as outlined by Doddridge's most recent biographer—someone with a knowledge of the history of religious controversies; a tutor who had made use of the lectures in teaching and had updated the references with texts published in the forty years since Doddridge's death—while acknowledging that 'I do not completely answer to the whole of this description.'[21] There is something of a hall of mirrors at work in Kippis's preface, for the author of that biography, the originator of calls for a new edition of *A Course of Lectures*, was Kippis himself, and, the rather thin mantle of anonymity notwithstanding, readers familiar with the 1792 edition of *The Family Expositor* in which the biography appeared would have been aware of that fact. His other activities in the wider world of polite literature identified him as a man interested in preserving intellectual endeavour in print. He edited the periodical *New Annual Register*, and was commissioned to co-edit the second edition of the *Biographia Britannica* (1778–95). Kippis believed a key function of the *Biographia Britannica* was to record the notable publications of its subjects:

[21] *A Course of Lectures* (1794), I, sig. a3.

it is part of our plan to give copious accounts of the writings of learned men, if they have been in any degree eminent. This is the only way of doing them that full justice, to which, by their merits, they are entitled. From the accumulation of new books, and the revolutions of literary fashion, even works of no small reputation come to be neglected.[22]

Kippis reproduced his biography of Doddridge from *The Family Expositor* in volume V of the *Biographia Britannica*. His attention to Doddridge's work and life in his literary endeavours prior to his editorship of *A Course of Lectures* suggests that keeping Doddridge's memory alive using print was a long-standing project for him, as the biography contains very full summaries of Doddridge's teaching and publications. Republishing *A Course of Lectures*, Kippis is attempting to do Doddridge 'that full justice' of having his activities and principles remembered late in the century. But more than preserving a record of a book 'of no small reputation', he is using Doddridge's work as a vehicle for his own contribution to the contemporary study of ethics and theology by adding new references to the work. In this respect he is acting in a similar way to Belsham (whose heterodox views in some areas he shared) but he sets his adaptation of Doddridge on a public stage rather than within the academy environment.

In his biography of Doddridge, Kippis emphasized the intellectual value of updating *A Course of Lectures*, saying: 'it would be extremely useful to enlarge the list of references, by introducing the names and productions of those writers who have treated upon the several matters in question since the Doctor's decease'.[23] Here he follows the example of Samuel Clark, who noted that 'a few references have been added particularly to some books published since the Author's death'. There is a difference in the intensity of claims for novelty, as Kippis announces in stronger terms that his edition augments what has gone before. He says that the changes to the course 'will be particularly apparent to any one who shall take the trouble of comparing the catalogue of authors inserted at the end of the present work with that which is given in the former editions'.[24] Indeed, he notes that this updated edition contains more references than a student could possibly consult, and this admission is the point at which Kippis's ideas about the purpose of the course diverge from Clark's and Doddridge's. He shares with his former tutor a vision of the work being used as a repository of references for 'future enquiries' to which ministers can turn even after they have competed their academic studies. But for Kippis, unlike Doddridge, it is not necessary to follow up each reference:

---

[22] *Biographia Britannica*, IV, sig. b.   [23] *Biographia Britannica*, V, 301.
[24] *A Course of Lectures* (1763), sig. A2, *A Course of Lectures* (1794), I, sig. a3v.

It is not to be expected that in their state of pupilage they should be able to pay a due attention to one half of the books here specified... it may be of great importance to know where hereafter to apply for fresh stores of knowledge.[25]

Nor do the 'fresh stores of knowledge' belong only to some hypothetical future lean winter. The book itself is full of these 'fresh stores'; so full of new material that it cannot strictly be considered as Doddridge's alone, a point underlined by Kippis's inclusion of the other tutors whose references he has incorporated. Kippis hints that the augmented nature of the course might lead to tensions in the text, saying, 'it is no part of my design... either to confirm or gainsay the opinions of Dr Doddridge'.[26] This leaves open the possibility that his new edition, in adapting and extending ideas from Doddridge's course, might introduce positions with which Doddridge would have disagreed.[27]

Samuel Clark had insisted that despite any changes, this course remained Doddridge's in its fidelity to the important feature of its flexible, evolving form. In a development of this point, Kippis notes that he has incorporated additional references, some from his former colleague Samuel Morton Savage (theology tutor at Hoxton academy) taken from the Benjamin Edwards's copy of Savage's lectures and others from James Mannings's copy of Samuel Merivale's lectures given at Exeter Presbyterian academy between 1761 and 1771. Kippis names all these men, emphasizing that this edition is created out of the work of tutors at academies with different denominational affiliations. Shared endeavour among dissenting tutors is celebrated in the paratexts and references of *A Course of Lectures*, and Kippis's preface publicly attests to the ongoing utility of Doddridge's lectures at academies both orthodox (like Hoxton) and heterodox (like Exeter) and transforms 'Doddridge' into an authorial figure through which to embody those practices. In another instance of the rich interconnections of manuscript and print cultures, teaching copies of the lectures that nourish academy practice circulate within a community of dissenting educators and inform a new printed edition of Doddridge's lectures while both the lecture manuscripts and the new edition draw on Clark's printed edition of the lectures. Kippis supplements the references in Doddridge's course with more recent printed texts but also with texts

---

[25] *A Course of Lectures* (1794), I, sig. a4.   [26] *A Course of Lectures* (1794), I, sig. a4.
[27] For example, in part VII ('The existence and nature of GOD, and the divinity of the SON and SPIRIT') Kippis adds substantially to the references to proposition 128 'God is so *united* to the derived nature of Christ... that... Christ may properly be called *God*', which he introduces with the observation 'Since these lectures were written, the question concerning the Divinity of our Lord has afforded matter for repeated, and almost perpetual discussion,' *A Course of Lectures* (1794), II, 170–6.

published in Doddridge's lifetime that Clark does not include. In the 'Definition' of the soul's immateriality that Belsham treated quite contentiously, Kippis reproduces all the references from the 1763 edition and adds four more, including Richard Price's sermon *The Nature and Dignity of the Human Soul* (1766) but not the exchange between Price and Priestley.[28] Even though he includes the additions of other tutors and recent books, and even though Belsham was his colleague at New College Hackney at this time, Kippis chooses not to include the most controversial relevant references at certain points in the course.

The sociable and intellectually generous nature of dissenting educators—their candour—has a high profile in Kippis's edition. He not only emphasizes the help he has received from various tutors in the production of the work but constructs the work itself as a beacon of tutelage, declaring that it can function as a resource for tutors in the future. It is to them that he addresses the remark 'It is the business of individual tutors to enlarge upon the Lectures in that way which accords with their own sentiments.'[29] In his edition, which does precisely this, Kippis provides a model for the use of Doddridge's lectures by later tutors: as a structure to which tutors could add their own references, and as a repository of sources. Kippis himself was a founding governor and tutor of New College Hackney, which did not impose any religious tests for entry and which developed a reputation for heterodoxy. His editorship of *A Course of Lectures* creates a connection between Doddridge's pedagogy (especially the principle of liberality of thought) and the educational and intellectual practices of heterodox dissenters, though Kippis himself is careful to distinguish between Doddridge's course and his own contributions in order to make it clear that Doddridge himself was theologically orthodox.

Kippis presents the edition as following Doddridge's method and supplementing his content. But that serene portrayal of fidelity was challenged by Doddridge's nineteenth-century editor Edward Williams (Congregationalist minister, tutor at Oswestry academy and later Rotherham College), for whom Kippis's extensive additions to Doddridge's text were problematic. In the 'Advertisement' to the third English version of *A Course of Lectures*, published in volumes IV and V of the *Works* (the whole collection edited jointly with Edward Parsons), Williams distances Kippis's edition from Doddridge's lectures. He announced that this edition contained all the references from Clark's version of the lectures but retained only some of Kippis's, and while Clark's 'Advertisement' is reproduced in full, only three

[28] *A Course of Lectures* (1794), I, 328–9.
[29] *A Course of Lectures* (1794), I, sig. a4.

paragraphs of Kippis's preface appear. In the text itself, where Williams does include some of Kippis's additions, these are relegated to one source among many for additional references. These moves reassert the strength of Doddridge's orthodoxy and diminish the presence of Kippis (associated with New College Hackney and heterodoxy) in Doddridge's lectures.

Kippis is not erased from the work, however. Throughout the text, Williams attributes references to the particular tutor responsible for them: 'The notes...are marked by the initials of their authors respectively, DODDRIDGE, CLARK, SAVAGE and KIPPIS.'[30] He represents the resource of the references as a collective endeavour developing over time and with the contributions of educators at various academies, as Kippis had done. This can be seen as one of the key traditions of the lectures in print: successive editors add substantially to the original content. Clark's 'Advertisement' identifies this as a procedure authorized by Doddridge himself by explaining that Doddridge inherited the mathematical form and some of the references from his own tutor, John Jennings, 'but he has so much enlarged and improved on the original plan, that the whole may now properly be considered a new work'. This statement is included in all subsequent editions of the lectures, contributing to the sense of a tradition of innovation being perpetuated.

However, Williams's treatment of references changes Doddridge's lectures profoundly. The references are relegated to the 'the bottom of the page' rather than being interwoven with the content which separates the references (both Doddridge's and those of other tutors) from Doddridge's own words, thereby altering the emphasis of the course.[31] The references are no longer central to the conduct of the lectures, but are supplementary materials. The sequence of the course as a whole also appears very differently in this nineteenth-century version. The lectures are divided across two volumes and appeared in the middle of all Doddridge's other works, hardly a form that could readily be adopted for lecture room use. Here the lectures serve as a historical record rather than a contemporary resource. 'It should be considered as a *book of reference*, when investigating the *history of opinions* on Pneumatology, Ethics, and Divinity', he suggests, and proposes that it be understood as 'the most complete syllabus of controversial theology, in the largest sense of the word, ever published in the English language'.[32] The combination of superlatives and the

---

[30] Doddridge, *Works*, IV, 283. Williams's own additions are marked 'W'.

[31] Doddridge, *Works*, IV, 281.

[32] Doddridge, *Works*, IV, 281–2. The work was also classified under 'controversial theology' in the library of Manchester College in 1830.

emphasis on the national language situates the printed *Course of Lectures* as a work of national, and not merely dissenting, significance.

3. EUROPEAN EDITIONS, 1768–1773

Printing the lectures was not only an English activity, however. Between the first and second English editions of the lectures came two independent translations of the work, both published in the Netherlands. The first was a four-volume octavo edition in French. The anonymous translator provided an introduction explaining how the lectures had been modified to make them appropriate for a Roman Catholic audience—particularly students at Jesuit seminaries such as the one in Liège, where the work was printed—and declaring that this version of the lectures contained substantial additions to Doddridge's original.[33] While comparing the Liège edition with the London one of 1763 does not entirely bear out this claim, it is certainly the case that the French editor has restructured the course far more freely than any of its English editors, who sometimes add materials, but never change the order of the lectures. For example, proposition 90 ('Various definitions of miracles examined') constitutes lecture 101 in the printed English edition (the beginning of part V of the course) and lecture 126 in the French (from part VIII of that version). The French editor has omitted some parts of Doddridge's course entirely (parts VIII, 'Of the fall of human nature', and X, 'The Scripture doctrine of good and bad angels, and of a future state'). He has reduced other aspects; for example, much of the material to do with Jewish customs and the Old Testament in part VI of the English course is omitted. Other sections are expanded, so that lectures on civil government become an entire part of the course (part IV) rather than a section of part III, as they are in the English. This editorial freedom marks a strong disjuncture with the practice of the editors of the English printed text.

On the whole, though, the French translation follows Clark's edition closely in terms of content, and in particular it includes almost all those references. Often a reference gives the English title of a work (Locke's *Posthumous Pieces*, for example, and Samuel Chandler's *On Miracles*) but sometimes the French title is provided: Samuel Clarke's 'Boyle Lectures' (as the work is titled in *A Course of Lectures*) is identified as 'Démonstration de l'Existence & des Attributs de Dieu' in part VI of the course,

---

[33] See 'Préface de l'Éditeur', in *Cours de lectures... du D. Doddridge*, 4 vols (Liège, 1768), I, i–viii.

proposition 90.[34] The choice reflects the language in which a work was available: if it had been translated into French, the French title is given. The French edition retains the page numbers of Doddridge's references where he reproduces a title in English. When a French title is used, there are no page references. This reference to French editions of works raises one of the many questions surrounding this version of the lectures: just how likely was it that French-speaking Roman Catholic theology students would have access to the English Protestant religious works which make up the bulk of the references in *A Course of Lectures*? And why did the editor not replace Doddridge's references with French, Roman Catholic authors? Given the anonymous editor's stated desire that the lectures be introduced to French-speaking seminaries, colleges, and universities it seems strange that he did not use works more likely to be available to students and tutors in these institutions.[35] Frustratingly, these questions have proved almost impossible to answer. Extensive investigation has not yielded the identity of the translator or evidence for the lectures' use in Jesuit colleges or even any clues as to how French-speaking Jesuits found out about Doddridge's lectures in the first place.[36] The translation of the lectures into French did contribute to Doddridge's reputation in the continental world of letters, for entries in nineteenth-century biographical dictionaries list the English and French versions of *A Course of Lectures* among his significant works.[37]

The fullest information about this edition of the lectures comes from correspondence between Mercy Doddridge and a former student at Northampton named Benjamin Sowden, minister of the English Reformed Church in Rotterdam from 1748 to 1778. Like several of Doddridge's former students he wrote occasionally to his tutor's widow. In Sowden's case the letters provided religious and literary news from the continent and asked for updates from home. It was he who appraised the Doddridge circle of this French edition by sending extracts from the preface with translations, and who told them that it was associated with the English Jesuit

---

[34] *Cours de lectures*, III, 8–14. Clarke's work had been translated into French by the Protestant Pierre Ricotier.

[35] 'Préface de l'Éditeur', viii.

[36] There were several tutors at the English Jesuit College at Liège who might have translated the work, but it has not proved possible to positively identify the translator or to establish how a copy of *A Course of Lectures* reached the college. One possible route is via William Strickland, a Jesuit priest from Warrington. I am grateful to Maurice Whitehead for this suggestion.

[37] Doddridge was included in several nineteenth-century French biographical dictionaries, which listed the English and French versions of *A Course of Lectures* among his significant works. See *Biographie universelle ancienne et moderne*, 85 vols (Paris, 1811–1862), XI, 388.

college in Liège.[38] He was also involved in the publication of a Dutch translation of the lectures, which came five years after the French version (in 1773). This publication has been neglected by scholars, both of Doddridge and of the international dissemination of academy teaching materials.

Unlike the French edition, the Dutch version of *A Course of Lectures* did not face the challenge of explaining how Doddridge's Protestant course had been transformed for a Roman Catholic audience. Indeed, in contrast to the French editor's somewhat overstated insistence that the lectures were more or less a new work, the Dutch version took pains to demonstrate its fidelity to Doddridge's lectures as delivered in his own lifetime. The lectures followed the structure of the 1763 English edition and the references in the samples I have studied are identical. Unlike the French edition, the titles of works are not translated. Where an English word can only be rendered imperfectly in Dutch, the English word is included as a footnote.[39] Such textual fidelity and editorial transparency corroborate the strong statements of commitment to Doddridge's words and work in the prefatory materials. As well as translations of Doddridge's introduction and Samuel Clark's advertisement explaining the genesis of the lectures and his editorial procedure (both from the English version), the Dutch edition carries a translation of a letter from Clark whose purpose is to endorse this particular edition and reaffirm the lectures' authenticity for a Dutch readership.

Clark's letter reaffirms and strengthens the statements from his English preface that any changes are to the style and not the content of the lectures. He insists that any additional references do not alter the sense of the work, and specifies that most changes are in the theology section of the course.[40] His argument in support of the publication's authenticity is made in terms of moralistic declarations of his own fidelity and by naming the former Northampton students Thomas Greaves and Benjamin Sowden (both residents of Rotterdam) to forge a direct connection between Doddridge's academy in the 1740s and the lectures' publication in the 1760s and 1770s. In a statement which bespeaks great confidence in

---

[38] DWL MS NCL L.1/9/24–5.

[39] For example 'werkkragt' translates 'machinery', 'samengesteld' translates 'very complex', and 'astrekking' translates 'abstraction'; all in Philip Doddridge, *Verzameling van Akademische Lessen*, 3 vols (Rotterdam, 1773), I, 12.

[40] Clark claims he 'makes not even the slightest change in the author's meaning' ('zelfs niet de allergeringste verändering maakt in des Auters meening'), and states that any changes that have been made are 'mainly in the theology part of them [the lectures]' ('wel voornamelijk in het Godgeleerd[heid] gedeelte van dezelve'). Samuel Clark, 'Uittreksel van eenen Brief', in *Verzameling van Akademische Lessen*, I, n.p.; paragraph 2.

the consistency of student transcriptions of Doddridge's lectures, he notes that Greaves and Sowden have their own manuscript copies from North-ampton academy which can be used to check the printed text.[41]

Greaves and Sowden's names reappear in the very long list of subscribers. They are the only English subscribers to the work, but are far from being the only ministers listed. The religious plurality of Doddridge's readers is strongly attested and so is their learning: numerous professors, lecturers, and students from institutions including the universities of Groningen and Franeker, and scholars from smaller towns (many in Friesland) including Leeuwarden, Sneek, and Zwolle. Pastors, preachers, and teachers from various Protestant groups are listed, including Men-nonites, Lutherans, Remonstrants, and adherents to the Augsburg Con-fession. Booksellers across the United Provinces from all the towns previously listed, many smaller settlements such as Zierkzee, Arnheim, and Nijmegen, the civic centres of Amsterdam and Rotterdam, and the university towns of Groningen, Leiden, and Utrecht subscribed to the publication, some of them purchasing dozens of copies.[42]

Clark's additional letter for the Dutch edition indicates there was uneasiness about the publication in some quarters which Doddridge's supporters sought to forestall. Perhaps this is related to an earlier regional controversy about theological orthodoxy in which antagonists implicated Doddridge's works in a more specific and heated way than had ever occurred in England.[43] Clark's statement that ministers should be granted more latitude when delivering lectures in the privacy of a lecture room to students they knew well than they might be granted when preaching anticipates Belsham's free adaptation of Doddridge's lectures to articulate controversial doctrines that was not registered in Kippis's printed edition of the lectures.

The Dutch attempt to neutralize the controversial potential of the work was apparently successful. The large number of subscribers from different denominations and districts suggests that Doddridge's lectures were wel-comed by Dutch speakers who considered the risks of exposure to het-erodox opinion to be worth running in order to receive an educational and theological compendium of such diversity. However, there was no second edition of the work. The lectures had a burst of Dutch support twenty

[41]   Clark, 'Uittreksel van eenen Brief', paragraph 5.

[42]   *Verzameling van Akademische Lessen*, I, sig. 2*–10*v.

[43]   For details of the debates about religious toleration and the risks of deism, see J. van den Berg and G. F. Nuttall, *Philip Doddridge and the Netherlands* (Leiden, 1987), 60–2. For Doddridge's popularity among ministers from different groups in the Netherlands see Joris van Eijnatten, *Liberty and Concord in the United Provinces: Religious Toleration and the Public in the Eighteenth-Century Netherlands* (Leiden, 2003), 437–46.

years after Doddridge's death and a decade after their English publication, but it does not appear as though they were absorbed into the mainstream of theological education in the United Provinces.[44] In this respect, the European reception of both Netherlands editions of Doddridge's lectures are similar, even if the circumstances of their translation could not be more different in terms of the religious affiliation of the anticipated audience.

In every edition of the *Course of Lectures* the editor offered his perspective on how the lectures should be used and understood, but each time this personal interpretative gesture is counterbalanced by the presence of Doddridge's own 'Introduction' which is included in every edition except the French one. This statement explains the content and sequence of the course and also the method to follow: to look up the references as soon as possible after the lecture or, in the case of the printed text, immediately after reading throughout a given section. In Clark's edition, a footnote to the heading 'Introduction' explains it is:

> to be considered as the Author's address to his own pupils, when they entered upon this course of Lectures, which will shew the propriety of some of the directions, which might otherwise appear too particular and minute.[45]

Clark emphasizes that publishing Doddridge's 'Introduction' presents the guiding principles of the course in their originator's own words. This establishes their cultural authority by reaffirming the author's personal presence in a posthumous, printed text and locating the lectures in a specific time, place, and method of study. Doddridge's editors were relocating his course to a public forum, away from the lecture room in which the words were originally delivered, and including Doddridge's advice meant that an expression of the author's intentions for the text remained available to readers. Doddridge's complicated, unfamiliar, and, to some, controversial method required the explanatory voice of its originating author and the framework for reception of their original use, and his editors were eager to provide this even as the lectures were being translated into a new language or religious context, or when their structure was being radically altered.

In the fifty years between Doddridge's death and the final edition of the *Course of Lectures*, the lectures were presented to different reading publics in a variety of ways. Originally the core theological education at his own dissenting academy and its successor, they continued to exert a strong

---

[44] This is also the conclusion of van den Berg and Nuttall, see *Philip Doddridge and the Netherlands*, 70.

[45] *A Course of Lectures* (1763), sig. b.

influence over dissenting education both as lectures delivered to students and as a printed text that served as a repository of references to theological debates from the later seventeenth to mid-eighteenth century. Printing the lectures consolidated their purpose as a work of reference and made that resource available to a wider audience.[46] The audience for the printed lectures were not confined to one denomination, nation, or language group. Their reach extended into Europe via developments of Doddridge's own personal connections. While they were primarily of interest to Calvinist Protestants, ministers and students in the Church of England, Roman Catholic colleges, and heterodox Protestant environments made use of the lectures, amply demonstrating Doddridge's own claim that they were a flexible and copious repository.

4. 'LECTURES ON PREACHING': ANXIETIES ABOUT PUBLICATION

In the provisions Doddridge made for the publication of his educational works in his will, he paired his theological lectures with the shorter course of lectures on preaching which came at the conclusion of the academy course, declaring that he wished both to be printed. He ends the section of his will dealing with the practical matters of publication with a statement about ministerial seriousness and responsibility. Combining instruction and exhortation, he demands that a copy of the lectures be given to students leaving the academy for their first ministerial post and that it should be accompanied 'with a Solemn Charge as before God and the Lord Jesus Christ that they seriously attend to the Contents of them so far as they are in their Consciences convinced of the agreeableness of those Advices to reason and to the Word of God'.[47] In this statement on education Doddridge reaffirms his belief that rational thought and the revelation of the Gospels are complementary aspects of religious knowledge, a view later echoed by editors of his *Course of Lectures* in their prefaces. In a testamentary act that issues authoritative directions for their use, he provides instructions for the reception of the 'Lectures on Preaching'. Rather than being a set of rules, they model the behaviour ministerial students should be guided by their own consciences to follow. Doddridge's idea that the published 'Lectures on Preaching' should be

---

[46] For a discussion of Williams's and Parsons's intentions in their version of *A Course of Lectures*, and an account of how they changed his mathematical method more significantly than either Clark or Kippis, see Rivers, *The Defence of Truth*, 24–6.

[47] TNA: PRO PROB 11/791, sig. 332.

placed after *A Course of Lectures*—connected yet distinct—is consistent with their appearance as the final volume in the ten-volume series of shorthand lecture notes made by Samuel Henley at Daventry and in the reports of how the lectures were introduced at Northampton academy found in Doddridge's 'Life of Thomas Steffe' and Job Orton's biography of Doddridge himself.[48] Doddridge imagined that the lectures in print would follow the pattern of their manuscript use.

Despite Doddridge's instructions, the 'Lectures on Preaching' were not published until the nineteenth century. Though in his will he emphasized their connection to the other lectures, and though the relationship between the two courses of lectures was preserved in academy teaching long after his death, the publication histories of the two courses were very different. And though the lectures themselves were short, the debates they generated in dissenting circles were of long duration. This was partly because of their content but also because of general religious and social principles they were seen to represent. To Doddridge's heirs these lectures were not simply a practical set of instructions or a valuable resource for new ministers (though they were both of those things). They were emblematic of ministerial attitudes towards the dissenting laity and to ministerial forebears, and raised the question of what sort of ministry was being espoused by those who recommended or used these lectures.

The state of the manuscript lectures was also problematic when it came to their publication, the question of which had first arisen in 1763 as *A Course of Lectures* was being published under Samuel Clark's stewardship. Mercy Doddridge, attempting to carry out Doddridge's wishes, seems to have requested Job Orton's opinion on how to proceed with publication of the 'Lectures on Preaching'. Orton acknowledged that '[t]he Author intended the preaching Lectures sh^d be printed' but questioned whether the lectures as they stood were in a good enough state for that, telling Mercy Doddridge, 'I know he intended to have transcribed them & thrown them into quite a different Form.' The practical difficulty was that the lectures had not been edited for publication by their original author: they were private and unpolished. But this was only the start of Orton's anxieties:

> As they stand at present, to print them w^d be the greatest Injury to his Reputation & Memory—to the dissenting Interest in General & the Credit of our Academies in particular; for there are many particular Remarks upon Authors yet living, many Cautions & Directions about ye prudential part of

---

[48] Samuel Henley's lecture notes 1759–1761 (DWL MSS 28.35–44) show that Doddridge's progression from theological lectures to lectures on preaching was preserved at Caleb Ashworth's academy. See Doddridge, 'Life of Thomas Steffe', xix–xx and Orton, *Memoirs*, 95–6.

his Pupils Conduct, which were given to the pupils in Confidence, & by no means fit to appear in the world—as Nothing w^d please ye High Church Men & narrow People among the Dissenters more, than to have an Opportunity to expose the D^r & his pupils & Instructions, as they w^d have a Handle for doing, were his private advices exposed.[49]

Orton's concern that the lectures might distress those at either end of the ecclesiastical spectrum is striking. He wished not to associate Doddridge with controversial views or actions but to construct his mentor as a reliable, orthodox authorial figure who could represent moderate dissent and appeal to all denominations within dissent and outside it. Orton would not risk publishing work under Doddridge's name which might lead to him becoming associated with heterodox ideas, enthusiastic impulses, or impolite manners. It was not a question of authenticity—the lectures, after all, were undoubtedly Doddridge's—but of propriety. Having appealed to Mercy Doddridge's sense of decorum by reminding her that the printed lectures must serve as a memorial to her husband for good or ill, Orton invoked the consensus of other dissenters, saying 'I have consulted all my Fellow pupils, to whom I had Access on this Subject & they all strongly remonstrated against printing them.' He evidently considered this collective opinion a strong claim, for he reiterated the point that 'among all my Brethren to whom I have fairly communicated this Affair, there is not <u>one</u> but agrees with me that it w^d be [in] every way wrong to print ye preaching Lectures'.[50] Emphatically though this point is made, Orton is not simply deploying an argument of strength in numbers. Collective agreement was valued highly among religious dissenters. New ministers were ordained after examination by a group of ministers, congregations selected their pastor by taking a vote of their members, and ministers (including Doddridge) often appointed groups of deacons to advise them on pastoral matters. By presenting Mercy Doddridge with the considered opinion of Doddridge's former students, Orton is invoking the principle of collective decision making. He hoped to persuade her to accept his advice by telling her that those best qualified to judge the merits of publication (all of them ministers, all of them men) had sided with him.

Orton acknowledged the importance and purpose of Doddridge's lectures, but questioned the seemliness of transposing lectures which had not been revised for publication from the private realm of personal interaction in the lecture room to the public arena of print. His particular anxieties were that private conversations between Doddridge and his

[49] Job Orton to Mercy Doddridge, 11 April 1763. DWL MS NCL L.1/8/48.
[50] Job Orton to Mercy Doddridge, 11 April 1763. DWL MS NCL L.1/8/48.

students should not be made public and, with respect to the content of the lectures, that writers still living were treated too brusquely and honestly for general reading. A further issue that Orton avoided fully articulating was that to overcome all of these problems, the 'Lectures on Preaching' would have to be carefully revised and edited, and Orton did not want to take on the task. Orton's opinion must have carried weight with Mercy Doddridge, for there is no further evidence in extant correspondence that she pursued the possibility of publishing the 'Lectures on Preaching' in her lifetime.

Lectures on preaching and pastoral care rounded off ministerial education in dissenting academies into the nineteenth century, and manuscript copies of Doddridge's lectures were being made and circulated right up to the moment a printed version of the text was published.[51] In a private setting among dissenters and guided by approved teachers these lectures were an acceptable resource; indeed a respected one. But granting readers who did not understand how Doddridge's academy was conducted access to his unmediated views on puritan and dissenting divines and Church of England clergymen concerned Orton (and rightly so, it would turn out). While dissenters may not have faced prosecution or persecution routinely in the eighteenth century, their anxieties about the content of some of Doddridge's works suggests that they feared the consequences of publicizing their teaching.

5. 'LECTURES ON PREACHING' IN PRINT

The preaching lectures first appeared in full, in book form, and in English in volume V of Williams and Parsons's edition of Doddridge's works, published in 1804. These editors expressed no qualms about the publication. In contrast to Orton's anxiety, they declare that the lectures 'secure the deserved reputation of Dr. DODDRIDGE' and assert their 'excellence' in three respects:

> In them we discover a great insight into human nature, an uniform regard to religious, moral, and civil propriety of conduct, ardent wishes to benefit mankind by promoting vital and practical religion.[52]

---

[51] DWL MS 28.124 is named and dated inside the front cover 'Timothy Davis 13 March 1802 Carmarthen' and ends 'Finis Nov^{br} 4th 1801', fol. 158.

[52] Williams and Parsons, 'Advertisement' to 'Lectures on Preaching' in Doddridge, *Works*, V, 424. Though both men are named as editors of the works as a whole, Williams was probably the sole editor of these lectures, as he was for *A Course of Lectures*.

In this précis the attributes for which Doddridge himself was praised are applied to the lectures, whose suitability for student and public perusal is extolled. No reason is given for the long delay in publication, nor do the editors note that at last Doddridge's wishes are being met. Indeed, there is no indication that they were familiar with the terms of Doddridge's will for they observe that 'the author has intimated no prohibition'.[53] This seems strange: if the lectures were such an honourable addition to the Doddridge canon, why had they not been published before and why did the editors choose neither to address that question nor to account for the gap? Striking too is the flurry of editions in the early nineteenth century following forty years of silence after Orton's strong injunction against their publication. There were six separate editions of 'Lectures on Preaching' in the first few decades of the century and the lectures were also included in three collections of Doddridge's writings.[54] Before these book publications of the whole body of lectures, extracts from the 'Lectures on Preaching' appeared in the *Universal Theological Magazine* and in an appendix to a collection of sermons compiled by Doddridge's editor Edward Williams, *The Christian Preacher* (1800).

Three factors can account for the late flourishing of the lectures. First, the passing of time obviated Orton's fears about the propriety of discussing living preachers so candidly. Second, the diversification and proliferation of print, which reached a high rate in the early decades of the century. The diversity of outlets for these particular lectures attest to the lively print culture for educational works of piety: they appeared in a periodical, within a multi-volume collected works, and as separately published, relatively inexpensive student editions. Finally, by the turn of the nineteenth century Doddridge's high reputation was secure. This was due to the passage of time and the resources of print and it acted as a spur to further publications (including the lectures) and reprints of existing works. Because of Doddridge's reputation there was a market for all his books, be they titles that had consolidated that reputation, or previously unpublished material.

---

[53] Doddridge, *Works*, V, 424. They were unlikely to have known the content of Doddridge's will.

[54] Separate editions were published in London in 1807, 1821 and 1822. The 1821 edition was simultaneously published in Edinburgh. The Boston edition was published in 1808. These collections in which they appeared were the *Works* and later *The Devotional Letters and Sacramental Meditations of the Rev. P. Doddridge, with his Lectures on Preaching* (London, 1832) and *The Miscellaneous Works of Philip Doddridge, D.D.*, ed. Thomas Morrell (London, 1839). On 11 April 1758, Job Orton wrote to Mercy Doddridge to say that he and Samuel Clark did not think the sacramental meditations were suitable for publication: see CHCN Doddridge MS.

These lectures' emergence into print cannot be fashioned into a single story. The different versions have different editors; and they identify (and treat) different 'problems' within the lectures. Each version must therefore be described in order to present a full picture of the discursive, adaptive, and often discontinuous construction of an official body of materials attributed to a particular author which took place posthumously and over many decades. It is also impossible to fix on an incontrovertible starting point for the process. The first version treated here is extracts that appeared in a volume of sermons by various authors edited by Edward Williams because that work constituted a kind of trial run by the editor of the first printed full version of the 'Lectures on Preaching'.

In *The Christian Preacher: or, Discourses on Preaching*, Williams collected together sermons by Doddridge, John Jennings and Watts, John Wilkins, and the seventeenth-century French Protestant minister Jean Claude, and a discourse by the Halle Pietist August Hermann Francke, all on the subject of preaching.[55] The compendium of sermons by English, German, and French ministers of different Protestant denominations provided ministers at work in the nineteenth century with examples of preaching and strictures on homiletic practice from earlier generations. By bringing these authors together as preachers on preaching, Williams was constructing a tradition of European evangelical orthodoxy and including Doddridge within it. The exemplary sermons were supported by an extensive bibliography in an appendix entitled 'The Preacher's Library'.[56] The list of books (which Williams developed over successive editions) begins with remarks about the value of reading and advice on where to discover which books have been published and their likely price. It lists titles and authors according to forty-seven categories, starting with editions of the Bible and biblical commentators and ending with poetry and music. Section 27 lists 'English Practical Writers' in the manner of lectures II–IV of the 'Lectures on Preaching'. Williams flags the point that the arrangement of writers follows Doddridge's ordering and that he incorporates some of Doddridge's comments:

> We may, with Dr. Doddridge, distribute them into the Puritans, the Nonconformists, and Episcopalians. Those writers of works which he has characterized shall be noticed in his own words, when they suit my purpose, distinguished by inverted commas.[57]

---

[55] Edward Williams, *The Christian Preacher: or, Discourses on Preaching* (Halifax, 1800).
[56] A second appendix of further reading was added in the fifth edition of 1843.
[57] Williams, *The Christian Preacher*, 467.

While the list does not correspond exactly with that of the 'Lectures on Preaching', there are sequences where the names of the writers appear in the same order as they do in the lectures. The printed list thus follows the manuscript tradition of incorporating these parts of Doddridge's lectures into materials produced by other tutors. Williams states in a footnote that his source is Doddridge's 'Preaching Lectures in Manuscript; of which I have two copies. When these differ, as they often do, the character which appears most just is given'.[58] Significant additions to Doddridge's lists include entries for George Whitefield ('a genius naturally sublime, sanctified by sovereign grace') and Doddridge himself ('Doddridge excels in distinctness of method, & scripture phraseology').[59] The entry on Doddridge is absent from the full 'Lectures on Preaching' as published four years later, perhaps in order to preserve the idea that the text is as close to Doddridge's words as possible. Whitefield does not appear in the printed 'Lectures on Preaching' either, perhaps because Williams was consciously avoiding including any controversial figures. Not carrying forward later additions to the lectures indicates that Williams was careful to make the published lectures keep as close to the authors noticed by Doddridge as possible.[60] Such fidelity is perhaps more important in a collected edition of an author's works than in extracts appended to a text written by another author.

Under Williams's stewardship, extracts from Doddridge's 'Lectures on Preaching' formed an increasingly significant component of a popular guidebook for preachers that promoted evangelical orthodoxy. Concurrently, extracts from the 'Lectures on Preaching' appeared in the Unitarian periodical the *Universal Theological Magazine*. In autumn 1803, two issues carried Doddridge's comments on Bible commentators, and two contained his sketches of the preaching style of puritan, dissenting, and established church preachers.[61] These extracts correspond very closely to

[58] Williams, *The Christian Preacher*, 452.
[59] Williams, *The Christian Preacher*, 470, 476. The remarks on Doddridge are not the same as those which appear in BBC MS G 93 and DWL MS NCL L.29/24.
[60] No evangelical Anglican preachers appear in Doddridge's 'Lectures on Preaching', even though Whitefield preached from his pulpit, Wesley lectured to Doddridge's academy students once, and both were among the most significant preachers of the age.
[61] The letter which introduces them begins, 'In those Lectures of Dr. Doddridge, which are denominated his *Preaching Lectures*, and which were never printed, are brief characters of the most celebrated commentaries,' *Universal Theological Magazine*, 9 (1803), 82. Commentators on the Bible are the subject of lectures XIV and XV (see 'Lectures on Preaching' in Doddridge, *Works*, V, 471–7). The notes on commentators appear in the *Universal Theological Magazine*, 9 (1803), 82–8 and 127–33; the second version of Doddridge's notes on practical writers (which correspond closely to lectures II–IV of the 'Lectures on Preaching' in Doddridge, *Works*, V) are printed in *Universal Theological Magazine*, 9 (1803), 195–202 and 237–45. The *Universal Theological Magazine* was

those in manuscript copies of the 'Lectures on Preaching' as well as the version printed in the *Works*. An earlier extract was rather different. In June 1803, a letter from 'Rusticus' had been printed which announced:

> I am induced to send you two other pieces, transcribed from a Course of MS. Lectures on ORATORY, which were used in the seminary over which Dr. Doddridge once presided. I apprehend a great part of them were drawn up the Doctor; but the copy from which I transcribed mine had evidently received additions.[62]

This first instalment comprises 'A brief account of ancient and modern moral writers' (a survey of Greek, Latin, French, and English orators) and comments 'On Style in Writing', which gives sketches of the style of various poets and preachers. The first set of remarks do not appear in any other manuscript or printed copies of 'Lectures on Preaching', and though some of the writers referred to in the second set appear in the preaching lectures, the range and order of the names bears little relationship to the manuscript 'Lectures on Preaching' which pre-date it, or to subsequent printed versions. The comments on the writers are often exactly the same as in eighteenth-century manuscript copies of the 'Lectures on Preaching' (for example, the remarks on John Tillotson's 'beautiful simplicity', which Doddridge borrows from Jennings) or the same idea is expressed in different words.[63]

How does the decision by 'Rusticus' and others to send extracts from Doddridge's lectures to the *Universal Theological Magazine* relate to Edward Williams's activities? The periodical setting is significant: 'Rusticus' presents his activity as part of the project to gather together and publish materials representative of dissenting culture in the previous century.[64] But while denominational magazines often published letters from, and anecdotes and opinions about, deceased ministers and tutors, presenting previously unpublished lectures in this way was unusual.[65]

---

founded in 1802 by William Vidler and continued as the *Monthly Repository* by Robert Aspland from 1809. The title continued until 1836. See Francis E. Mineka, *The Dissidence of Dissent: The Monthly Repository, 1806–1838* (Chapel Hill, NC, 1944), 80–1.

[62] *Universal Theological Magazine*, 8 (1803) 301–9. 'Rusticus' has been identified as the Unitarian minister Edmund Butcher, who had been educated at Daventry academy: see Alexander Gordon, 'Butcher, Edmund (1757–1822)', rev. M. J. Mercer, *ODNB*.

[63] Doddridge, *Works*, V, 435.

[64] 'As a literary curiosity, and as I think containing some very just remarks, I send an Extract for insertion in your liberal and useful Work,' wrote Rusticus in a letter dated 1 March 1803, and published in August that year. *Universal Theological Magazine*, 9 (1803), 82.

[65] 'Rusticus' also sent two lectures on eloquence by Andrew Kippis because they appeared in the same manuscript as the extracts of Doddridge's lectures. These were the only other lectures to be printed in the magazine. *Universal Theological Magazine*, new ser., 1 (1804), 192–6, 255–63.

Moreover, publishing extracts of Doddridge's lectures on oratory and preaching in this particular magazine introduced Doddridge's advice to appreciative readers from a specific demographic: ministers interested in controversial theology. The contributors and editor were publishing materials which had circulated widely in manuscript for decades, presenting it as the first time the material had been printed, and making no connection with the other recent appearance in print of similar extracts, those in Williams's *Christian Preacher*. The *Universal Theological Magazine* may have had the aim of establishing them as a legitimate and valuable part of the Doddridge corpus, but given that it only offered decontextualized extracts, a more obvious purpose was to align Doddridge and his teaching with a dissenting group that was rather different from Williams's own. Denominational differences may account for this. The *Universal Theological Magazine* was a relatively learned Unitarian journal whose readers were mostly ministers, but they might not have been in sympathy with Williams, who was an orthodox Congregationalist unsympathetic to the heterodoxy that Unitarianism supported. Including extracts from Doddridge's lectures here claims him as a forebear to a different tradition of dissenting education from the one Williams wrote for and to which he belonged.

In the period just before their publication in complete form in Doddridge's *Works*, dissenters from different theological parties who all viewed Doddridge as an influence apparently wanted to make his teaching materials available. They did not, however, issue complete publications: extracts from the 'Lectures on Preaching' appeared in peripheral locations of appendixes and periodicals at first. Perhaps those responsible were testing out the lectures' suitability for print publication, and hoped to gauge responses to the publication of extracts before publishing the whole course. At least one response to the activities of the 1800s indicates that Orton had correctly anticipated objections to the 'Lectures on Preaching' all those decades earlier. 'P. H.', a correspondent to the *Universal Theological Magazine*, observed that 'DR. DODDRIDGE'S Preaching Lectures were never intended for the press, and are in many views unfit for publication; otherwise they would have been published with his other Lectures.'[66] This correspondent insists that the magazine should not print further extracts, nor should the editors of the *Works* publish the 'Lectures on Preaching'. Though the two locations treat the lectures differently, 'P. H.' believes that nowhere in print is appropriate for the 'Lectures on Preaching'.

[66] *Universal Theological Magazine*, 9 (1803), 297–9.

In the case of the 'Lectures on Preaching', print follows manuscript precedents very closely. Both Williams and the *Universal Theological Magazine* published the same parts of the Doddridge course: the comments on preachers. This was also the material from Doddridge's lectures which academy tutors appended to their own lectures on preaching. The parts of Doddridge's course dissenters were most likely to circulate were among the parts of it Job Orton thought should be suppressed. They are both controversial and important to generations of ministerial students.

Williams and Parsons claimed that by publishing the lectures in the *Works* they were responding to a demand from the reading public. In fact, they claimed that a desire to forestall any improper appearance of the lectures in their entirety drove them to include them in their edition:

> it is well known that there are many mutilated and very imperfect copies abroad; and it is not improbable that, from some motive or other, a copy might find its way into the press in a form calculated to reflect but little credit on either the publisher or the author.[67]

The editors may have had the first extract to appear in the *Universal Theological Magazine* in mind as one such 'imperfect' copy and 'Rusticus' himself had noted that the copy in his possession could not have been a transcription of lectures delivered by Doddridge himself. 'Rusticus', however, was at ease with the process of circulating manuscripts and adding materials to them: he described how his copy was taken from another manuscript copy, not made while following the lectures in person, and he noted that two lectures by Kippis had been included in the manuscript. Williams and Parsons were not able to endorse this flexible way of combining materials from different sources in one document. As the editors of Doddridge's complete works, their project was to define and reproduce the corpus of Doddridge's writings. To assert that their version was not only the official one, but also the only one that should be trusted to convey Doddridge's words most accurately and comprehensively, they stress the thoroughness of their editorial practice. 'For the purposes of collation the Editors are in possession of four copies'; they wrote, and listed the dates to prove the authenticity of each of the manuscripts.[68] Their emphasis on the variety of manuscripts available and the extent to which their content varied does not conform to the evidence provided by manuscript copies extant today (for the lectures correspond in arrangement and

---

[67] Doddridge, *Works*, V, 424.
[68] Doddridge, *Works*, V, 423. Williams writes in *The Christian Preacher* that he is in possession of two copies of the 'Lectures on Preaching', indicating that he borrowed two more in preparing the edition of the lectures for publication.

content with surviving manuscript copies) but it may be a rhetorical justification for the publication of the lectures and a claim for the usefulness of having an established version in print.

Following the publication of Doddridge's *Works*, the 'Lectures on Preaching' were published separately a number of times. The first such edition was published in 1804 in London, by Robert Ogle, who was one of the booksellers responsible for the *Works*.[69] The immediate appearance of a separate, small-format edition of the lectures may have been to forestall piracy.[70] The editorial statement which precedes the text in each separate edition of the lectures is an excerpt from the 'Advertisement' by Williams and Parsons, described as 'the respectable Editors'.[71] The lectures are presented as an educational work, and this particular edition as an economical version designed to serve the needs of divinity students and ministers who do not possess a copy of Doddridge's *Works*. Students and readers outside dissenting academies could now possess a copy of Doddridge's 'Lectures on Preaching', and those within it need not make a handwritten copy of the lectures. The publication carried the authority of Williams's and Parsons's version of the lectures beyond the collected *Works* into separate, affordable books.

Similar reasons for publication are stated in a unique Dutch edition of the lectures, published much earlier than these English editions and extracts. This edition is a publishing curiosity: it preceded English printed versions of the lectures by many decades but was not directly associated with any of them, nor with the Dutch publication of *A Course of Lectures*. The originator of this version was a former student of Doddridge's named Thomas Greaves, who was assistant pastor to Sowden at Rotterdam from 1752 and later a subscriber to the Dutch *Course of Lectures*. The Dutch edition ends with a date: '*Northampton den 28ste van January* 1745', which is consistent with the dates Greaves attended the academy.[72] As a register of the year he transcribed the lectures, it is a vestige of the lectures' manuscript origins included as an attestation of this work's authenticity. Greaves's preface begins with a strong assertion of Doddridge's authorship which anticipates Clark's prefatory statements included in the later Dutch

[69] While the 1804 and 1821 editions were published by Ogle, the 1807 edition was published by Richard Edwards, who was not connected with the *Works*, and the 1808 edition by Manning and Loring.

[70] The *Works* cost £2 in boards, according to an advertisement in the 1805 edition of *The Family Expositor*. On authors and publishers favouring swift reprints of a work in a small format to forestall piracy, see Sher, *The Enlightenment and the Book*, 84.

[71] Doddridge, *Lectures on Preaching* (London, 1807), iv.

[72] Philip Doddridge, *Lessen over het Samestellen en Uitspreken van Predickatien* (Rotterdam, 1770), 144. The surviving manuscript copy of 'Lectures on Preaching' from Doddridge's academy also has 22 lectures. DWL MS NCL L.29/22.

edition of the *Course of Lectures*. Greaves notes that the lectures are unpublished in either English or Dutch and acknowledges that this might cast doubt upon their authenticity. He declares, therefore, his own role as the trusted conveyor of true materials when he describes 'having heard them from his own mouth, and have copied them from his own handwriting, when I found myself under his care for the five years I was in his house'.[73]

The body of the text is astonishingly close to the 1804 English printed edition right from the start. Both begin with a direct, oral address 'Gentlemen...' or in Dutch, 'Mynn Heeren'. The Dutch lectures contain nothing that is not also present in contemporary English manuscripts and later printed versions of the lectures. Very occasionally references are missing from the Dutch edition. For example, in lecture II students are advised to avoid natural religion as a topic, but to introduce aspects of it in the context of an evangelical sermon, and the Berry Street Lectures are used as a reference. In the Dutch version, the advice is there but the Berry Street example is not, possibly because Doddridge had not added it to his lectures at the point Greaves attended them, or because the title was not available in Dutch. Even idioms and figurative phrases are translated literally into Dutch, for example 'It is feeding the people with roots rather than fruits' is rendered as 'dewyl het niets anders is dan het volk met de wortels in plaatz van met de vrugten in voeden' and 'Painting and carving are learned by imitation' (to express reasons for taking notes of sermons heard and reviewing them in private) becomes 'Schilderen en Beeldhouwen word geleerd door navolging.'[74]

The only significant change is the number of lectures: twenty-two in the Rotterdam edition, twenty-five in those published from 1804 onwards. The difference here is in arrangement rather than content. In the printed English version, lectures 2, 3, and 4 are 'On the Use and Character of Practical Writers', 'The Character of Dissenting Writers in the Present Age' (i.e. since 1700), and 'The Character of Writers of the Established Church', whereas this material occupies only two lectures in the Dutch version. The English lecture 5 ('Rules for Composing Sermons') thus corresponds to the Dutch lecture 4. The Dutch lecture 7 ('On selecting thoughts and their arrangement') combines lectures 8 and 9 from

---

[73] 'als hebbende dezelve uit zynen mond gehoord en naar zyn eigen handschrift gevolgt, toen ik my onder zyne Academische zorg bevond en myn verblijf, vyf jaren lang, in zyn huis had.' *Lessen over het Samestellen*, sig. *2.

[74] Doddridge, *Lectures on Preaching*, lecture 5, § 4, 36 and lecture 1, §13; compared to *Lessen over het Samestellen*, 20 and 5.

the English version.[75] Therefore the Dutch lecture 8 corresponds to the English lecture 10. In terms of content, there is virtually no difference. The element of the lectures which did vary slightly in English—the lists of preachers and their qualities—is consistent with English published versions. The lists of preachers (puritans, nonconformists, dissenters, and members of the established church) are identical between the Rotterdam edition in 1766 and the Boston edition in 1808.[76] The affinity between the Dutch printed edition, translated from a copy of the lectures given by Doddridge in the mid-1740s, and the editions based on Williams's and Parsons's version in the nineteenth century indicates that all the editors took the manuscripts from the period of Doddridge's own academy as their copy text. None of the printed editions registers the additions and slight variations incorporated in later manuscript copies as described in Chapter 2. In this respect the content of the lectures reflects the editorial statements insisting on fidelity, as far as possible, to Doddridge's own words. Editors who knew nothing of each other's work followed a very similar approach in editing these materials for publication.

6. INTENTIONS AND EFFECTS

It was partly in order to demonstrate the thoroughness of dissenting education that *A Course of Lectures* was published, and dissenters from different traditions used it to claim Doddridge as a learned and respectable figurehead for their own educational and religious schemes in the late eighteenth and early nineteenth centuries. This single work was published in three distinct versions by dissenting ministers with different editorial agendas. One wanted to fulfil the wishes of his former tutor, another to confirm Doddridge's place in the Republic of Letters, and the third to reassert Doddridge's role within dissent as a learned author of an earlier age. This text is a representative example of a work that goes from having a long life as a coterie item scribally published within a particular community, to a public contribution to the Republic of Letters.

The publishing history of the lectures on preaching was rather different: excitement at finding and transmitting previously unpublished Doddridgeana motivated the diffusion of the lectures in periodicals, while the lectures were included in the *Works* in order to contribute to the production of a

---

[75] Lecture 7 is titled 'Over de verkiezing van Gedagten en derzelver Schikking' in Dutch; *Lessen over het Samestellen*, 45.

[76] The only change is that in the 1808 edition, Charnock appears later in the list of nonconformists and Clarke earlier in the list of preachers from the established church.

complete record in print of Doddridge's writings. These discursive and editorial activities were motivated primarily by the idea of Doddridge as an individual author, but the positive consequences of Doddridge's reputation for the standing of dissent more generally, and the education of dissenting ministers in particular, were evidently in the minds of those who participated in the debates. The named author as an identifiable individual both bestows legitimacy on an ongoing tradition and is himself afforded significance by the present-day participants in that tradition.

Intentions for publishing these educational materials ranged from obedience (fulfilling the request of the deceased) through memorial (preserving the legacy of the dead using print) to polemic (claiming Doddridge for one group among competing dissenting interests). They were also motivated by antiquarian interest in denominational history and pride in the traditions of religious dissent. In these respects, both courses of lectures are comparable to the posthumously published and collected works which are discussed in Chapter 6, and broader questions about authorship and editorial procedure will be pursued there.

This chapter has investigated publication patterns for educational works originating in dissenting academies. While the facts about the publication processes can be stated with a considerable degree of certainty, the conclusions to be drawn about the project's influence are tentative, largely due to the fact that the publication of theological and homiletic lectures was unusual throughout this period. Doddridge might have been an influential teacher but the publication of his teaching materials was not so, either in terms of curriculum or as a model for other tutors. Motivation can be established more definitively than influence. These materials were published with the aim of providing educational materials for new generations, but an increasingly powerful purpose was to establish an intellectual heritage for dissent that could be articulated through the figure of Doddridge as an exemplary author: the 'celebrated Dr Doddridge'.[77]

Chapters 1–3 of this book have delineated the cooperative temper of education and publishing among men associated with orthodox dissenting academies in some detail. In order to broaden the picture of dissenters' textual engagements to facilitate learning, Chapters 4–6 will turn to the ways in which dissenting precepts animated books for heterogeneous audiences, by examining the work Doddridge's friend Watts.

---

[77] Notice of Mercy Doddridge junior's death in *Gentleman's Magazine*, 75 (1805), 1080.

4

Isaac Watts, Educationalist

Isaac Watts's name is most likely to be known today to those who have spent time in British or North American churches, where 'When I survey the wondrous cross' remains a devotional staple across the denominations. Watts's crucial role in the development of English-language hymnody has been amply discussed by scholars.[1] While there is increasing awareness of Watts's central role in the development of educational writings for children and theories of commonplacing, and important accounts of pedagogic texts that connect Watts to Locke, a tendency persists to describe him as a poet or hymn writer.[2] In doing so, historians imply that Watts was an influential educationalist simply or primarily because he was well known for his hymns.[3] This chapter will suggest instead that Watts's work as a pedagogue in prose was neither divorced from nor subservient to his activities as a hymnodist.[4]

Certainly the bibliographic evidence for his importance as a poet is very strong: more than twenty editions each of *Divine Songs Attempted in Easy Language for the Use of Children* (1715) and *The Psalms of David Imitated in the Language of the New Testament* (1719) were published in Watts's lifetime, and at least thirty separate editions of *Horae lyricae* (1709) and over 150 editions of *Hymns and Spiritual Songs* (1707) were published in the eighteenth century alone.[5] He was portrayed primarily as a hymnodist

---

[1] Most significantly in Louis F. Benson, *The English Hymn* (London, 1915), Davie, *A Gathered Church* and 'The Language of the Eighteenth-Century Hymn', in *Dissentient Voice*, 67–82 and J. R. Watson, *The English Hymn: A Critical and Historical Study* (Oxford, 1997).

[2] See, for example, Lucia Dacome, 'Noting the Mind: Commonplace Books and the Pursuit of the Self in Eighteenth-Century Britain', *Journal of the History of Ideas*, 65 (2004), 603–25 (614) and Andrea Immel, 'Children's Books and School-Books', in *CHBB*, V, 736–49 (737). An excellent study of children's literature that attends to Watts's role in this burgeoning category is E. Jennifer Monaghan, *Learning to Read and Write in Colonial America* (Worcester, Mass., 2005).

[3] Monaghan, *Learning to Read and Write*, 220.

[4] John Hoyles makes a similar point in *The Waning of the Renaissance 1640–1740* (The Hague, 1971), 143–4, though his aim—to trace a shift within literary culture between 'the age of Marvell and the age of Blake' (p. xii)—is quite different to mine.

[5] These are very conservative estimates: a full bibliographic analysis is difficult, partly because there are no surviving copies of many editions of these texts. We may imagine the

in nineteenth- and twentieth-century biographies, which styled him 'the father of English hymnody' and claimed 'no other [hymn] writer of this order approaches near to him in the elevation, not merely of expression, but of sentiment'.[6] Watts's hymns united ardent Christians in deathbed narratives and were sometimes the only religious instruction received by children in poorhouses.[7] They were also crucial for congregational worship and private reading in colonial and post-Revolution America.[8] Watts's hymns were a daily presence in pious lives.

While eighteenth-century characterizations of Watts certainly do not ignore this aspect of his work, his reputation in his lifetime and the decades immediately following his death was a more rounded one, as a man of letters active in many fields. Watts was identified on title pages as 'that justly celebrated Divine, Philosopher, Moralist and Poet', and collections of his 'Beauties' mixed poetry and prose, imaginative writing and sermons, hymns and philosophical definitions.[9] In the first book-length biography of Watts, his prose works are discussed before his lyric poetry, hymns, and metrical psalms, and the extensive survey of 'Respects paid to him at his Decease'—taken from sermons and letters—shows that contemporaries mentioned his hymns no more frequently nor fulsomely than they did his work as a minister and philosopher. While the cultural power of Watts's hymns is undeniable, it was through his activities across numerous genres and among different social and intellectual milieux that his reputation as a man of learning was established.

For Watts, scriptural and moral poetry, discourses on private piety, textbooks of geography, astronomy, and logic, and treatises on ministerial

print runs were large, for Watts said that *The Psalms of David* had sold 'some thousands in a year's time', 'Preface', *Hymns and Spiritual Songs* (London, 1720). See Selma L. Bishop, *Isaac Watts's Hymns and Spiritual Songs (1707): A Publishing History and a Bibliography* (Ann Arbor, Mich., 1974), esp. xv–xviii and J. H. P. Pafford, *Isaac Watts: Divine Songs* (London, 1971) esp. ch. 5 (61–79); and charts of suggested numbers of editions, 70–1. The rate of publication of all these works increased enormously from the later eighteenth century onwards, partly because they came out of copyright.

[6] James Hamilton, *Christian Classics: Readings from the Best Divines, with Notices Biographical and Critical*, 4 vols (New York, 1859), III, 306; Edwin Paxton Hood, *Isaac Watts: His Life and Writings, his Homes and Friends* (London, 1875), 103.

[7] See Richard Burnham, *Pious Memorials, or, the Power of Religion upon the Mind in Sickness and at Death*, rev. George Burder (London, 1820), 276–84; Charles Kegan Paul, *William Godwin, his Friends and Contemporaries*, 2 vols (London, 1876), I, 6; Hamilton, *Christian Classics*, III, 302–3. A sixteen-year-old boy in a workhouse who was familiar with Watts's hymns was interviewed by Henry Mayhew in 1859 (*Reading Experience Database* record 1289).

[8] See David D. Hall, 'The Uses of Literacy in New England, 1660–1850', in *Printing and Society in Early America* (Worcester, Mass., 1983), 1–47 and Kevin J. Hayes, *A Colonial Woman's Bookshelf* (Knoxville, Tenn., 1996), 26, 32–9.

[9] For example, *The Beauties of the Late Revd. Dr. Isaac Watts* (London, 1782).

conduct all contributed to the same project of reforming the methods and materials for attaining understanding of God and the world. Watts repeatedly makes this point in his prefaces by highlighting the improving aim of his works and declaring the interconnected nature of branches of understanding. Taking Watts's own cue to consider the intellectual connections among his works allows for an analysis of particular groups of texts (in this chapter, educational and philosophical works) that is sensitive to their collective function. It does not isolate works according to their genre, or consider them as either secular or religious, for only adults or children, and in this respect it approaches Watts's works with due consideration for the way he wrote them, recognizing that he sought to break down literary and intellectual divisions. This approach also acts as a reminder that current perceptions of Watts might impair a clear view of the type of writer he was considered to be in his own time. One reason for Watts's importance in eighteenth-century culture is that he wrote works in many areas, through which he introduced diverse and large audiences to rational educational practices that were devoutly Christian. The learning, piety, and liberal thought that have been explored with relation to Doddridge in earlier chapters are also important themes in this delineation of Watts. Given the friendship between the two men, it is hardly surprising that intellectual and social candour—openness of engagement—characterized the educational and religious approaches of both.

1. WATTS'S METHODS IN CONTEXT

In his lifetime, Watts's educational works attracted the attention of participants in the learned world. In July 1741, the *History of the Works of the Learned* recommended that readers 'ambitious of appearing with any *éclat* in the Republick of Letters' should consult Isaac Watts's recently published *The Improvement of the Mind* (1741).[10] The review identified Watts's work by its subtitle '*a Supplement to the Art of Logick*', highlighting its relationship to Watts's earlier textbook *Logick* (1725), a survey of the operations and applications of human reason which by 1741 was in use at the universities of Oxford and Cambridge as well as at dissenting academies. The use of the word 'éclat' in this complimentary summary positions *The Improvement of the Mind* as a work for the confident neophyte who wishes to command attention. The *History of the Works of the Learned* provided abstracts of new works of history, theology, and

---

[10]   *History of the Works of the Learned*, 10 (1741), 1–28 (28).

natural philosophy, and published debates between learned authors. Watts's text was less self-declaredly scholarly than other material covered in the journal, and in this respect the *History of the Works of the Learned* might appear an unlikely place to read about a compendium of study methods, recommended reading, and desirable comportment produced by a dissenting minister.[11] But Watts had said that his hope for *Logick* was 'that the gentleman, and the christian, might find their account in the perusal [of it], as well as the scholar', and the attention to its sequel in the *History of the Works of the Learned* suggests that his aim of situating his works within a polite as well as a pious milieu was supported by review journals.[12] Watts's strategies for drawing a range of audiences together in particular printed works were part of a wider task to demonstrate and encourage reading and learning. This project had its roots in dissenters' educational and literary culture, but Watts also addressed readers from beyond his own tradition, and this chapter will investigate the range of ways in which he did both.

The attitude to print culture of the seventeenth-century Presbyterian divine Richard Baxter provided an important model for Watts and other dissenters of the eighteenth century. Baxter energetically published works that promoted daily piety and spiritual self-learning, and he saw publishing as an extension of his ministry, for, as he put it, 'lively Books may be easilier had, than lively Preachers'.[13] Baxterian preaching was emotionally engaging ('affectionate') and easily understood. It was experiential and firmly located in scripture. Baxter addressed particular texts (and even sections of texts) to certain readers in order to meet the spiritual needs of diverse constituencies. His *Christian Directory* (1673) includes lists of books suitable for poor students, less poor students, and for family reading.[14] Watts similarly sought to open up his works to varied and extensive audiences. He imitated Baxter's practice of writing simply and offering advice to specific groups of Christians. Doddridge also declared his esteem for Baxter in his correspondence, and the 'Lectures on Preaching' emphasized the model for eloquence and effective ministry that

---

[11] M. O. Grenby notes that children's books were sometimes reviewed in the monthlies, but his examples date from the 1780s onwards. Watts's works for young people were being reviewed almost half a century earlier than this, indicating another aspect of publishing for the young in which he was a pioneer. See M. O. Grenby, *The Child Reader 1700–1840* (Cambridge, 2011), 187.

[12] Watts, *Works*, V, iii. Mee, *Conversable Worlds*, 73.

[13] Baxter, *The Christian Directory*, in *Practical Works*, I, 454. Quoted in N. H. Keeble, *Richard Baxter, Puritan Man of Letters* (Oxford, 1982), 34. See also Rivers, *Reason, Grace, and Sentiment*, I, ch. 2.

[14] Baxter, *The Christian Directory*, in *Practical Works*, I, 717–22; 454–5 respectively; Keeble, *Richard Baxter*, 36–43.

Baxter provided to young dissenting ministers: 'A manly eloquence, and the most evident Proofs of amazing Genius, with respect to which he may not improperly be called The English Demosthenes...Few were the means of converting more souls than Mr Baxter.'[15] Watts and Doddridge both looked to Baxter as the exemplary author, the supreme orator and clearest teacher from an earlier age of nonconformity, and borrowed his approaches in their efforts to shape educational, learned, and religious culture in the eighteenth century with distinctively dissenting attributes.

Watts's pedagogy appealed to a variety of audiences and, as the presence of the review in the *History of the Works of the Learned* suggests, these prose works—characterized by straightforward aims and modes of presentation, and promoting empirical methods of rational enquiry—were read by adults as well as young students. The expansion of the realm of learning has been identified as one characteristic of enlightenment culture, and numerous published texts addressed the purpose and matter of education.[16] Watts's works contributed to pedagogic ideas and practice within and beyond dissenting education, not least because he adapted and repackaged John Locke's educational principles and was a favourite author of Samuel Johnson.[17]

Locke's treatise *Some Thoughts Concerning Education* was reprinted steadily throughout the eighteenth century and his 'Of the Conduct of the Understanding' was appreciated by educators (among them John Jennings) for the cues it gave on developing strategies for learning. Unlike Locke, Watts did not confine his remarks to the education of gentlemen or make specific demands about structures for education or the characters of educators that addressed only wealthy men and members of certain intellectual circles.[18] Investigating the audiences Watts addressed and

---

[15] Doddridge, *Works*, V, 431. *Calendar* 155, 185.

[16] Educational treatises published or republished in the period include John Locke, *Some Thoughts Concerning Education* (1693; 11th edn, 1745) and numerous conduct manuals include *The Polite Student* (London, 1748). Learned texts aimed at mass audiences are treated as examples of 'popular enlightenment' in Germany in Jonathan B. Knudsen, 'On Enlightenment for the Common Man', in *What is Enlightenment? Eighteenth-Century Answers and Twentieth-Century Questions*, ed. James Schmidt (Berkeley and Los Angeles, 1996), 270–90.

[17] Both Robert DeMaria and Richard Yeo have noted Watts's role as a popularizer of Locke who was read by Samuel Johnson, and DeMaria identifies Watts's educational ideas as informing the structure and content of Johnson's *Dictionary*: see Robert DeMaria, *Johnson's Dictionary and the Language of Learning* (Oxford, 1986), 19–20, 36–7; Richard Yeo, *Encyclopaedic Visions: Scientific Dictionaries and Enlightenment Culture* (Cambridge, 2001), 73–4, 158. James McLaverty, 'From Definition to Explanation: Locke's Influence on Johnson's Dictionary', *Journal of the History of Ideas*, 47 (1986), 377–94.

[18] John Locke, *Some Thoughts Concerning Education*, §93 and §94. See also Paul Schuurman, 'Locke's Way of Ideas as a Context for his Theory of Education in *Of the Conduct of the Understanding*', *History of European Ideas*, 27 (2001), 45–59 (57).

the physical formats of his books (often duodecimo or even smaller) leads away from the scenes of scholarship and scientific investigation thought to characterize enlightenment culture and towards a more diverse, and dispersed, set of mediations. Importantly, Watts's texts—which combined lively forms of direct address, practical questions about and explanations of philosophy, and invitations to open debate—were encountered by children as well as students and adults. The young were a particularly important audience for Watts.

M. O. Grenby has argued that it was through the innovative marketing strategies of John Newbery and other early children's publishers that 'children's literature as a new taxonomic category' emerged from the 1740s.[19] In terms of content and format, several Watts titles are significant precursors to that trend. The ideas of John Locke provided the principal intellectual source for that market. Watts shared his pragmatic view of the need for improved teaching materials, and, as Andrea Immel explains, his works represent an early stage of the development of the genre.[20] As well as Immel's example of *Divine Songs* (designed to inculcate understanding of religious doctrines and promote positive ethics), *The Art of Reading and Writing in English* (1721), *Logick* (1725), *The Knowledge of the Heavens and Earth Made Easy* (1726), and *A Short View of the Whole Scripture History* (1732) disseminated Watts's principles of free enquiry within the parameters of a Christian education (an important way in which he modified Locke) and declared the intellectual importance of historical and philosophical learning from an early age. Because they recommending continued reading and training, these books created a demand for more books; demand that booksellers like Newbery met (and cultivated further) with his own publications. Thus Watts should be understood as an important conduit between Lockean educational psychology and Newbery's business.

The presentation of information to children in simple language and through inexpensive books which Watts championed was one aspect of a culture of informal education enabled by print, at the other end of the spectrum in terms of format and price to monumental encyclopedic works such as Ephraim Chambers's *Cyclopedia* and Samuel Johnson's *Dictionary*. Richard Yeo has described encyclopedias as instruments of the burgeoning Republic of Letters that, from the seventeenth century onwards, facilitated

[19] Grenby, *The Child Reader*, 4.

[20] Immel, 'Children's Books and School-Books', 737. Children's literature from the seventeenth century that may have influenced Watts is discussed in Harry Escott, *Isaac Watts, Hymnographer: A Study of the Beginnings, Development, and Philosophy of the English Hymn* (London, 1962), 199–206.

the dissemination of knowledge through alternative channels to the universities. This new community of learning was imagined in inclusive terms as one in which well-informed discourse could be undertaken by all those with appropriate mental training.[21] Such training was provided by Watts's works which describe and enact methods for intellectual preparation in simple language. The boundaries of the 'Republic of Letters' (an imagined community of the seventeenth century that continued to be evoked throughout the eighteenth) were flexible, its principles not necessarily uniform, and the kinds of books and types of readers it encompassed were heterogeneous to say the least. Watts used print to disseminate his ideas about education and his mode of address widened the potential readership for his own works. As such his publishing activities consciously extended dissenting educational ideas beyond dissenting academies: a point he made himself when he noted that his sermons '[are] now published, not with any design to inform the learned world, but to serve the vulgar Christian'.[22]

Watts often presented the quest for improvement as being his motive for going into print. In the preface to *Hymns and Spiritual Songs*, he notes three areas of devotional life in need of reform:

> Perhaps the Modes of Preaching in the best Churches still want some Degrees of Reformation, nor are the Methods of Prayer so perfect as to stand in need of no Correction or Improvement. But of all our Religious Solemnities *Psalmodie* is the most unhappily manag'd.[23]

Across a series of publications (including *Two Discourses, A Guide to Prayer* and *A Humble Attempt for the Revival of Practical Religion among Christians*, and *Hymns and Spiritual Songs*) Watts sought to remedy each of these deficiencies by offering a model for religious worship that spurred the intellect and the stirred emotions. These publications and other hymns and prose works all sustained a religious community dispersed across a range of Protestant denominations that was committed to evangelical action, universal education, and community endeavour. This chapter, therefore, will show that principles of ethical living and religious understanding were repeated, explained, and given a philosophical grounding in Watts's prose works. His poetry is not the central object of study here because it has tended to receive more critical attention than the prose

---

[21] Yeo, *Encyclopaedic Visions*, 34–46. For a Republic of Letters that was a rather more exclusive community, see Goldgar, *Impolite Learning*, 2–3, 6–7, and 239–42.

[22] Watts to Colman, 11 April 1723, in MHS, *Proceedings*, 339.

[23] Isaac Watts, *Hymns and Spiritual Songs* (London, 1707), iv.

works even though the latter had just as significant an effect on education, international self-understanding, and schemes for national improvement.

2. WATTS AS CONDUIT: EDUCATIONAL WRITINGS

Watts had a broad view of what constituted instructive writing. He pursued a project for mental and spiritual improvement across his poetry and prose. He considered the former to be a particularly effective means of teaching children the principles of religious practice, setting out four reasons for this in the preface to *Divine Songs* (1715). First, 'There is a greater delight in the very learning of Truths and Duties in this way', second 'What is learnt in *Verse* is longer retain'd in Memory', meaning that hymns form the 'constant Furniture for the Minds of Children'. This presence of hymns in the memory acts as a prompt to meditation and thinking of God when children are alone, as an alternative to the negative effects of 'the loose and dangerous Sonnets of the Age'. Finally, these hymns can form part of 'daily or weekly' family worship, and to that end Watts has 'confined the Verse to the most usual Psalm Tunes', thereby making it possible for the instruction contained in his poetry to take place in various circumstances, namely private reading and family prayer, and to reach adults as well as children. The preface reassures parents and teachers that 'you will find here nothing that savours of a Party: The Children of high and low Degree, of the Church of *England* or Dissenters, baptised in Infancy, or not, may all join together in these songs'.[24] Identifying three contentious divisions of social status, religious affiliation, and doctrinal commitment and insisting that *Divine Songs* will transcend these boundaries, Watts imagines the text creating a united chorus: rather than individual children reading, a collective sings together. This image provides a motif for the work, which espouses an open-minded concept of religious practice and encourages shared intellectual activity. These aims, and a similar optimism of tone, can be found across Watts's educational writings.

Such works include *Logick*, *The Improvement of the Mind*, and *Philosophical Essays* (1733) as well as more simply presented texts such as *The Art of Reading and Writing English* (1721) and *A Short View of the Whole of Scripture History* (1732). Specifically religious instruction was offered in

---

[24] Isaac Watts, *Divine Songs Attempted in Easy Language for the Use of Children* (2nd edn, 1716), not paginated.

sermons, an annotated edition of the Westminster Assembly's catechism, and *An Humble Attempt* (1731). Watts also recommended the works of others and became a textual figure presiding over practical texts he had neither written himself nor given a preface. Doddridge dedicated his 'Course of Serious and Practical Addresses' entitled *The Rise and Progress of Religion in the Soul* (1745) to Watts, partly because the topic was one Watts himself had wanted to address. He wrote letters encouraging Doddridge to write the work, and had tested out sections of the text on his household and servants to ensure that it was comprehensible to the full range of 'persons of every Character and Circumstance' invoked on the title page.[25] The dedication is a tribute to Watts in which Doddridge praises him for the reach of his influence, his grasp of different forms, and his ability to use these forms to address different readers. In a metonymic move, Doddridge depicts Watts's texts undertaking Watts's tasks:

> While You are in a Multitude of *Families*, and *Schools* of the lower Class, condescending to the humble, yet important Work of forming Infant Minds to the first Rudiments of Religious Knowledge and devout Impressions by your various *Catechisms* and *Divine Songs*, You are also daily reading Lectures of *Logick*, and other useful Branches of *Philosophy* to studious Youth . . . I congratulate you, that You are teaching no doubt Hundreds of *Ministers*, and Thousands of *private Christians*, by your *Sermons*, and other *Theological Writings*.[26]

Watts is presented as a personal teacher and adviser to children, ministers, university students, and 'thousands of private Christians'. To Doddridge it is the combination of the specificity of personal engagement with each reader at the same time as the wide range of audiences addressed across a variety of genres which is the key feature of Watts's works. Through his affectionate address, Doddridge is emphasizing the particularity of Watts's approach. At the same time, he is presenting a moment of shared endeavour undertaken by members of the same community to the wider world. Perhaps there is an element of expedience here—Doddridge is advertising one person's writings in the preface to his own and hence widening the potential audience for both—but a second, more complex, aim is being enacted too. Doddridge and Watts were not unique for their desire to spread the ideas and practices of dissent beyond their own community, while presenting the rational and evangelical character of dissent as guiding their work.[27] But unlike dissenters who wrote learned works aimed at

---

[25] *Calendar* 945, 963.
[26] Doddridge, *The Rise and Progress of Religion in the Soul* (London, 1745), v–vi. See also Rivers, *Reason, Grace, and Sentiment*, I, 174.
[27] Rivers, *Reason, Grace and Sentiment*, I, 165.

scholarly audiences, they addressed ordinary people in texts which encouraged their readers to unite spiritual and daily life.[28] Watts and Doddridge did not only address the learned and polite, and they attempted particularly to show their audiences ways of approaching their works.

In his dedication to *The Rise and Progress of Religion in the Soul*, Doddridge expresses a wide conception of what constitutes a 'work', and encompasses a community of participants in its production. He stresses that a single work is not a solitary act but part of a network of texts, writers, readers, and listeners. This sense of collectivity—so characteristic of dissenters' self-presentation explored throughout this book—partly accounts for Watts's emphasis on the importance of method and the clear arrangement of texts under 'heads': if dissenters are producing new kinds of texts, which encourage and diffuse new kinds of religious and intellectual experiences, a secure way of encountering them is required. If freedom of enquiry is to be encouraged (as it was by John Jennings and Philip Doddridge in their academies) those engaged in the enquiry must be trained in appropriate methods for accessing and understanding materials. They must learn 'the right use of reason', in the words of the subtitle to *Logick*.

In *The Strength and Weakness of Human Reason* (1731) Watts discusses 'whether reason is an adequate guide to religion, morality and happiness'.[29] This topic lies at the heart of Watts's writings and his conclusion, broadly, is that it is. Watts understood the purpose of reason differently depending on whether the context was religious or secular understanding: in his religious poetry, for instance, Watts emphasizes that reason alone is not sufficient for full religious understanding.[30] Rivers points out that while Watts claims his decision to cast the enquiry in *The Strength and Weakness of Human Reason* in the form of a dialogue between 'an inquiring deist' and 'a Christian divine' invites debate and the use of reason on the part of his readers the static actuality of a printed text does not, in fact, permit his conclusions to be questioned. This is true of all printed dialogues, of course. Watts is here using the form to dramatize the intellectual question and the heart of religious knowledge and to model courteous and informed debate for readers to imitate.

---

[28] Printed works designed in part to showcase dissenting learning include Daniel Neal, *The History of New England*, 3 vols (London, 1720) and *The History of the Puritans*, 4 vols (London, 1732–1738); Nathaniel Lardner, *The Credibility of Gospel History*, 2 vols (London, 1727). In its final form, this work ran to twelve volumes (London, 1748–1760).

[29] Rivers, *Reason, Grace and Sentiment*, I, 180.

[30] J. R. Watson, 'The Hymns of Isaac Watts and the Tradition of Dissent', in *Dissenting Praise: Religious Dissent and the Hymn in England and Wales*, ed. Isabel Rivers and David L. Wykes (Oxford, 2011), 33–67 (40–2).

Watts's works train readers to think critically, a project he frames within an investigation of two key terms for intellectual enquiry that have figured large in this book: 'reason' and 'method'. It is in order to create an intellectual climate of curiosity-driven investigation and aversion to dogmatic acceptance of received opinion that Watts devotes himself to training the mind in the 'right use of reason' and open-minded discussion. This has been described as an attitude of compromise and assumed to have been a pragmatic means of avoiding the vicious divisions of seventeenth-century political and religious life primarily in England.[31] But this irenic approach was not unique to English Protestantism and cannot be explained exclusively in terms of a reaction to the civil wars in the Three Kingdoms, for Dutch Reformed ministers also sought it, and there is evidence that English dissenters followed the Dutch example.[32] Watts's rational evangelicalism should be thus be seen as part of a pan-European culture of practical learning. As well as the affinities with the Halle network to be described in Chapter 5, there are resonances with the 'enlightened evangelicalism' that Jonathan Yeager finds in the activities of the Scottish minister John Erskine.[33] Empirical knowledge gathering, social activism, and international exchanges of books were components of the optimistic and open-ended religious culture of learning in this period, which operated across denominations.

Watts's hope that reason and method will be used to seek out truth underlies his educational textbooks such as *Logick* and *The Improvement of the Mind* as well as his works of advice to preachers and congregations such as *An Humble Attempt*.[34] The philosophy training text *Logick* was designed to provide readers with the tools for developing their own critical enquiries. It guides students through the principles of free enquiry and gives examples of how to apply these to their own thought rather than abstractly theorizing the operations of the mind. As such it is very different from logic as it was studied in the English universities, and appears to respond to John Locke's complaint in *Some Thoughts Concerning Education* (1693) that 'I have seldom or never observed any one to get the skill of reasoning well . . . by studying those rules that pretend to teach it' and his insistence that 'Right reasoning is founded on something else than the

---

[31] Hoyles, *The Waning of the Renaissance*, 151. Hoyles presents Watts as representative of a polite, Protestant enlightenment based on intellectual compromise in order to argue for the ultimate weakness of classicism and enlightenment as cultural forces.

[32] Tessa Whitehouse, 'Intellectual and Textual Entrepôts: Moses and Aaron, Hermann Witsius and the International Transmission of Educational Texts', *English Studies*, 92 (2011), 562–75 (563–5).

[33] Yeager, *Enlightened Evangelicalism*, 19–21 and ch. 8.

[34] Rivers, *Reason, Grace, and Sentiment*, I, 180.

predicaments and predicables.'[35] Watts's four-part structure resembles that of the Port Royal logic of 1662, while the categories into which it divides logic—perception, judgement, argumentation, disposition—echo Jean Le Clerc's *Logica* (1692), which introduces the theory of ideas, judgement, method, and argument.[36] Both these texts opposed Aristotle, and in his preface to the *Philosophicl Essays* of 1733, Watts also writes of 'the slavery of Aristotle and substantial forms... and words without ideas'. Naming Newton, Gassendi, Bacon, and Boyle as his heroes, because 'They taught mankind to trace out truth by reasoning and experiment', Watts locates his intellectual efforts elsewhere, within a tradition of empirically-based natural philosophy guided by rational enquiry.[37] As his choice of English exemplars suggests, this tradition was identified with the work of the Royal Society, which gained its charter in 1662. The Protestant intellectual culture of exchange central to the working of the Royal Society was not one from which Watts considered himself excluded, despite its Stuart origins: indeed, he became one of the key eighteenth-century promoters of its principles.

Logick provided a framework for applying the empirical principles Watts advocated, whose purpose he articulates in a phrase which conflates the discipline and his book: 'Logick helps us to strip off the outward disguise of things.'[38] The book draws on Locke's *Essay Concerning Human Understanding* (1690), takes Locke's enquiries as the starting point for each section, and follows the Lockean method of providing a series of examples to illustrate the workings of particular operations.[39] Watts reconfigures Locke's *Essay* into an educational sourcebook by making the examples simpler, more direct, and more frequent, and by paraphrasing Locke's text and giving references to it (particularly Book II 'Of Ideas').

[35] Locke, *Some Thoughts Concerning Education*, §182.
[36] Antoine Arnauld and Pierre Nicole, *Logique, ou l'art de penser* (Paris, 1662). The first edition published in England was *Logica, sive ars cogitandi* (London, 1674); the first edition in English was published in 1685; the last English edition in 1727. See also Jean Le Clerc, *Logica, sive ars ratiocinandi* (London, 1692). Le Clerc was used at several dissenting academies. I am grateful to Mark Burden for providing information about Arnaud, Le Clerc, and logic teaching at dissenting academies. For the different categories into which acts of reasoning could be divided and the significance of that choice in the period, see John P. Wright, 'The Understanding', in *The Oxford Handbook of British Philosophy in the Eighteenth Century*, ed. James A. Harris (Oxford, 2013), 149–70, esp. 152–4.
[37] Watts, *Works*, V, 502.   [38] Watts, *Works*, V, 2.
[39] 'The line from the Port Royal to the logic of Watts... goes straight through Locke's *Essay* and his *Conduct*', John W. Yolton, *Perceptual Acquaintance from Descartes to Reid* (Minneapolis, 1984), 113. For the ongoing influence of this milieu on English religious educationalists, see Anne Stott, 'Evangelicalism and Enlightenment: The Educational Agenda of Hannah More', in *Educating the Child in Enlightenment Britain: Beliefs, Cultures, Practices*, ed. Mary Hilton and Jill Shefrin (Farnham, 2009), 41–56.

In a significant modification of Locke's purpose, Watts emphasizes the religious applications of the process by inserting throughout *Logick* examples which speak to contemporary denominational conflicts. For example, the proposition that all ideas must be true or false is illustrated by contrasting Roman Catholic and Protestant understandings of the words 'church' and 'sacraments'.[40] In an account of the inexact relationship between words and ideas he uses the word 'bishop' and its French form 'evêque' and discourses on the function of an episcopate.[41] Elsewhere, Watts's examples reaffirm the majesty of God rather more triumphantly than occurs in Locke's *Essay*, and the whole work is framed by Watts's opening declaration that '*Reason*, as to the *Power and Principle* of it, is the common Gift of God to all Men.'[42] This optimistic conviction is central to Watts's practice of weaving together religion and education and in *Logick* Watts uses Locke's methods to develop a method of logic training which embraces evangelical nonconformity. This religious reorientation of Locke was one of the primary channels by which Lockean ideas were disseminated to an educated reading public. *Logick* was used in dissenting academies and at colleges in America. It also won recognition in the English universities: as Watts wrote to his friend Benjamin Colman, 'Even Oxford & Cambridge break thro' their bigotry & hatred of yᵉ Dissenters, & use my Logic, my Astronomy, & my Poems.'[43] This is important evidence for the religious and tolerant character of transatlantic educational culture in the period.

Watts's philosophy texts demonstrate the outcomes of reasoning as well as the methods for it and as a dissenter one such application of logic was to argue that religious toleration has an emphatically rational basis. To this end, Watts invokes Locke in the preface to *Philosophical Essays*:

> His admirable Letter of *Toleration* led me as it were into a new Region of Thought, wherein I found myself surprised and charm'd with Truth. There was no Room to doubt in the midst of Sun-beams [and it] taught me to allow all Men the same Freedom to chuse their Religion, as I claim to chuse my own.[44]

These *Essays* pay close attention to evidence of God in the natural world, and Watts's recurrent favouring of natural metaphors uses a particular lexical set to knit together Locke's arguments in favour of religious toleration and the subjects addressed in the *Philosophical Essays*. Watts

---

[40] Watts, *Works*, V, 24.   [41] Watts, *Works*, V, 26–7.
[42] Watts, *Works*, V, 1.
[43] Watts to Colman, 8 May 1728, MHS, *Proceedings*, 341.
[44] Watts, *Works*, V, 503.

ignores any separation between different categories in this case, between questions relating to ontology and natural philosophy on one hand, and arguments for the separation of church and state on the other. Instead, he argues that Locke encourages complete freedom of enquiry:

> The man who has laboured to lead the world into freedom of thought, has thereby given a large permission to his readers to propose what doubts, difficulties or remarks have arisen in their minds, while they peruse what he has written.[45]

Here Watts articulates the potential of Locke's ideas for new modes of intellectual engagement, while the essays themselves demonstrate how this might be done. The twelve essays make connections between the physical and the spiritual worlds by interrogating the origins of ideas, the existence of spirits, and the activities of the soul, as well as investigating the nature and workings of light, plants, and animals. The aim of the *Philosophical Essays* is partly to introduce Lockean ideas to a new audience, but particularly to explore how Locke's challenges to epistemology might affect traditional ways of thinking about the relationship between religion and knowledge of the world.

In Watts's scheme, knowledge of the natural world is important for how it helps man to understand God and as a demonstration of God's omnipotence and wisdom, and Watts pursues questions about the world according to an experiential method of enquiry. For example, in the course of a discussion of Locke's views on vitality and identity, Watts asks: 'When the graft of a pearmain has grown three months or even years upon the stock of a crab, is it the same tree?'[46] In choosing this example of the practice of using the hardy crab variety as the rootstock for mealy fleshed eating apples for his query, Watts is, like Locke, rooting his enquiry in the visible natural world. He opens up the work to the experiential knowledge of readers and his questioning style invites their responses.[47]

3. WATTS IN USE

Watts's discursive mode was readily adopted by one reader of the *Philosophical Essays*, Hester Thrale Piozzi. Between 1798 and 1800, she

[45] Watts, *Works*, V, 503.   [46] Watts, *Works*, V, 627.

[47] Pratt gives examples of students noting their approval for the *Philosophical Essays* on its pages, such as 'the Man that Liketh not this Book is a Whipple-swick': see Anne S. Pratt, *Isaac Watts and his Gift of Books to Yale College* (New Haven, 1938), 25.

annotated an early edition of the *Philosophical Essays*. This accorded with her regular practice as described by H. J. Jackson: a 'serious and voracious reader, Piozzi was accustomed to make notes for herself as she read'.[48] Piozzi's annotations to Watts's text are striking for the breadth of knowledge on theological, artistic, horticultural, and social topics she applied to the ideas developed in the text. For example, alongside Watts's question about the pearmain she observes:

> A *Crategus Aria Theophrasti* will grow in England no way—but inoculated into a Thorn: in three or four years like the Cuckoo it kills its Parent, and flourishes up a fine king of the Poplars. I planted several so myself at Streatham Park.[49]

Her response to Watts's question is grounded in her own horticultural experience, while her conclusion is expressed figuratively through the trope of the cuckoo. This combination of practical knowledge and imaginative engagement with the ideas is evident throughout her annotations, which consistently address Watts personally. At points, her copy of the text takes the form of a dialogue with the *Essays*' author. In a discussion of the operations of plants, Watts writes: 'Colouring in its original Glory and Perfection triumphs here; Red, Yellow, Green, Blue, Purple, with vastly more Diversities than the Rainbow ever knew, or the Prism can represent.'[50] Piozzi responds in a playful tone that insists on factual accuracy: 'Not so my dear Doctor; In the Prism & Rainbow *every* colour is contained, and you know that better than poor H.L.P. only the Subject runs away with you.'[51] Direct replies follow Watts's questions in 'A brief scheme of Ontology': 'Is a bat a bird or a beast? Is every monster to be called a man which is born of a woman?', to which Piozzi responds: '(i) A beast (ii) Yes.'[52] Elsewhere she uses anecdotes to provide additional perspectives on the points raised, as when Watts writes, 'there are some original Particles of an animal Body, which continue from its birth to its death . . . and these may probably continue the same even till the great resurrection', and she notes: 'Mr. Hogarth told me that the Eye never grew larger from Birth to Death, and in effect we see children with fine eyes as we call them—a Thousand Times for once that we admire Men's and Women's eyes; only (as he said) because they looked larger and finer among the infant's features, than among the features of a grown person.'[53]

---

[48] H. J. Jackson, *Marginalia: Readers Writing in Books* (New Haven, 2001), 104.

[49] James P. R. Lyell, *Mrs. Piozzi and Isaac Watts* (London, 1934), 41.

[50] Watts, *Works*, V, 595.   [51] Lyell, *Mrs. Piozzi and Isaac Watts*, 37.

[52] Watts, *Works*, V, 641. Lyell, *Mrs. Piozzi and Isaac Watts*, 42.

[53] Watts, *Works*, V, 631. Lyell, *Mrs. Piozzi and Isaac Watts*, 42.

Following Watts's analogy between space and shade, Piozzi writes:

> Much of our Difficulty (as Beattie says) proceeds from Language: We use the
> word Nothing in a positive sense one Minute, in another Minute we treat it
> as mere Privation—yet to the *Grammarian* as to every other SCHOLAR The
> *Thing* Space is incomprehensible, be the Words what they may be in which
> we discourse upon it.[54]

Here she is drawing on ideas from a work published after Watts's death to
interrogate the reasons for disparity between definitions of 'space'. Her
incursion into the discourse does not answer Watts's query, but puts
Beattie (like Watts, both a poet and a philosophical writer) into contact
with Watts. Hogarth's artistic eye and Beattie's moral philosophy contribute to Watts's observations via her annotations, and populating
Watts's discourses with fashionable and learned individuals of her own
day is a means of continuing the debate in which personal encounters (her
anecdote from Hogarth) have comparable status to published claims like
Beattie's. In these respects, Piozzi followed Watts's practice of dissolving
social and generic boundaries around a text and among its readers.

Piozzi was a wealthy patron of artists and an unusually highly educated
woman; a female adult actively reading the *Essays* at the turn of the
nineteenth century, seventy years after their publication. Piozzi's notes
on Watts are consistent with her reading practices as outlined by Jackson,
and *Philosophical Essays* was by no means the only book that Piozzi
annotated.[55] Surviving books with her notes include an edition of *Bax-
teriana* (1815) that she gave her nephew as a gift and into which she wrote
some notes, and a 1786 edition of the Bible, both of which indicate
ongoing commitment to practical religion on the part of this *salonnière*.[56]

But, importantly, Piozzi's questioning and correcting notes on Watts
are also consistent with reading practices encouraged by Watts himself.
In *The Improvement of the Mind* Watts advises the reader to 'Deal freely
with every author you read...if he does not explain his ideas or prove
his positions well, mark the faults or defects and endeavour to do it
better...in the margin of your book.'[57] As well as giving plenty of
similarly practical advice, Watts reminds readers to reflect on the manner
and purpose of their learning. At the beginning of 'The Conduct of the

[54] Watts, *Works*, V, 519–21. Lyell, *Mrs. Piozzi and Isaac Watts*, 26. James Beattie, *An
Essay on the Nature and Immutability of Truth* (Edinburgh and London, 1770),
'Introduction'.
[55] Jackson, *Marginalia*, 65–110.
[56] Many of Piozzi's books are in the Donald and Mary Hyde Collection of Dr Samuel
Johnson at Houghton Library, Harvard University.
[57] Watts, *Works*, V, 207.

Understanding', Locke remarks, 'it is easy to perceive that Men are guilty of a great many Faults in the Exercise and Improvement of this faculty of the Mind, which hinder them in their Progress and keep them in Ignorance and Error all their Lives'.[58] In *The Improvement of the Mind*, Watts shows students how to avoid these faults. The book encourages wide reading, diverse conversation, and the exercise of the intellectual faculties; the kinds of understanding that Piozzi demonstrates in her responses to the *Philosophical Essays*.

Piozzi responded to Watts's *way* of thinking as much as to the specific ideas, and she synthesized different types of knowledge to address abstract questions. She practised just the kind of engagement that Watts's pedagogy, with its emphasis on individual reasoning, invited; and her copy of the book became a site of enquiry. This approach supports Jackson's claim that Piozzi can be used to infer ways of reading in the period, because she is following prescriptions: her example shows that reading theory and practice were often in harmony, with productive intellectual effects.

Piozzi's friend Samuel Johnson valued *The Improvement of the Mind* for the moral edification it could offer, and recommended it to female acquaintances. In 1781 he wrote to Piozzi from Lichfield:

> I have here but a dull scene. Poor Lucy's health is very much broken. She takes very little of either food or exercise, and her hearing is very dull, and her utterance confused; but she will have *Watts's Improvement of the Mind*. Her mental powers are not impaired, and her social virtues seem to increase. She never was so civil to me before.[59]

To which she replied:

> I am glad Watts's Improvement of the Mind is a favourite book among the Litchfield ladies: it is so pious, so wise, so easy a book to read for any person, and so useful, nay necessary, are its precepts to us all, that I never cease recommending it to our young ones. 'Tis *a la portée de chacun* so, yet never vulgar; but Law beats him for wit[.][60]

Johnson's formulation implies that his stepdaughter 'Poor Lucy's' ill health and reading of Watts have combined to improve her 'social virtues'. Piozzi's response makes it clear that the qualities she admires in the work are its simplicity and its piety. A compendium of study skills could be read as a guide to moral comportment. The title invites such a use, for in this

---

[58]   Locke, 'Of the Conduct of the Understanding', 6.

[59]   Samuel Johnson to Hester Thrale, 31 October 1781. *Letters to and from the Late Samuel Johnson*, ed. Hester Piozzi, 2 vols (London, 1788), II, 211.

[60]   Hester Thrale to Samuel Johnson, 2 November 1781. *Letters*, II, 214. Thrale refers to William Law, *A Serious Call to a Devout and Holy Life* (London, 1729).

period 'improvement was not just a matter of civility', as Mee has shown by sketching the social, moral, and educational capacities of the concept.[61] In this example, a seventy-two-year-old man encourages a woman in her sixties to read a book for students written forty years earlier, and another adult woman compares it to William Law's work of practical piety. The scenario demonstrates the varied audiences for Watts's pedagogic writings and the different uses to which they could be put.

Watts intended his works to be understood and used by non-specialist readers. The fact that he mediated Locke's ideas for an audience who may well not have read Locke themselves, for example, means that his own strategies and positions were as likely to influence the people reading them as were the works to which Watts responded. This is particularly important given that Watts does not uncritically simplify Locke but contests some of his conclusions, and shapes Locke's arguments about the centrality of reason and observation around his own evangelical priorities for promoting practical religion. He disseminates Locke's methods while modifying his ideas, and explicitly invites his readers to do the same. Watts's call to readers even of the lowest station to reason freely, viewed in conjunction with the effect of diffusing Locke's ideas to readers not originally addressed by Locke, generates an accessible intellectual culture. Some of Watts's biographers praised him for this, including Samuel Johnson:

> He has provided instruction for all ages, from those who are lisping their first lessons, to the enlightened readers of Malbranche and Locke; he has left neither corporeal nor spiritual nature unexamined[.][62]

Watts was not consciously conducting a radically equalizing project. One of the first things he says in 'A Discourse on the Education of Children and Youth' (1753) is:

> I limit these instructions... by the *station* and *rank in life* in which children are born and placed by the providence of God. Persons of better circumstances in the world, should give their sons and their daughters a much larger share of knowledge and a richer variety of instruction, than meaner persons can or ought.[63]

This conventional reiteration of the requirement to behave appropriately to one's station can be understood with reference to Watts's imagined uses

[61] Mee, *Conversable Worlds*, 68.

[62] Samuel Johnson, 'Life of Watts', in *The Lives of the Most Eminent English Poets: With Critical Observations on their Works*, ed. Roger Lonsdale, 4 vols (Oxford, 2006), IV, 105–10 (109). First published in *Prefaces, Biographical and Critical, to the Works of the English Poets*, 10 vols (London, 1779–81), VIII, 1–24.

[63] Watts, *Works*, V, 360.

of John Reynolds's *A Practical Discourse of Reconciliation* (described in Chapter 5), for Watts situates Reynolds's book in both the workshop and the closet, and insists that it is equally suited to both as long as its readers in each location approach it in a fitting manner. Learning, to Watts, is available to all as long as its primary purpose is kept in mind: it must deepen the reader's understanding of God's work.

But despite his conservative claims, in both his words and the physical appearance and dissemination of his works, Watts does make learning more widely available. Small, relatively cheap editions of his works were published, which he distributed freely.[64] He reached great numbers of people because of the variety of genres in which he chose to write, so that a university student unlikely to read a dissenter's sermon, for example, would encounter Watts in an educational text, or a devout woman of the middling 'rank' (in Watts's term) unlikely to peruse the *Philosophical Essays* could learn from *A Humble Attempt*.[65] His preaching (though often interrupted by ill health) was another channel through which Watts could spread his ideas, and his hymns and *Divine Songs* were of course extremely important vehicles for the transmission of his religious and moral principles. This combination of forms and modes accounts for the extraordinary reach of Watts's ideas and affirms Doddridge's assertion in the dedication to *The Rise and Progress of Religion in the Soul* that 'You are teaching no doubt Hundreds of *Ministers*, and Thousands of *private Christians*.'[66]

4. CONDUITS OF WATTS

As well as the numerous reprints of his individual works Watts's ideas spread through other kinds of texts from the mid-eighteenth century onwards and his words continue to circulate separately from his books today: he provides 914 quotations in the present *Oxford English Dictionary*.[67] Watts's presence there today was anticipated in the eighteenth

[64] Watts sent a 'large packett' of copies of *The Improvement of the Mind* to Colman 'to be distributed to many persons among you'. Isaac Watts to Benjamin Colman, 14 July 1741. MHS, *Proceedings*, 385.

[65] Readers of Watts's *Logick* listed in the *Reading Experience Database* include Elizabeth Gurney (later Elizabeth Fry) who read it in 1798 aged eighteen (*Reading Experience Database* record 22323); Thomas Green, an Anglican gentleman who read it in 1799 at the age of thirty (*Reading Experience Database* record 13222); and Joseph Jenkinson, a Methodist artisan who read it in 1839 at the age of twenty-nine (*Reading Experience Database* record 9851).

[66] Doddridge, *The Rise and Progress of Religion in the Soul*, vi.

[67] Watts is the 493rd most frequently quoted source in the *Oxford English Dictionary* according to the 'Sources' feature on *OED Online*.

century by the numerous extracts (particularly from *Logick* and *The Improvement of the Mind*) used to illustrate terms and topics in the 'Supplement' (1744) to John Harris's *Lexicon technicum* and in Johnson's *Dictionary* (1755). As Robert DeMaria points out, Watts's ideas influenced Johnson's conception of the *Dictionary* as a single book that would perform multiple functions as an encyclopedia, an educational text, and a work of moral guidance. Johnson attempted where possible to provide quotations for definitions which would 'besides illustrating the meanings of words, teach fundamental points of morality'.[68] Thus Watts influenced both the content and the concept of Johnson's *Dictionary*.

The editors of the supplement to *Lexicon technicum* held Watts in similarly high regard to Johnson: his name appears third (after Locke and Berkeley) in their long list of new authors brought in to illuminate 'Physics, Metaphysics, Ethics, Logic, Grammar, Rhetoric, Poetry, History, Music, Painting, Sculpture, Policy, Botany, Medicine, Surgery and other miscellaneous Subjects'.[69] These encyclopedic works took Watts as a source for straightforward definitions of specialist terms and used his words to articulate and endorse a philosophical approach to ordering knowledge. Watts's principles are broken down into units (phrases, extracts, examples) and fitted into monumental volumes that house an all-encompassing epistemological project. His educational and ethical guidelines are presented across the books' entries with the result that his influence permeates a genre which in format, content, and tone is quite distinct from his own works.

Even further from these encyclopedic works than Watts's own were books intended for children not only to read, but also to covet. John Newbery's considerable importance in the children's book industry is well documented, but he is usually considered as a businessman, as an imaginative entrepreneur who pursued innovation principally for profit, and who unabashedly marketed works within works.[70] He certainly did so, but the

---

[68] DeMaria, *Johnson's Dictionary*, 20. McLaverty shows how Johnson used Watts to implement definitions in the *Dictionary* that followed a theory of language different from Locke's in key respects, particularly in that it distinguished between definitions of names and definitions of things, see 'From Definition to Explanation', 388.

[69] *A Supplement to Dr. Harris's Dictionary of Arts and Sciences* (London, 1744), 3. Watts is named ahead of Francis Bacon, Robert Boyle, and Richard Steele.

[70] Accounts of Newbery appear in J. H. Plumb, 'The New World of Children in Eighteenth-Century England', in *The Birth of a Consumer Society: The Commercialization of Eighteenth-Century England*, ed. Neil McKendrick, John Brewer, and J. H. Plumb (London, 1982), 286–315 (301–6), Barbara Benedict, *Making the Modern Reader: Cultural Mediation in Early Modern Literary Anthologies* (Princeton, 1996), 185, and Grenby, *The Child Reader*, 41–6. See also S. Roscoe, *John Newbery and his Successors, 1740–1814: A Bibliography* (Wormley, 1973).

pedagogic principles he thereby disseminated warrant consideration. One of his early children's publishing successes was the *Circle of the Sciences* series (1748), which offered pocket sized introductions to English language, grammar, poetry, rhetoric, logic, ontology, chronology, mathematics, and geography. The topics of these tiny volumes match the subjects being added to Harris's *Lexicon technicum* at the same time (the two works were published four years apart), showing that booksellers' strong interest in making information on these topics widely available in print at the midpoint of the eighteenth century crossed boundaries of genre, format, and intended audience. This suggests not only a strong demand for works of practical and intellectual self-improvement in this period, but also that booksellers and editors relied on Watts's words to supply these texts. The *Circle of the Sciences* series as whole owes a great deal to Watts.[71] In several volumes, his principles and even words are reproduced wholesale and only sometimes is this debt acknowledged.[72] The volume on logic borrows his arrangement of the subject, many of his examples, and plenty of his actual words, arranging them in an engaging question-and-answer format that Watts himself often used. There were five editions of this series in the eighteenth century, through which Watts's pedagogical principles were directly addressed to children and readers who may not have known they were encountering Watts's ideas.

Books which contained Watts's words and facilitated the approaches to knowledge he recommended were circulating among different print purchasing and reading groups from the 1710s onwards. His ideas and methods were a significant part of the intellectual landscape right through the eighteenth century because of the variety of formats and modes of presentation in which they circulated. These texts catered to and perhaps exacerbated the widespread hunger for intellectual improvement: in these terms, Watts's words were a key enabling factor in the proliferation of printed materials that Clifford Siskin has identified as a condition of enlightenment culture.[73] Though Watts tends to be thought of as a religious or evangelical writer his education writings sought to synthesize religion and reason. The repeated reprinting of his educational works, and

---

[71] Kleeman explores the connections between Newbery and Locke (but omits Watts) in 'The Matter for Moral Education'. An earlier article notes that the volumes on logic and rhetoric in the *Circle of the Sciences* 'would have met the disapproval of Locke', see Robert Bator, 'Out of the Ordinary Road: John Locke and English Juvenile Fiction in the Eighteenth Century', *Children's Literature*, 1 (1972), 46–53 (48). Bator assumes (mistakenly, in my view) that when the author praises 'a modern logician, to whose excellent writings we own ourselves indebted' he is referring to Locke (52).

[72] John Newbery, *The Circle of the Sciences*, 7 vols (London, 1748), V, xxiv.

[73] Clifford Siskin, *The Work of Writing* (Baltimore, 1997), 4–12.

the fact that extracts and ideas from his works appear in encyclopedias, compendia, and children's books attests to the widespread influence of his approach in the milieu of informal education and self-improvement in both intellectual and religious terms. Watts actively encouraged his readers to follow his practices, and this led to his continued presence in print throughout the eighteenth and nineteenth centuries as his works were adapted for new audiences by editors following his example. The informal, self-improving intellectual culture of the period typified by the proliferation of 'very useful books' was significantly shaped and propagated by Watts.[74]

[74] The term 'very useful books' is from Klein, 'Politeness for Plebes', 367.

5

Isaac Watts, Publisher

As a supporter of dissenting academies, author of catechisms, and promoter of practical divinity, Isaac Watts was an active participant in the educational world of dissent. He set an important example to dissenters as an author whose reach in print extended far beyond the ministerial contexts set out in preceding chapters and in this respect, as well as in more practical ways, his methods certainly influenced the publishing projects of Doddridge, Orton, and others.[1] In addition to his own writing, Watts's textual endeavours encompassed editing, recommending, and distributing the works of others. Such projects both disseminated and enacted his belief in the principles of convivial international intellectual and practical engagement which characterize dissenting education for the ministry and the broader religious contexts to English religious enlightenment culture in this period.

One of the principal mechanisms for the international circulation of ideas by which English readers and writers encountered discourses beyond an exclusively anglophone frame was religion, and the example of Doddridge recommending texts by Buddeaus and Lampe in his 'Life of Steffe' registers the scholarly, theological side to this.[2] Through his work as an editor Watts disseminated information about religious practice to other communities, across national borders and not only within a clerical culture. In these respects his activities anticipated those of the Scottish minister John Erskine, whose 'primary contribution to evangelicalism was not as a minister, but as a disseminator of information, primarily through the sending and propagating of religious ideas through books', according

---

[1] In a letter to Doddridge about *The Rise and Progress of Religion in the Soul* he joins with Lady Abney in urging Doddridge to 'make the best bargain with your Bookseller for Yourself'. Isaac Watts to Philip Doddridge, 10 April 1744, *Calendar* 963.

[2] W. R. Ward, *The Protestant Evangelical Awakening* (Cambridge, 1992). Work pursuing the implications of Ward's ground-breaking research into religious awakening in an international context includes Michael A. Haykin and Kenneth J. Stewart (eds), *The Emergence of Evangelicalism: Exploring Historical Continuities* (Nottingham, 2008) and Mark A. Noll, *The Rise of Evangelicalism: The Age of Edwards, Whitefield and the Wesleys* (Downers Grove, Ill., 2003).

to his most recent biographer.[3] Taking the examples of Watts and Erskine
in conjunction suggests that efforts to communicate knowledge about
religious developments were considered by their clerical participants
to constitute an important contribution to international religious and
intellectual enlightenment for, as Jonathan Yeager notes, 'Erskine and
other British and American evangelicals would not have viewed the
Enlightenment as counterintuitive to faith, at least prior to the 1790s.'[4]
Because of his educational and philosophical concerns, Watts wished to
encourage approaches to the religious revivals that spread across Europe
and the Atlantic world in the 1730s and 1740s that balanced the dangers
of enthusiasm with judicious rational enquiry and biblical understanding.[5]
In such a framework, the content of published texts and their modes of
dissemination bridged the distance between religious revival and enlightened exchanges of learning. Watts not only sought to connect different
conditions of experience (insisting that individual spiritual encounters
should be informed by scripturally founded preaching) but he did so
through varied textual means. His work in print often came about because
of his personal relationships, many of which were sustained through
letters.[6] The multi-stranded project of what Yeager terms 'enlightened
evangelicalism' was pursued by Watts and characterized by both affective
bonds of friendship and pragmatic processes of print publication.

Watts presented collaborative efforts within the dissenting ministerial
community and with religious associates in Germany and New England to
a broadly imagined reading public and introduced foreign writers to
English readers. He helped shape a community of godly learning through
prefaces and recommendations as a crucial part of his project to connect
audiences in different religious and social groups and of different nation-
alities through print. His eighteenth-century biographer Thomas Gibbons

[3] Yeager, *Enlightened Evangelicalism*, 11.
[4] Yeager, *Enlightened Evangelicalism*, 16. Erskine notes that James Bradley and Dale Van
Kley present an overview of the nineteenth-century French historiographical origins of the
enlightenment as a secularization narrative in *Religion and Politics in Enlightenment Europe*
(Notre Dame, Ind., 2001).
[5] For the characteristics of religious evangelicalism in this period of 'revivals' or 'awakening', see Isabel Rivers, 'Writing the History of Early Evangelicalism', *History of European
Ideas*, 35 (2009), 105–11 (105). Rivers notes that Ward sees evangelicalism as a 'pre-
enlightenment' phenomenon (107).
[6] Though Robert Darnton insists on a clearly demarcated enlightenment of *philosophes*
alone, declaring that 'to equate the Enlightenment with the totality of Western thought is to
get it badly wrong', it is striking that virtually all of the characteristics he attributes to the
philosophes (campaigning, collective action, diffusionism, a commitment to writing and
especially letters, an emphasis on rational enquiry) can be found among the English
dissenters and their friends in Europe and America. See Darnton, *George Washington's
False Teeth* (New York, 2003), 6–7 and 80–1.

speculated that Watts did this 'from an hope of doing public service', wishing 'to give a wider diffusion to pious and useful compositions than they would in all probability have obtained without it'.[7] Thanks to his high reputation, the advice he gave about reading significantly shaped transatlantic intellectual life throughout the eighteenth century. A particularly important aspect of this project was that he demonstrated how to collaborate by editing texts and suggesting the publication of fresh works, and he used his own reputation to endorse other writers. The effect of these activities was to bring new narratives and ideas to new audiences. Putting separate texts into contact with each other widened his readers' horizons and spread learning, in some cases across continents. But what was the complexion of the literature Watts promoted and how did his interventions affect the cultural world he inhabited?

The works Watts recommended were mostly books of practical piety and sermons, including works by John Mason, John Reynolds, Samuel Clark, Matthew Henry, Benjamin Colman, and Edward Hitchin. He also promoted narratives and biographical works such as Jonathan Edwards's account of religious awakening in his town, *A Faithful Narrative* (1737), and Thomas Halyburton's *Memoirs* (1718), and religious meditations like Elizabeth Rowe's *Devout Exercises of the Heart* (1738).[8] The diversity of genres represented might suggest that these works do not necessarily share many features, yet Watts's introductions repeatedly articulate key themes of usefulness, learning, and religious purpose, and always carefully identify the different groups of readers he hopes the work will reach. In the prefaces he wrote, Watts set out his project: to use print to enhance people's spiritual lives at the same time as promoting positive mental habits for different categories of readers. He repackaged and condensed works, introduced texts from Germany to New England (and vice versa, via England), bought copies of cheap tracts to distribute to the poor, sent books to colleges overseas, and recommended particular writings in his sermons. These approaches contributed to the project enacted by Watts's own publications across different genres (including hymns, sermons, and essays) which sought to develop their readers' faculty of understanding, and as such they constitute a significant aspect of Watts's literary work.

For Watts, books are powerful communicative agents but human readers are by no means passive in reception. Pleasure is a valid and valuable component of literary response: Watts expresses 'Satisfaction' and 'sensible Pleasure' at the experience of first reading and then

---

[7] Thomas Gibbons, *Memoirs of the Rev. Isaac Watts D.D.* (London, 1780), 133–4.

[8] For a list of recommendations and prefaces written by Watts see A. P. Davis, *Isaac Watts: His Life and Works* (London, 1948), 279–81.

publishing John Jennings's advice to ministers *Two Discourses*, and his
delight that 'this wonderful Discovery' of religious awakening is made
public in the form of Jonathan Edwards's *A Faithful Narrative* is not only
because of the future benefits he anticipates (the text will 'incourage our
Faith and Hope') but also because it will reinforce scripture history.[9] The
expression and transmission of ideas (and readers' engagement with them)
takes place through the circulation of relatively inexpensive volumes which
mark the movement from private acts of reading, writing, and prayer to
public acts of worship and discussion. To Watts, the social life of religious
education proposed by and figured in these works should extend into
the wider world, and this enabling vision of literary endeavour was one of
the most positive tendencies to emerge in enlightenment-era religious
publishing.

1. THE EDITOR'S ROLE

Watts's prefaces repeatedly re-imagine reading communities with the
purpose of making the work in question more directly relevant to the
lives of potential readers and prompting those readers to self-examination.
The examples here—which range from collections of useful sayings about
God to accounts of philanthropic projects—show the variety of educational platforms Watts constructed and how he did it; their significance
within and beyond dissent; and their role in creating a culture of learning
shaped by both philosophical empiricism and affective evangelicalism. In
the case of Watts, it is not easy or necessarily helpful to separate these
strands, for the two impulses often coexist in a single text.

In the recommendation to the *Select Remains* (1736) of the millenarian
Church of England clergyman John Mason, Watts suggests that parents
teach their children Mason's proverbs, extends the potential audience for a
piece called *Serious Advice to Youth* beyond the group proposed by its title
to 'all who sincerely desire to maintain a conscientious *Walk with God*',
and suggests that 'The *Directions* and *Signs*, &c. may be useful to doubting
and discourag'd Christians; and to all who make Conscience of the great
Duty of Self-Examination.'[10] These readers are not grouped into discrete
categories—of the young, of ministers, of the learned, and so on—but are

[9] Isaac Watts and John Guyse, 'Preface', in Jonathan Edwards, *A Faithful Narrative of
the Strange Surprizing Work of God in the Conversion of Many Hundred Souls in Northampton*
(London, 1737), viii and Watts, 'Advertisement', in John Jennings, *Two Discourses: The
First of Preaching Christ, the Second of Experimental Preaching* (London, 1722), xii.
[10] Isaac Watts, 'Preface', in John Mason, *Select Remains* (2nd edn, 1742), xviii–xix.

identified by their spiritual needs. While addressing anticipated readers is a conventional strategy for any recommendatory preface, the consistency of Watts's approach of grouping readers together and telling them how to use the work is remarkable, as is the unusual degree of specificity with which he addresses these groups. Introducing Mason's *Select Remains*, Watts reconfigures categories of readers and visualizes the locations for reading which a particular work might enter:

> I have often tho't, that this Collection of short Sentences, under various Heads, are very proper to attend Christians of the middle Rank of Life, either in the Parlour or the Kitchen, in the Shop or the Work-House; and for that End I have been a frequent Purchaser of them, to distribute in Families, among private Christians.[11]

Watts had a strong sense that the key aim of writing was the improvement of the reader, and that a single text might improve readers of differing educational experiences. Here, by imagining different scenes of reading, he proposes a range of circumstances in which the book might be useful. As well as directing the text to the 'Shop or the Work-House' and the mercantile and artisan readers such locations suggest, he proposes that 'serious Persons may find sufficient Matter to furnish them with frequent pious Meditations . . . and they may be as happily useful in the Retirements of the Closet'.[12] Not only do the locations for reading a work change according to the occupation of the reader, but so does the manner of reading. This is why Watts repeatedly praises the style of arranging a work under various 'heads'.[13] By offering a method and a clear outline, a writer can address a diverse range of readers without fearing they will interpret the work incorrectly. As with Doddridge's academy lectures, encountering new ideas is to be encouraged but heterodox thinking is not.

In the preface to John Reynolds's *A Practical Discourse of Reconciliation between God and Man* (1729) Watts gives a detailed statement about the responsibilities of the editor and of readers. He specifies the ways in which he has changed Reynolds's text by rearranging the material into sections and altering the title page and reveals that he has given the work a new title. Reynolds had called it the *Compassionate Letter to the poorer Part of the Christian World* but, says Watts, 'I must confess I saw nothing in the Book which should confine it to the *Poor*', so he retitled it *A Compassionate Address to the Christian World*. In the preface to this new edition he

[11] Watts, in Mason, *Select Remains*, iii–iv.

[12] Watts, in Mason, *Select Remains*, iv.

[13] In *The Improvement of the Mind*, Watts advises, 'Whatever you would betrust to your memory, let it be disposed in a proper method, connected well together, and referred to distinct and particular heads.' See Watts, *Works*, V, 280.

declares, 'I thought it might be very useful to Persons of all Ranks and Degrees in the World, and especially to the younger Parts of Mankind.' Having identified a much wider potential audience for the text and retitling the work so as not to exclude them, Watts tells his wealthier readers how they can ensure the continued usefulness and further diffusion of the text: 'I hope it will yet see the Light in many more Editions, by the charitable Benefactions of those who are dispos'd to spread abroad useful Books to promote the common Salvation.'[14] Metaphors of light and diffusion are here applied to the distribution of inexpensive texts in a manner that connects salvation and enlightenment via usefulness and publishing.

In his directives to readers and description of editorial process we find several ways in which Watts understood religious textual culture as collaborative. He confidently declares that the editor has the freedom to intervene in the content and presentation of a work and in this he is following as editor of printed prose works a pattern he had advocated in relation to the public performance of hymn singing in the preface to his own *Hymns and Spiritual Songs* (1707). There, certain stanzas are placed within square brackets and the minister is directed to decide which stanzas should be sung and which omitted.[15] Written texts seek to echo the oral, communal life of worship out of which they emerged by replicating structural patterns familiar from sermons—such as arranging a discourse under 'heads'—and reanimating the communal environments of prayer and hymn singing by evoking multiple, diverse, and participatory audiences. This is a distinctive culture in which models of authorship and literary ownership are flexible and literature is a common resource.

Watts's editorial work should be understood as an aspect of his ministry and, particularly, as an educational 'public service' (in Gibbons's term) that extended his personal interventions in dissenters' own educational projects by introducing them to a wider public. One book that Watts promoted in order to forge a connection between dissenting education and a national and international project to improve education and religious understanding is John Jennings's *Two Discourses: The First of Preaching Christ and the Second of Experimental Preaching* (1723).

[14] John Reynolds, *A Practical Discourse of Reconciliation between God and Man* (London, 1729), x. The *Compassionate Letter* was a staple text of the Society for Promoting Christian Knowledge among the Poor; see Isabel Rivers, 'The First Evangelical Tract Society', *Historical Journal*, 50, (2007), 1–22 (9). In September 1736, Watts sent two copies to a missionary in New England to help in his work converting American Indians. MHS, *Proceedings*, 351.

[15] Isaac Watts, 'Preface' to *Hymns and Spiritual Songs* (London, 1707), xiv.

2. *TWO DISCOURSES*: INTERNATIONAL
SCHEMES FOR MINISTERIAL IMPROVEMENT

Two Discourses is a small book that has received little attention in studies of education and religious training, but it was considered by its promoters to be very important. It crossed denominational and national boundaries and over numerous editions it grew to contain instructive prefaces, letters, and a biographical narrative as well as the discourses announced by the title. The work described and enacted the polite discourse, evangelical action, and intellectual commitment that it recommended. These writings began life as lectures on practical religion delivered to the students at Jennings's academy. In his 'Account of Mr Jennings's Method' Philip Doddridge described how, one Friday in every month, students and tutor would unite in a day of devotion, fasting, and contemplation in preparation for the Lord's Supper that Sunday. At ten o'clock they would gather in the chapel:

> after some time spent in the Offices of Devotion Mr Jennings gave us a Lecture from the Pulpit on some Topick which was peculiarly Suitable to us as Students. These he compos'd with great Care and Exactness... The incomparable Discourses of preaching Christ, and of experimental Preaching, which he publish'd to the World just before his Death were drawn up and preach'd on such Occasions.[16]

In Doddridge's account, the printed text emerges out of community religious practice, which it also sustains. Watts's recommendatory preface to the printed version explained that the discourses could be useful beyond the academy context for which they had been composed, for 'if in the *middle Age of Life* we should examine our Performances by the Light of this Treatise, 'tis possible we and our People might be gainers by it'.[17] As he later would for Reynolds's *Address*, Watts explicitly resituates the work spatially and temporally, suggesting it should be used as an enlightening guide by experienced ministers as well as students and thereby imagining the educative function of the text reaching beyond the dissenting academy in which it began. The first discourse takes the requirement for 'careful and rational enquiry' best approached by study of the Gospels and expository works and the need for sermons to keep Christ at their centre as a starting point from which to outline a programme for composing intellectually rigorous sermons that are emotionally affecting.[18] The second discourse

---

[16] Doddridge, 'An Account of Mr Jennings's Method', fol. 37.
[17] Jennings, *Two Discourses* (3rd edn, 1736), x–xi.
[18] Jennings, *Two Discourses*, 15.

addresses the need to cultivate serious piety among the laity and here Jennings identifies a role for print in shaping the devotional character of local communities: by publishing these discourses he could speak to individual readers who would not be seen in his meeting house.

Watts's recommendatory preface sets out the value of the discourses in terms of liberality. He anticipates the work 'will spread its good Influences as far and wide as it finds Readers' and, further, it 'will become a more extensive Benefit' as sermons influenced by John Jennings's ideas reached illiterate hearers.[19] The work's interdenominational usefulness further invokes openness: these particular discourses 'are founded upon the general Principles of Christianity, and therefore invite the Perusal of All, being written without the narrow Spirit of a Party'.[20] Within a frame that invites readers to identify themselves as tolerant and by refusing to specify limits for the work, Watts proposes a reformation in preaching. He asserts the importance of evangelical and experimental preaching as the best way of stemming the 'the Growth of *Deism* and *Infidelity*' and encouraging true religion.[21] His conception of the work of preaching corresponds to Doddridge's views on reading: liberal thought protects religious orthodoxy rather than challenging it.

Watts had international ambitions for this project from early on. He sent copies of *Two Discourses* to (among many others) the influential minister in Boston Benjamin Colman and Gotthilf August Francke, Pietist minister and son of August Hermann Francke, founder of the charitable institutions at Halle. In return, Francke sent a copy of a letter on preaching written by his father in Latin which David Jennings (brother to John) then translated into English and included in a new edition of *Two Discourses* in 1736. In an additional 'Advertisement' to this new version, Watts emphasizes the familial and social ties connecting the different materials contained in the book: the translator of the letter is identified as 'my valuable Friend Mr. David Jennings, the surviving Brother of the Author'.

In his own preface to Francke's letter, David Jennings participates in Watts's collective approach to book publishing. Jennings's preface reinforces the ideas expressed in Watts's by outlining the publishing history of the *Two Discourses* in Scotland and Germany.[22] As well as advertising the popularity of the discourses, this information forges a practical connection between Francke's letter and Jennings's discourses in addition to Watts's thematic connection between the two. Jennings presents *Two Discourses* as having several different centres of influence connected by print trade

---

[19] Jennings, *Two Discourses*, vii.
[20] Jennings, *Two Discourses*, vii.
[21] Jennings, *Two Discourses*, viii.
[22] Jennings, *Two Discourses*, 75–6.

networks of import, export, and distribution and by the individuals who promote each work to a new audience. He gives the social and institutional context of the publication by describing Francke's projects at Halle and explaining the significance of Francke and Jennings being published together. The preface highlights instances of small-scale endeavours within communities with strong familial and affectionate connections influencing the spread of ideas internationally. Rather than simply serving an already connected international community, the book attempted to generate wider awareness of ventures being undertaken in the cause of promoting religion in different places.

The intellectual and social impulses animating this new edition were strongly international and interdenominational, reflecting the fact that, as W. R. Ward has argued, 'British churches... were subject to important continental influences' that shaped the development of religious revival in the British Isles and colonies.[23] The work Watts undertook in print was inspired and supported by activities that began outside England and had enduring international significance. Chief among these were the charitable institutions in Halle, Germany, set up by August Hermann Francke at the end of the seventeenth century. The Halle complex (including an orphanage, printing house, dispensary, and educational establishment) inspired religious and educational activists of different denominations in Great Britain, and the attitudes shared by Pietists and dissenters such as Watts led to especially productive exchanges, though these have been overlooked.[24]

Seventeenth-century religious exchanges in the Atlantic world have received considerable attention from historians, as have wider European encounters into the eighteenth century, particularly as seen from the perspective of Boston.[25] However, the role of eighteenth-century English dissenters (particularly Congregationalists such as Watts) in international networks has been less thoroughly reconsidered in light of new interpretative models which emphasize communication and cooperation among different groups.[26] The example of Pietism was a particularly generative

---

[23] Ward, *Protestant Evangelical Awakening*, 296.

[24] For the connections between Halle and England, see Daniel L. Brunner, *Halle Pietists in England: Anthony William Boehm and the Society for Promoting Christian Knowledge* (Göttingen, 1993); W. R. Ward, 'German Pietism, 1670–1750', *Journal of Ecclesiastical History*, 44 (1993), 476–505; and Tessa Whitehouse, 'Godly Dispositions and Textual Conditions: The Literary Sociology of International Religious Exchanges, c.1722–1740', *History of European Ideas*, 39 (2011), 394–408.

[25] Susan Hardman Moore, *Pilgrims: New World Settlers and the Call of Home* (New Haven, 2007); Carla Gardina Pestana, *Protestant Empire: Religion and the Making of the British Atlantic World* (Philadelphia, 2009); Peterson, 'Theopolis Americana'.

[26] For nonconformist groups who did not prioritize an educated ministry (particularly Quakers and Baptists), social and educational relations between America and Europe were

one for English dissenters, who compared themselves and their ante-cedents to the Pietists active in Germany in the early eighteenth century. They did so both in terms of the attitude of the establishment towards them (Watts pointed out that 'Pietist', like 'Puritan' was originally a 'Name of Reproach') and with reference to the activities and priorities of both groups.[27] Watts's continued involvement in publishing and distrib-uting books in England, America, and Germany demonstrates that he contributed to an expansive project of instruction and discourse about religious conduct and ways of accessing God. His editorial activities and his own writings connected Halle, London, and New England both pragmatically (through publishing news and texts from one place in others, and by sending news and texts from one place to others) and psychically (by drawing the inhabitants of these sites and beyond into an imagined community).

Readers participated in the collaborative exchange of the work which the prefaces encouraged. The respective acts of translation by G. A. Francke and David Jennings generated a series of book exchanges between London and Halle.[28] In 1739, Watts sent copies to Benjamin Colman in Boston, and requested that he give one to Harvard College 'for I think it a very usefull book for students, and wish they were more dispersed'.[29] Colman took this as a cue to publish an edition of the work in Boston, to which he added a statement describing the range of books donated by Watts which have 'inrich'd both our *Colleges*'.[30] The paratexts continued to reflect the international dimension of the peda-gogic relationships valued by the participants in the publication, and the presence of the text in educational institutions in Germany, England, and New England attests to their belief in its practical value.[31] The 1744

rather different. See Carla Gardina Pestana, *Quakers and Baptists in Colonial Massachusetts* (Cambridge, 1991), esp. 14, 116–18.

[27] Isaac Watts, *An Essay Towards the Encouragement of Charity Schools* (London, 1728), 49. For the importance Halle Pietists attached to epistolary networks, see Thomas P. Bach, 'G. A. Francke and the Halle Communication Network: Protection, Politics and Piety', in *Pietism and Community in Europe and North America, 1650–1850*, ed. Jonathan Strom (Leiden, 2010), 95–110.

[28] Some correspondence between English dissenters (particularly Watts) and Halle Pietists survives at AFSt/H: see MS C 504:3, 7, 11, 14 and 16 and MS K 22.

[29] Watts to Colman, 13 November 1739, in MHS, *Proceedings*, 371.

[30] Jennings, *Two Discourses* (Boston, 1740), 14. Colman sent a copy to Watts who thanked him for reprinting the work. Watts to Colman, 18 March 1741, in MHS, *Proceedings*, 380.

[31] Nineteen copies were listed in the Yale College library catalogues, see Pratt, *Isaac Watts and his Gift of Books*, 65–6. Jonathan Edwards read the English translation of Francke's letter, see Peter J. Thuesen (ed.), *The Works of Jonathan Edwards XXVI: Catalogue of Books* (New Haven, 2008), 222.

Boston version of the materials was described on the title page as 'published by David Jennings' and 'Recommended by Isaac Watts'.[32] As well as John Jennings's discourses, Francke's letter, Watts's two prefatory statements, and David Jennings's prefaces, this edition includes an abridgement of a biography of Cotton Mather (the seventeenth-century religious leader in New England) written by his son Samuel and introduced by David Jennings.[33] The addition of this text consolidates all the themes and aims of the earlier versions of the work. Family bonds are again reasserted as a driving force behind printed texts. Along with the content of the work, this reaffirms the importance of community ties in pious projects, and the presence of the biography in the volume extends the network of knowledge and influence beyond Europe. The biography offers a practical pattern for Christian living and as such supplements the advice on preaching contained in John Jennings's discourses and the model of charitable behaviour embodied by Francke. The capacity for the volume to be viewed as a handbook of resources is reflected in the new title: *Instructions to Ministers*.

The project as a whole can be seen as an enlightened evangelical activity in various senses: activism is a key aspect of evangelicalism while attention to individual action within sociable norms is characteristic of enlightenment. Along with other endeavours in this period, this project embodied both.[34] Shared commitment to the benevolent diffusion of information and expertise binds the two movements together, as exemplified by *Two Discourses*. Through this text, its editors sought to connect new ideas with new audiences internationally in order to deepen understanding of connections between religion and society via the exchange of information and ideas.

The extent to which Watts's hope that the work should both enhance people's rational and emotional engagements with religion and dissolve denominational boundaries was achieved cannot easily be measured, but the fact that the work was regularly reprinted suggests a sustained interest in its content, belief in its usefulness, and a long-standing commitment (shared by readers and editors) to the principles espoused in and by the work. Thus the religious and intellectual network depicted in the prefatory and biographical parts of the work offers a model for piety and community that addresses the history and ambitions of the reading community of the

---

[32] *Instructions to Ministers*, ed. David Jennings (London, 1744), title page.
[33] The original edition was Samuel Mather, *The Life of the very Reverend and Learned Cotton Mather D.D. & F.R.S.* (Boston, 1729), which was only published in Boston.
[34] Bruce D. Hindmarch, 'Reshaping Individualism: The Private Christian, Eighteenth-Century Religion, and the Enlightenment', in *The Rise of the Laity in Evangelical Protestantism*, ed. Deryck W. Lovegrove (London, 2002), 67–84 (67).

work itself. Ever since the earliest days of Calvinist practice, notions of community (including concern for the intellectual and spiritual welfare of all its members, and a belief in the centrality of family prayer and free discussion to develop religious understanding and godly living) had been foundational to the self-understanding of gathered churches. These principles, which survived partly by being propagated and reinforced through print (notably by Richard Baxter) in a period when freedom of worship was severely curtailed, were now represented and enacted through an international ministerial culture which sought to facilitate widespread improvement through print and preaching. Textual models served to reinforce and extend personal interactions. This example points to the influence of long-lived religious traditions on so-called enlightenment practices and provides strong evidence that processes understood today in terms of enlightenment often emerged out of religious culture and not in opposition to it. It was not only rational dissenters such as Joseph Priestley and learned, 'Latitudinarian' divines of the established church who decisively shaped the English enlightenment. Moderate dissenters such as Watts contributed to this intellectual culture in important ways, aided by their educational structures and existing international associations.

Across many reprints, in three significantly revised versions, and in different countries, *Two Discourses* acted as a site for publicizing religious projects. Its authors, translators, and editors sought to reform preaching to make it practical, affectionate, yet not enthusiastic, and to introduce these aims to students and clerical audiences within dissent, in the Church of England, and particularly in Europe and New England.[35] They hoped to extend the audience for dissenting ideas about incorporating the example of Christ into one's daily life to the 'politer sort' (as John Jennings put it) and to international audiences. Its creators saw the book as embodying in print a significant aspect of dissenting culture which prized the use of personal communications between friends to express shared goals.

Overlapping cultures of publishing, friendship, and news brought events and texts, writers, readers, and listeners from northern Europe, the British Isles, and North America into contact and shaped the ongoing publication and reception across three decades of *Two Discourses*. In its later incarnations the text was disseminated within a context of religious revival it had arguably contributed to shaping. Its power in an international evangelical context is most fully understood when it is placed

[35] Dissenters, among them Watts, were extremely wary of the charges of enthusiasm levelled at George Whitefield and other revival preachers, from whom many dissenting ministers sought to distance themselves. See Davis, *Isaac Watts*, 46–9.

alongside a related endeavour: Watts's efforts to publish Jonathan Edwards's account of religious revival in his community, *A Faithful Narrative of the Strange Surprizing Work of God* (1737). Across these two texts we find strong correspondences in evangelical purposes, determination to modify enthusiasm, and yet respect for affective religion and the desire to inculcate it. The two examples of international educational religious publishing can be compared in terms of the importance of friendship, the significance of institutions, and the anticipated readership and utility of the works in question to refine our understanding of the conjunction of affection, trade practices, and literary endeavours across texts in the religious revivals of the 1730s and 1740s.

3. *A FAITHFUL NARRATIVE*: PUTTING AWAKENING INTO PRINT

A Faithful Narrative and *Two Discourses* both originated in coterie engagements and were given a renewed life in the public sphere in printed forms that drew attention to their origins in religious friendship networks. Despite some similarities between the publications (both were fairly inexpensive and widely available), their content and ostensible purpose are rather different.[36] *A Faithful Narrative* was published in order to communicate news about edifying and extraordinary instances of religious awakening that began among a small community in Massachusetts and spread through the local area. The publication was presented as a response to the wishes of the laity, a dissenting congregation in London who had heard an epistolary account of it read out at a meeting and wanted more information. It was primarily news. Conversely, *Two Discourses* was an explicitly top-down effort from senior ministers and tutors to trainee ministers to congregations. The basis for the publication was Watts's belief that preaching practice needed to be reformed and that ministerial educators and leaders were responsible for training junior ministers to preach well so that the laity could understand the Gospel and thereby be open to religious experiences. It is a text that sought long-term effects. The international dissemination of both works was facilitated by religious correspondence networks that had historical resonances as well as contemporary existence.

It was because of Watts and Colman's existing and long lasting association that Jonathan Edwards's *Faithful Narrative* was published in

---

[36] Early editions of *Two Discourses* cost sixpence and *A Faithful Narrative* one shilling.

England in 1737. This particular process is well known and usually described from the perspective of American religious history.[37] As Susan O'Brien has shown, the international religious community that publicized the awakenings of the 1730s and 1740s drew on the traditions and practices from seventeenth-century puritan and nonconformist culture and added new modes of communication (such as weekly papers) in order to represent and disseminate religious news.[38] O'Brien argues that these established networks were invigorated by the new religious impulse given by awakenings, but the full span of the correspondence between Watts and Colman shows that their epistolary friendship was an active one even in less exciting religious times. Additionally, the tone of the letters shows very clearly that though they were moved by the reports of awakenings, they were anxious for accounts to be verified and presented plainly. There were rationalist impulses animating their correspondence as well as evangelical ones.[39]

Considering the publication of Edwards's *Faithful Narrative* in the context of Colman and Watts's personal history and the wider participatory network of which it is a part, it becomes clear that while the 1740s were certainly a 'crucial moment' of transatlantic correspondence, not only were existing communications networks instrumental to the dissemination of news about and analyses of revival (as O'Brien has shown) but the manner of those discourse influenced the process of news exchange too.[40] The moderate, affectionate, and pious epistolary conduct of ministers from England and America provided a model for the intellectual exchanges prompted by events that were ostensibly anti-rationalist and experiential. In conjunction with appropriate reading, the practice of letter writing was a means of developing rational, analytical, and conversational methods for assessing the new and strange evidence presented in the letters themselves. Epistolary culture provided the methods and materials for gathering and analysing new knowledge across continents.

[37] See Pratt, *Isaac Watts and his Gift of Books*, 28–50; C. C. Goen (ed.), *The Works of Jonathan Edwards, IV: The Great Awakening*, (2009), 32–46; Jon Butler, 'The Plural Origins of American Revivalism', in *Awash in a Sea of Faith: Christianizing the American People* (Cambridge, Mass., 1990), 164–93; Frank Lambert, 'The First Great Awakening: Whose Interpretive Fiction?', *New England Quarterly*, 68 (1995), 650–9.

[38] Susan O'Brien, 'A Transatlantic Community of Saints: The Great Awakening and the First Evangelical Network, 1735–1755', *American Historical Review*, 91 (1986), 811–32 (823–31).

[39] See W. R. Ward, 'The Relations of Enlightenment and Religious Revival in the Early Eighteenth Century', in *Reform and Reformation: England and the Continent c.1500–c.1750*, ed. Derek Baker (Oxford, 1979), 281–305 (283, 285–6) and Lucia Bergamasco, 'Évangelisme et Lumières', *Revue française d'études américaines*, 92 (2002) 22–46, esp. 31–5.

[40] Hall, 'Learned Culture in the Eighteenth Century', 411–33 (414).

Watts and his fellow minister John Guyse heard the news of extraordinary religious experiences among Edwards's congregation via Colman,
who sent them the abstract of Edwards's letter to him which had been
published at the end of a volume of sermons by Edwards's uncle William
Williams in December 1736. Watts and Guyse originally thought the
account should be published in Boston, and sent £5 each for this purpose.[41] In the end, it was printed in London with a preface by the two
English dissenters. As soon as it was published, they sent:

> one hundred books in sheets as a present to New England, 50 of them to be
> disposed of by you, & 50 by Mr Edwards. If we have time to bind up any we
> have orderd 6 to be gilt (viz) 1 for ye Governor, 1 for Dr Colman, 1 for M^r
> Edwards, 1 for Mr Williams who preachd ye sermons, 1 for Harvard College,
> & 1 for Yale College.

The Faithful Narrative may have been an extraordinary tale of an aston-
ishing series of events, but its publication and dissemination fitted with
Watts's usual book-giving practice in New England. Individual recipients
(here, the key participants in the account originally being published) were
named, the colleges were to receive their own copies, and Watts and
Guyse provided extra books for Colman to distribute. Immediately after
these practical instructions, Watts declared:

> May ye same spirit of grace that wrought that mighty work empower the
> Narrative of it to convert more souls & to make us min[iste]rs more zealous
> in our labours![42]

The first of these two intended purposes is consistent with that articulated
in the printed preface, dated the previous day. As Watts and Guyse wrote
there, 'This Account of the extraordinary and illustrious Appearance of
divine Grace in the Conversion of Sinners, is very like by the Blessing of
God to have a happy Effect, towards the Honour and Enlargement of the
Kingdom of God.'[43] In the published preface, Watts and Guyse frame the
consequences of the account in terms of possibility ('is very like') rather
than certainty and express those consequences in the language of moderate
politeness, as producing a 'happy Effect' of 'Honour and Enlargement',
rather than the rather more muscular and explicit declaration that the
'spirit of grace that wrought that mighty work' should 'convert more
souls'. Ideas expressed in documents addressed to a wide public on one
hand and a named individual on the other are very similar, but there is a

---

[41] Isaac Watts to Benjamin Colman, 2 April 1737, in MHS, *Proceedings*, 256.
[42] Watts to Colman, 13 October 1737, in MHS, *Proceedings*, 357.
[43] Watts and Guyse, 'Preface' to Edwards, *Faithful Narrative*, viii.

difference of emphasis. In the letter to a fellow minister, Watts singles out ministers as a group who should be particularly spurred to action by the text. The published text, meanwhile, deliberately excludes material that might limit its audience (either by specificity of address or stridency of expression), for Watts was alert to the social and textual dynamics of public and private sites of discourse.

The cooperative publication of *A Faithful Narrative* should be understood as one collaboration among many undertaken over the course of a long lasting relationship between Watts and Colman. It was part of a diverse complex of activities which included the book exchanges described above and the spread of news about the revivals in Scotland and New England.[44] Watts provided updates about English and Welsh evangelicalism, related the Wesleys' rising and waning popularity, and replied to requests for information about George Whitefield's movements.[45] Though the tone and conduct of the discourse is friendly (Watts always signed himself 'your affectionate brother'), personal information about individual correspondents only ever occupies a line or two of each letter. By contrast, the diversity and quantity of individuals, books, places, and occasions described is remarkable. The flow of cross-currents is also strong (each man had numerous other correspondents in Britain and America), suggesting that the 'isolated correspondence of individual ministers' identified by O'Brien had developed into a community aware of its connections by the eighteenth century.[46] As the English editor of A. H. Francke's letter on preaching, David Jennings was one of several English ministers who appeared in the correspondence as an intellectual broker.

The active transatlantic correspondence network of Congregationalist ministers was a decentred one in which participants shared information about each other and news was not filtered through restrictive channels or transmitted at the behest of individual figureheads. Watts, for example, frequently expressed a hope of learning more about American revivals but, even though his name was attached to *A Faithful Narrative*, he did not insist on controlling the spread of news; instead, he suggested that people in New England take the lead:

> I should be glad to see some short account from one or two more of ye ministers in New Engl[an]d who were eye & ear witnesses of this great work in some of the neighbouring towns, printed in Boston, & if they were judiciously done I am sure some hundreds of them might be sold in London as a further testimony to this great work of God in Hamshire.[47]

---

[44] MHS, *Proceedings*, 375, 387, 395–9.
[45] MHS, *Proceedings*, 383, 387, 391–2, 394.
[46] O'Brien, 'A Transatlantic Community of Saints', 813.
[47] Watts to Elisha Williams, 7 June 1738, in MHS, *Proceedings*, 335.

Watts's confident projection of sales for such texts suggests that he assumed that it was not only ministers who had an appetite for further news of awakening, and his desire for 'eye & ear witnesses' attests to the advantage of participation in an epistolary community: that one could gather numerous reports and assess them by careful comparison. The fact that he appeared to prefer ministerial accounts to any by the laity indicates, however, quite a limited view of who was qualified to participate in these culture of knowledge exchanges. Although this international web of informal learning encompassed many individuals in various locations, it was not an open world and a hierarchy of transmission from the more to the less educated was preserved. In such a context, the ministerial duty to preach and teach well expounded in *Two Discourses* was paramount.

As well as contributing to projects designed to spread dissenting preaching and ministerial methods to trainee ministers, established ministers, and the laity within dissent and within England, Watts had international, interdenominational hopes. *A Faithful Narrative* and *Two Discourses* represent a significant attempt to connect learned evangelical communities across the Atlantic and Europe.[48] O'Brien identifies several 'revival means' which increased lay self-determination, including 'weekly sacraments . . . prayer societies, the practice of itinerant preaching, and coordinated prayer days—all of which were recognized as potentially threatening to a minister's control'.[49] In these terms, the emphasis ministerial authors placed on the instrumental role for sermons in generating the correct conditions for emotionally affecting, rationally guided religious experience can be seen as an effort to reassert the central place of rigorous, evangelical preaching in religious experience which would assure the minister's continued control. While they may have been responding to a perceived weakness in preaching provision, the tenor of the discourses and the pattern of their publication offer a generative, expansive, and participatory model for improvement appropriate to principles of self-directed intellectual and social engagement. The sudden 'surprizing' surges in religious experiences related informally and—after Edwards's *Faithful*

---

[48] Jonathan Edwards, *A Faithful Narrative of the Surprizing work of God . . . In a Letter to the Revd. Dr. Benjamin Colman* (London, 1737). See Watts's letters to Benjamin Colman concerning the publication of the work in MHS, *Proceedings*, 349, 353, and 356–7; Goen, *The Works of Jonathan Edwards, IV: The Great Awakening*, 32–46; Susan O'Brien, 'Eighteenth-Century Publishing Networks in the First Years of Transatlantic Evangelicalism', in *Evangelicalism: Comparative Studies of Popular Protestantism in the North America, the British Isles, and Beyond 1700–1900*, ed. Mark A. Noll, David W. Bebbington, and George A. Rawlyk (Oxford, 1994), 38–57 and 'A Transatlantic Community of Saints', 815 and 819.

[49] O'Brien, 'A Transatlantic Community of Saints', 821.

Narrative—in print should therefore be understood in the context of an ongoing project of instruction in the appropriate conduct and learning for religion directed at ministers and the laity which *Two Discourses* embodied and which was strongly influenced by Halle Pietism. Open minded British religious leaders looked east and west for models, stories, and positive signs and, as the range of texts promoted by Watts indicates, religious revival emerged in a context that valued educational, sociable, and international exchange very highly.

4. INTERNATIONAL AND INTERDENOMINATIONAL TEXTUAL SOCIABILITY

The emotional fervour associated with religious awakening was surrounded by, connected to, and shaped by a less strident but sustained and powerful educational programme through the network of texts, agents, and distribution. One way, therefore, of thinking about evangelical awakening in the context of enlightenment culture is to adopt a wide conception of education. Many of the texts Watts promoted evinced and shaped enlightened aims through their driving concern for conduct and knowledge and because they sought answers to the question of how to exert a benign influence on the behaviour and morals of people who might well not read the texts in which those ideas were expressed.

The situation of literary sociability described here provides a starting point for understanding how a collaborative temper of improvement moderated strident enthusiasm in narratives of evangelical revival. For while it is true that 'the Christian Enlightenment was heavily influenced by the type of "enthusiasm" it saw itself as combating', the writers Watts knew actively sought to incorporate positive aspects of enthusiasm into their own writing rather than reactively adopting some of its features in order to defeat it.[50] Attending to this mood expands existing understanding of the connections between print and awakening because it emphasizes the disposition of writing and dissemination as much as the news or information contained in those texts.

The international scope of Watts's work was facilitated by friendships and manifested in collaborative work to promote texts across languages and national borders. He sought to advance education and knowledge, politeness and piety in a manner characterized by candour, liberality,

---

[50] Helena Rosenblatt, 'The Christian Enlightenment', in *The Cambridge History of Christianity*, *VII*, ed. Brown and Tackett, 283–301 (297).

and optimism. Taking these factors together, not only does an open and generous religious international in the enlightenment period emerge, but so too does the distinctively communal literary culture of Watts's circle. The desire to disseminate educational practices and religious news around the public sphere was motivated by strongly evangelical commitments and effected by personal and public channels of communication. The textual engagements described here had powerful histories for their participants and an equally strong—though dispersed—effect over long periods and among scattered audiences. The decentred series of associations that Watts sought out were not simply pragmatic, but representative of the diverse and imaginative engagements that he, his correspondents, and his readers valued.

Wary of the limited conclusions to be drawn from taking a narrowly bibliographic view of influence and conscious of the fact that, as William St Clair notes, it is virtually impossible to estimate how many readers a particular copy of a book may have had, this chapter and Chapter 4 have taken a broad view of Watts's publishing activities.[51] By considering bibliometric evidence (such as number of editions) and evidence drawn from print culture (particularly his presence in other books) as well as by attending to particular engagements with certain texts, these two chapters have developed a qualitative as well as quantitative picture of Watts's role within the educational culture of dissent and beyond it, in British and international contexts. This approach might not entirely resolve the difficulty so eloquently described by Donald Davie when speaking of Watts's hymns, that:

> We...have no method by which to translate the quantitative facts of so many copies sold and printed year after year, into that qualitative consideration of how they conditioned the sensibility of the English people.

But it has nevertheless tried to bring together ideas about Watts's work in different areas in order to give as full a sense as possible of what Davie termed Watts's 'civilizing influence' (though the term preferred here is 'improving') and understand how and why this influence spread.[52]

Through his books and acts, Watts was a towering figure within dissent and a leading participant in the international culture of enlightened evangelicalism. He was useful to 'readers at the boundaries' of literacy (in William St Clair's phrase) and leaders of a moderate British intellectual culture such as Samuel Johnson and Philip Doddridge.[53]

---

[51] William St Clair, *The Reading Nation in the Romantic Period* (Cambridge, 2004), 235.
[52] Davie, *A Gathered Church*, 33.　　[53] St Clair, *The Reading Nation*, 343.

While his ideas circulated in tracts, extracts, and prefaces to the works of others, his stature as a substantial author for a learned dissenting tradition was—like Doddridge's—preserved through impressive physical editions that were posthumously published, and it is to these that Chapter 6 will turn.

6

Friendship, Labour, and Editing Posthumous Works

The reader sitting down to a morning in the library with the posthumously published multi-volume works of either Isaac Watts or Philip Doddridge finds herself in the company of a hefty body of work. She will probably have some trouble finding enough space to arrange all six volumes around her and will certainly require a range of reading aids: bookstand, page weights, lamp, desk, and chair. In this respect, her reading experience is already qualitatively different from reading their individual works in their separate editions. The appearance of the set as a set also signals a particular bibliographic context. The reader opening the first volume of Watts's *Works* in six crown quarto volumes—well bound in good calf with detailed double tooling in gold—is met with a diptych honouring Watts as a canonical author of English letters. To the right, a title page set in fine Roman type, elegantly and unambiguously arranged so that the author's name complete with honorary title and these volumes' claim to embody his complete 'Works' share the limelight, supported in smaller type by the names of the editors, David Jennings and Philip Doddridge. These are names recognizable for their own piety and learning in print and their presence endorses the work as an official publication. All is orderly and correct. This declaration of authorship (expressed typographically and through the morphology of the page) has a visual and mimetic counterpart in the engraved author portrait to its left. Here, the reader encounters a serene and neatly attired Watts, wig in place, clerical bands pressed and symmetrical, gazing out from an oval frame which is decorated with oak, laurel, and palm: leaves that symbolize wisdom, poetic excellence, and piety excellence respectively. Words and image construct a strongly laudatory authorization of these *Works* as the official monument to an important man of letters.

A similar encounter awaits the eager reader of the first complete edition of Doddridge's *Family Expositor* to be published in full after his death. Here, the title page of each generous quarto volume is rubricated, evoking the traditions of biblical scholarship to which this work contributes.

Though the name of any editor is absent, the posthumous nature of the work and its official sanction is verbally registered by a statement asserting that the edition is 'Printed by Assignment from the Author's Widow.'[1] As with Watts's *Works*, the title page of the first volume operates in concert with a frontispiece portrait. The illustrated page is abundantly decorated, with an elaborate frame around the central image in which *putti* bear aloft garlands of flowers, a devil-figure hides his face, and Doddridge's head, encircled by a halo of stars, is lifted to a heavenly realm by a group of female figures. These are identified in the caption as 'Faith & Piety accompanied by Benevolence' who holds his clerical coat and drops coins into the outstretched hands of a kneeling woman in simple attire while Faith rests a cross and book on her lap and points to Doddridge.[2] The author's face appears as an *imago clipeata*, a concept in portraiture that did complex representational work. A *clipetus* encourages an emblematic reading of the head, it indicates the literal absence (through death) of the depicted individual yet produces coherence in visual display and the interpretation thereof through the long history of the concept, used to draw together the absent and the present.[3] The *imago clipeata* bears both classical and Christian associations, for it was used in imperial Rome and Byzantium and to depict Christ in early Christian art, and in this frontispiece context its use presents Doddridge as a memorable worthy, a learned gentleman, and a figure who, though dead, lived on through his published work of classical and Christian erudition.

Both author portraits deploy a startling range of visual conventions in their efforts to represent the deceased author as dignified man of learning. Neither image quite conforms to a twenty-first-century reader's idea of how a dissenting minister might be figured in this bibliographical context: perhaps the portrait of Daniel Neal that accompanied the second edition of *The History of the Puritans* (1754) is closer to what she anticipates. Neal is bewigged and dressed for his profession like Watts and is framed within sculptural devices—also like Watts—though a scalloped centrepiece and framing of palm leaves and olive branches provide the only embellishment in this case. The image lacks the flamboyance and imaginative flourishes so abundant in Doddridge's portrait and present in Watts's too. The understated allegory of the leaves (both of which represent peace in the Christian tradition, indicating that Neal's narrative does not have divisive

---

[1] Philip Doddridge, *The Family Expositor*, 6 vols (London, 1761–1762), I, title page.

[2] Doddridge, *The Family Expositor* (1761–2), I, frontispiece. The design and execution of the image is attributed to Anthony Walker on the image itself.

[3] Marcia Pointon, *Hanging the Head: Portraiture and Social Function in Eighteenth-Century England* (New Haven, 1993), 65–6.

or incendiary intentions) is supplemented by a small cartouche bearing a sober scene of a woman seated, gesturing to an open book held open by a *putto* with a seated child turned towards her. This resembles allegorical depictions of education with the addition that the woman has a radiant circle at her neck: the sun in this position is associated with purity, perhaps a visual pun on the name of the 'puritans'.[4] Appropriately to a historian of the puritans, Neal is presented as a theological and historical author in keeping with seventeenth-century patterns of visual austerity, though there is a slight smile on his lips and his cloak is rather rumpled.

The varying styles of these printed author portraits illustrate the difficulty of framing questions about posthumous works in terms of an author's tradition or social setting. Watts, Doddridge, and Neal shared religious commitments that kept them outside the established church and a literary inheritance that sustained this identity, but all also enjoyed reputations beyond the world of dissent in which they had been nurtured as authors. As Seed notes, 'Neal's *History of the Puritans* can be placed alongside the hymns of his close friend Isaac Watts in its aspiration' to politeness and wide acceptance.[5] And yet the ways in which they were represented as authors after their deaths have little in common. That variety raises questions about what posthumous publication entailed and specifically of who was responsible for the different elements of posthumous works. Addressing the role of format, paratexts, and publication models in creating the utility and meanings of texts, this chapter will consider the production of Watts's and Doddridge's posthumously published works with reference to Doddridge's pivotal role in these processes, for he moved from author shaping his own works to editor of Watts to subject for posthumous glorification in his own right. Correspondence among friends, editors, and executors articulates the range of tasks posthumous editions were expected to fulfil and this evidence of variety and import informs the argument that these editions were testamentary acts which functioned as showcases for dissenting learning and as memorials.

In this narrative, the roles of particular individuals—authors, editors, booksellers, subscribers, relatives, friends—are important. Therefore, rather than providing a history of editions that treats their production and editing in philological or hermeneutic terms, the exploration of the canonical status conferred by posthumous editions that follows is social,

---

[4] Cesare Ripe, *Iconologia: or, Moral Emblems* (London, 1709), 26 (fig. 103). For this reading of a sun see 'Purity', 63 (fig. 253). The portrait of Neal bears particular comparison to that of Watts because the two editions were published only a year apart, in the same format, the dissenting booksellers James Buckland and James Waugh were involved in both publications, and the portrait was the work of the same engraver, Simon Ravenet.

[5] Seed, *Dissenting Histories*, 42.

biographical, and practical in nature: who wanted what to happen? How did the books get produced? What texts are included in posthumous works and on whose authority? Were processes of posthumous publication and the works that result shaped by distinctively dissenting traditions? Investigating books in these terms develops the picture of dissenting textual traditions presented so far by complementing the account of manuscript circulation, informal publication, and small, cheap editions with an explicit consideration of how dissenting authors and editors approached the weighty matter of posterity.

1. COLLECTED *WORKS*: IDEAS AND PRACTICE

Isaac Watts had long anticipated his death and when it finally came, his financial and literary affairs were in order. This is not surprising. His surviving letters are full of information about his publishing programme and over the years he offered advice to friends about their own publishing arrangements on several occasions. Authorial reputation and recompense were significant matters to him, perhaps because he continued to smart at having sold his copyright to *Hymns and Spiritual Songs* for £10. In his will he declared his intentions regarding how he should be memorialized as an author through a series of practical instructions. He appointed literary executors, authorized the sale of his copyright (which was done, to James Waugh, for £600), and named Philip Doddridge and David Jennings as his chosen editors. He explained where to find his unpublished papers, gave the editors freedom to do what they wanted with them, but stipulated that 'such as shall be published may have the Attestation of their names prefixed to satisfy the World they are genuine'.[6] Securing a credible literary legacy was unquestionably an important matter to Watts and he hoped to achieve it by associating his posthumously published writings with the names of two respectable ministerial associates who were authors in their own right.

His determined effort at authorial direction from beyond the grave seems—on the evidence of the complete *Works* finally published in six crown quarto volumes in 1753—to have been successful. This substantial monument to the well-known and prolific author encompassed the full range of his writings: a body of divinity intended to demonstrate theological orthodoxy and Christian living, the poet's voice modulated to a variety of genres, and the pedagogue and pastor's practical guidance

---

[6] TNA: PRO Prob 11/776, sig. 509.

expressed by means of educational guides, philosophical treatises, and sermons. As Jennings put it in the biographical account which prefaced the first volume, 'I question whether any author before him did ever appear with reputation on such a variety of subjects, as he as done, both as a prose-writer and a poet.'[7] Though Jennings's insistent use of adverbs of degree and frequency creates rather breathless prefatory hyperbole, the six hefty volumes do display a variety of subjects, and a diversity of forms and genres too. The range of topics and modes, of poetry and prose, might perhaps have been unusual for an author but it was not unique in this period. Watts's *Works* reminds twenty-first-century readers that he is comparable to other wide-ranging writers such as Jonathan Swift and Catharine Cockburn Trotter.[8]

However, there was perhaps something surprising about such a popular writer as Watts appearing in this grand physical form. The Watts of his *Works* was not especially recognizable as the Watts long known to the readers of his educational books or participants in oral cultures of hymn singing and family reading. Instead, the editors and booksellers involved in this publication drew on traditions specific to collected works to convey this posthumous figure of Watts. There were two principal lines of development in posthumous or collected works in this period: that of the theologian and that of the poet and, as the case of Watts illustrates, these could overlap.

Scholarly work on the form and content of collected works of eighteenth-century English authors has generally focused on poets, even though, as McLaverty has noted, the category of 'works' came to a fairly late flowering for literary writers in comparison to theologians, lawyers, and doctors. McLaverty suggests that it was through the efforts of book-sellers focused on belles lettres such as Bernard Lintot and Jacob Tonson that poets' collected works started to come into print, 'building on established public practice in relation to clergymen, lawyers, physicians, philosophers and a few established literary figures'. The crucial factor in developing such editions was the proof of a readership: 'There was an established readership, a public, for various forms of professional writing and evolved institutions of authorship; parallel arrangements were now being developed for literature.'[9] But rather than 'parallel' arrangements,

---

[7] David Jennings, 'Some Account of the Author's Life and Character', in Watts, *Works*, I, vii.

[8] See Stephen Karian, *Jonathan Swift in Print and Manuscript* (Cambridge, 2010), ch. 1 and Melanie Bigold, *Women of Letters, Manuscript Circulation and Print Afterlives in the Eighteenth Century: Elizabeth Rowe, Catharine Cockburn and Elizabeth Carter* (Houndmills, Basingstoke, 2013), ch. 4.

[9] James McLaverty, *Pope, Print and Meaning* (Oxford, 2001), 53.

the existence and appearance of collected *Works* of a variety of authors provides evidence of an interfused literary culture of monumental authorship which developed over the course of the eighteenth century. The patterns of publishing *Works* was not a one-way movement away from the ancient learned professions traditionally embodied in such collections and towards new figures honoured in a vernacular literary canon. The appearance and success of publishing models used by Alexander Pope for individual works and collected *Works*, for example, informed the posthumous and collective works of theological authors such as Doddridge that were highly successful publishing ventures in themselves.

To put it another way, the emergent national canon constructed through diverse modes of critical editing as delineated by Marcus Walsh was not fixed in terms of genre in the mid-eighteenth century. Watts is a transitional figure in this cultural shift, a reminder that a single author did not always fit into one category. Watts is figured in his *Works* as theologian, poet, and scientific writer. As Marcus Walsh argues, 'editorial activity in the eighteenth century . . . must be seen in the light of contested practices, constructions and representations of learning, scholarship and reading in the period'.[10] The way in which Watts's *Works* came into being helps clarify the nature of those practices and constructions and to identify where and why contestation might flare up. So does the publishing history of *The Family Expositor* following its author's death, a case which further illustrates the difficulties of harmonizing commercial, religious, and intellectual factors in the construction of pious and useful books.

2. WATTS'S *WORKS* 1748–1754: EDITORIAL NEGOTIATIONS

Four days after Watts's death on 25 November 1748, Nathaniel Neal wrote to Philip Doddridge saying that 'I could not, in friendship, avoid writing you a line, to inform you that the Doctor has made his brother Enoch and myself executors to his will.' Neal named Watts's heirs, gave the date of the will, and copied verbatim the section appointing Jennings and Doddridge editors of the remaining manuscripts. He concluded with a significant caveat regarding these materials: 'I question whether there are any left which he has ordered to be published.'[11]

---

[10] Marcus Walsh, *Shakespeare, Milton and Eighteenth-Century Literary Editing: The Beginnings of Interpretative Scholarship* (Cambridge, 1997), 29.
[11] Nathaniel Neal to Philip Doddridge, 29 November 1748. *Calendar* 1424; Humphreys, V, 84.

Early in 1749, David Jennings wrote to Doddridge to say that he could not yet send a list of Watts's manuscripts, but provided information about the financial and intellectual property arrangements:

> I suppose you know, that Dr. Watts has left Mr. Neal and his Brother, Mr. Enoch Watts, joint executors. I find Mr. Neal does not choose to meddle with the Manuscripts just at present. When he does, you will have immediate notice. I believe we shall not have near so much trouble in publishing the Doctor's Manuscripts as I expected, when he acquainted me with his design of committing them in part to my care; which was three or four years ago; for since then he has published most of the Manuscripts he designed for the press, so that, as I learn from Mr. Parker, there is little if any thing more remaining of that sort than the second part of the Improvement of the Mind. He tells me there are also some miscellaneous things in the manner of his Reliquiae Juveniles; but whether enough to make a volume, and whether intended by him for the press, I cannot say.[12]

Jennings's identification (on the advice of Watts's amanuensis Parker) of the second part of *The Improvement of the Mind* as the sole unpublished work of significance remaining explanation of the situation was close to Neal's view. Neal wrote to Doddridge a month later, saying: 'I immediately determined to send you a list of Dr. Watts's manuscripts, in order that you may consider with yourself and consult Mr. Jennings, when and how they shall be delivered to you.'[13]

Jennings certainly began the editing procedure in optimistic spirits ('there is little if anything more remaining'), and this positive view was echoed in Doddridge's final words on the subject too. Writing to his wife during a visit to London in 1750, Doddridge noted that he was at Jennings's house, where the two men had concluded that 'We shall agree mighty well about Dr Watts's manuscripts.'[14] But despite these positive expressions at the start and end of the process, there were some difficulties in between.

One hurdle was the condition of the manuscript of the second part of *The Improvement of the Mind*. Watts had promised the sequel in the preface to part one (1741) but it had never appeared. This was the manuscript that David Jennings identified as the sole outstanding work. Three months after Watts's death, the lawyer Nathaniel Neal (son of

---

[12] David Jennings to Philip Doddridge, 5 January 1748/9. *Calendar* 1437; Stedman, *Letters to and from... Doddridge*, 251.

[13] Nathaniel Neal to Philip Doddridge, 8 February 1748/9. *Calendar* 1447; Humphreys, V, 104. The list of manuscripts does not survive, but is reproduced in Stedman, *Letters to and from... Doddridge*, 379–80; and Humphreys, V, 103.

[14] Philip Doddridge to Mercy Doddridge, 2 August 1750. DWL MS NCL L.1/1/131; *Calendar* 1639.

Daniel Neal and nephew of Nathaniel Lardner) observed to Doddridge that 'I was very sensible the second part of Dr. Watts's Improvement of the Mind, would fall short of your expectation as a finished piece.'[15] It certainly seemed to have fallen short of Neal's, for he urged extensive revisions:

> High as Dr. Watts's talents were esteemed by me, I think you should make no difficulty of taking such liberties as may seem to you necessary; nay you seem expressly warranted to do it by the paper left with the manuscripts. You are not laying before the world his opinion on doubtful and disputed points, but his illustrations of acknowledged ones: and the defects in those illustrations, did not arise from his want of ability to discern, or rectify them, but to the works remaining unfinished, till the decays of his bodily constitution disabled him from exerting those abilities.[16]

At issue was the extent of editorial intervention desirable (or permissible) in the preparation of Watts's manuscripts for publication. The view on this depended on whether the works were considered complete or not and if not, why that was. Jennings thought the works had been finished by Watts, and were therefore in the state the author wished: hence there would be little to detain the editors. Neal advocated the opposite, taking the view that Watts's physical infirmity prevented the works being finished. He was very clear that he saw problems in the manuscript of the second part of *The Improvement of the Mind*: 'I think it, in all respects, imperfect, in matter and form.' Neal's proposals give an expansive view of what 'editing' a posthumous work might entail, one not confined to judicious cutting: 'It wants to be digested, in some parts reduced, in others (it may be) enlarged, in all methodized, connected, and polished.'[17]

Neal's statements further imply that Doddridge had himself expressed concern or dissatisfaction regarding the manuscript; a sense supported by evidence that the editing appears to have caused difficulty. The same month Doddridge confided to his friend Samuel Clark his anxiety: 'how I shall prepare for the press the second volume of Dr. Watts's Improvement of the Mind I cannot imagine', he said, and requested Clark's assistance in completing the work.[18] The inclusion of the second part of

[15] Nathaniel Neal to Philip Doddridge, 5 March 1749/50. *Calendar* 1589; Humphreys, V, 112. Nuttall, who does not include this passage, suggests a date of 15 March 1749/50.

[16] Nathaniel Neal to Philip Doddridge, 5 [or 15] March 1749/50. *Calendar* 1589; Humphreys, V, 112–13.

[17] Nathaniel Neal to Philip Doddridge, 5 [or 15] March 1749/50. *Calendar* 1589; Humphreys, V, 112–13.

[18] Philip Doddridge to Samuel Clark, 1 March 1748/9. *Calendar* 1455; Humphreys, V, 110. Clark replied 'I am glad you'll have ye opportunity of perusing Dr Watts's Papers & of

The Improvement of the Mind in Watts's collected *Works* is emphasized on the title page and in newspaper advertisements. It was this new work which was used to command the attention of the book-purchasing public. Neal was conscious that part of the aim of producing Watts's *Works* was to exhibit a representative dissenter's polite learning, hence his concern that this intention would be threatened if pieces lacking polish were admitted to the volumes; particularly pieces that were to be advertised on the title page and in the press.

Both Neal and Doddridge articulate friendship as a motivating force in the editorial activities being undertaken. Neal begins his first letter to Doddridge outlining Watts's instructions regarding his material and literary estate 'in friendship' while Doddridge confides his doubts about the project to a close friend early on and later highlights his concord with David Jennings. Behind these statements lies a powerful sense of the need for dissenting ministers to work for the benefit of their own tradition. Friendship in these circumstances was not a Ciceronian, disinterested bestowal of affection and virtuous deeds but personally and practically contingent, animated by feelings of obligation which in turn were born out of personal connections and a sense of one writer's place in a circle of fellow ministers and a tradition of dissenting writers. In this context, posterity is not only about securing the reputation of an exemplary writer such as Watts (though that was important, hence Neal's concern) but also requires the effort of those remaining. Friends left alive must take on new roles governed by tradition in relation to the memory of their associate as posthumous guardians of reputation and manuscripts.

There are ominous suggestions that the work begun in recognition of the responsibilities of friendship and framed by discourses of commitment to cordial relations was challenged by the nature of the tasks necessary. There was evidently risk of serious disagreements about the degree of editorial intervention required or desired in Watts's writings, for Neal wrote to Doddridge declaring that:

> The interposing between yourself and Dr. Jennings, in relation to Dr. Watts's MSS, is to me by no means an agreeable undertaking; but if he requests it (and if he does not it can answer no purpose) I shall be ready to do what I am able for the honour of the MSS as well as to prevent a misunderstanding between the Doctor and you.[19]

---

publishing w^t you may think useful, among wch perhaps may be found some wch he though more proper to be publish'd after his death,' [? May] 1749. Letter dated by Doddridge, CHCN Doddridge MS. See G. F. Nuttall, *Philip Doddridge: Additional Letters* (London, 2001), letter 1472A.

[19] Nathaniel Neal to Philip Doddridge, 11 April 1750. *Calendar* 1600; Humphreys, V, 154.

One of the more unpleasant duties of the literary executor was to resolve editorial disputes, in this case between friends. But attempts at further analysis of the editorial process are frustrated by lack of information. These men were too delicate to express in writing what in particular was wrong. Some problems with epistolary evidence about book publishing are well put by Donald Nichol, writing about William Warburton's editing of Pope:

> The main narrative available is epistolary, hence fragmented, and an inter-pretation...will be subject to such difficulties as hiatus (non-existent letters), imbalance (more of Pope's letters have been preserved than Warbur-ton's), irretrievable conversations and tonal inference (is the writer sneering behind his pen or is he serious?).[20]

Nichol's taxonomy of difficulties is certainly helpful as a checklist though it also offers some warnings for interpretative practices. His account, slipping from discussion of the editing of Pope's *Works* in particular to comments on the relationship between Warburton and Pope in general, exposes another complicating factor in the use of epistolary evidence, which is that because it performs the personal relationships that it also describes, readers follow it as a human drama and thereby risk losing sight of the books that were the starting point of the investigation. Caught up in Neal's social difficulties and his efforts to articulate them, the reader only realizes later that the moment of a crucial shift in the scope of the enterprise is missing from the epistolary record. When and by whom was it decided to present Watts's collected works in a series of volumes? When and by whom were the editorial duties of Jennings and Doddridge extended from preparing the text of unpublished manuscripts for publication to bringing together and ordering all Watts's published works too? The facts are not present in the surviving correspondence.

Another difficulty when investigating the intentions behind and out-comes of collected *Works* is that editors and executors are not the only agents. Grieving and impecunious relatives may want a certain kind of publication for financial or emotional reasons. Patrons, friends, and con-gregants may see a posthumous edition as a way of broadcasting a particular version of their client, companion, or minister to the wider world, and have views about what that version should look like. Subscribers to a multi-volume *Works* surely had an idea of the quality of paper, type, and workmanship they could expect for their money. The first volume of Watts's *Works* carries a list of 136 subscribers' names, including members of the Abney family, Watts's former student Sir John Hartopp, Thomas Secker (the Archbishop of Canterbury), the Countess of Huntingdon, and

---

[20] Nichol, *Pope's Literary Legacy*, xxxvii.

Aaron Burr and Samuel Sherwood (tutors of the College of New Jersey). The subscription lists publicly attest to support for the work from dissenters and members of the established church in England, and educators in America. Booksellers wanted a marketable product and the subscription list was in part a means to this end: by displaying the names of the wealthy and cultivated readers it had already secured, the book might attract more such readers. Another addition to collected *Works* that booksellers were beginning to demand was a biography because 'it has been so usual to prefix some account of an author's life to such a collection of his works as these six volumes contain' (as the preface explained) even though none of Watts's associates felt able to provide one.[21]

All these desires and intentions affect the work finally published and its reception. These compromised, complicated, and interwoven intentions are ultimately expressed to readers typographically and materially, through the selection and order of texts and 'bibliographical codes'; Jerome McGann's term for elements of a work which transmit meaning in non-linguistic ways, including typography and page layout, format, paper, binding, and price.[22] Attention to these aspects of book production can reveal the modes of editorial, authorial, and commercial communication in operation.[23]

3. WATTS'S *WORKS* AS OBJECT

Surviving copies of the six elegant and generously proportioned crown quarto volumes first advertised for sale in August 1754 are finely bound in good calf and embellished with intricate gold tooling: they are expensive objects, for display as much as for reading. The frontispiece image of Watts attributed to the 'virtuoso engraver' Simon Ravenet is an elaborately wrought celebration of a seemly man of genius, as noted in section 1.[24] Watts is accompanied by not one but two muses, Urania and Erato;

[21] David Jennings declined to write a full biography citing 'want of materials' so Neal approached Doddridge, who did not write one either. Volume I of the *Works* began with the biographical part of Jennings's funeral sermon. Nathaniel Neal to Philip Doddridge, 5 [or 15] March 1749. *Calendar* 1589; Humphreys, V, 111; Watts, *Works*, I, iii.

[22] McGann, *The Textual Condition* (Princeton, 1991), 57. For McGann, authors (and by implication, editors) do not have as full control over bibliographical codes as they do linguistic ones.

[23] 'Editorial communication' is an adaptation of Marcus Walsh's term 'scholarly communication' in 'Form and Function in the Eighteenth-Century Literary Edition: The Case of Edward Capell', *Studies in Bibliography*, 54 (2001), 225–42 (241).

[24] Sheila O'Connell, 'Ravenet, Simon François (1721–1774)', *ODNB*. The image was almost certainly commissioned specifically for the *Works*.

astronomy and lyric poetry. These muses and their accoutrements represent the range of Watts's learned and literary endeavours, his secular lyrics and hymns. They are subordinate in size and position on the page to Watts, who presides over the materials and sources for his literary creations, diffusing an enlightening glow over the figures and objects below. Everything is present and correct in an insistent—possibly even overdetermined—working of authorial presence.[25] Though Thomas McGrath has noted that 'the selection or commissioning of a portrait for a printed book was usually the responsibility of the editor' there is no evidence that Jennings (the sole surviving editor after 1751) played any role in this portrait.[26] Frontispiece portraits were, argues Janine Barchas, 'a caste label' which 'raised the price of a hand-press book'.[27] Given these factors, it seems likely that the booksellers were responsible, that they had a clear sense of the kind of authorial figure they wished the edition to portray, and that they were prepared to take on extra expense to achieve that.

This grand mode of authorial representation has a long history and many aspects of the Watts portrait are highly conventional (as David Piper observes, 'the artist cannot spell out and analyse qualities of mind and spirit . . . as can a biographer: his methods of characterization of anything other than the outer man are generally not very subtle') but this is not to say that these features are uninteresting.[28] Rather, the conventions that developed around engraved author portraits came from various sources in print and religious culture. One example is the metonymic operation of Watts's *Works* as a reflection of Watts the man, conveyed by framing of the portrait as though it could be a mirror. This is a commonplace that operates allegorically but also physically. The portrait precedes the works and prepares readers for them but is separate both spatially and technologically, as it is printed in a separate process. The figure of metonymy recalls sixteenth- and seventeenth-century *Works*, placing Watts in a tradition of worthy authors. More specifically, it evokes fellow nonconformist Richard Baxter's favoured concept of the 'speculum'; that the works of a great man should demonstrate exemplary Christian action and thought.[29] Watts's particular social and intellectual milieu as well as

[25] For analysis of the ways by which author portraits came to authenticate the works they precede in an earlier period, see Sarah Howe, 'The English Author Portrait, 1500–1640', *Papers of the Bibliographical Society of America*, 102 (2008), 465–99.

[26] Thomas McGrath, 'Facing the Text: Author Portraits in Florentine Printed Books, 1545–1585', *Word and Image: A Journal of Verbal/Visual Enquiry*, 19 (2003), 74–85 (76).

[27] Janine Barchas, *Graphic Design, Print Culture, and the Eighteenth-Century Novel* (Cambridge, 2003), 22.

[28] David Piper, *The Image of the Poet: British Poets and their Portraits* (Oxford, 1982), 22.

[29] Keeble, *Richard Baxter*, 122.

his place in a broader culture are visually and verbally displayed in this monument to polite learning in the eighteenth-century style.

That learning was carefully ordered within the works, which were grouped into volumes by category: three volumes of sermons and discourses (which could be purchased as a stand-alone set), one of hymns and poems, one of educational writings, and one of learned and controversial essays.[30] The original circumstances and contexts of writing and printing are not visible on the title pages or contents lists of the volumes, all of which follow the same layout in order to create an impression of uniformity. The individual volume title pages and lists of contents collectively and successively detail a compendium of religious and philosophical writings, educational pieces, poetry, and belles lettres. This monumental edition of all Watts's writings reinforces his status as an intellectual of the age and seeks the acknowledgement of learned audiences of some wealth.

These bibliographical elements might have encouraged book purchasers to place their Watts in company with John Tillotson (whose three-volume *Works* in folio with a new biography by Thomas Birch and a newly engraved portrait done by Ravenet was published in 1752) or with John Milton whose prose works in two crown quarto volumes were issued by Andrew Millar in 1753, and perhaps even Alexander Pope, whose nine-volume works in octavo edited by Warburton had appeared in 1752.[31] Format acts as a mediating element both in the sense that it mediates the reader's encounter with Watts's own words and that the crown quarto size places Watts, along with Milton, as an intermediary between Tillotson at the grand theological end and Pope at the companionable poetry end of the gentleman's library.

Watts's *Works* is steeped in the traditions of theological and nonconformist memorial editions but it is also an expansive and confident declaration of his place in the world of eighteenth-century polite letters. The apparatus of the *Works* highlights a Christian context for their composition but does not announce denominational particularity or draw attention to the precise contexts of composition. For example, the information that many of his educational works were originally produced for children, dissenting families, or students in dissenting academies is not presented here. The publication of the *Works* built on Watts's efforts in

---

[30] Prospective purchasers were informed that 'The three first Volumes, containing the Practical Works, may be had alone, Price neatly bound, 2l. 2s.', *London Evening Post*, 20–2 August 1754.

[31] *The Works of the Most Reverend Dr. John Tillotson, Archbishop of Canterbury*, ed. Thomas Birch, 3 vols (London, 1752) and *The Works of Alexander Pope*, ed. William Warburton, 9 vols (London, 1751). See Rosemary Dixon, 'The Publishing of John Tillotson's Collected Works 1695–1757', *The Library*, 7th ser., 8 (2007), 154–81.

his lifetime to dissolve boundaries around dissenting theology and behaviour, and to construct instead a cross-denominational literary culture of learning.

The private processes by which the public monument was constructed are not all recoverable, but those that are articulated in surviving letters are characterized by personal obligation, shared work, and candid exchanges. These features of friendly intellectual labour undertaken on behalf of others and as part of a collective are also found in the correspondence relating to the publication of Doddridge's posthumous works. Indeed, Doddridge's approach of seeking advice from trusted parties while preparing Watts's *Works* for posthumous publication at the end of the 1740s was followed by his own friends and former students in the 1750s as they completed *The Family Expositor*.

4. *THE FAMILY EXPOSITOR* IN DODDRIDGE'S LIFETIME

Philip Doddridge's *Family Expositor* was characterized by his biographer Job Orton as 'his Capital-work' which 'He had been preparing... from his Entrance on the Ministry'.[32] It was an ambitious compendium of New Testament translation, paraphrase, and commentary conceived by Doddridge as a learned work for family reading which would awaken and consolidate religious feeling.[33] The *mise-en-page* is highly unusual, consisting of a main text of Doddridge's own translation of the New Testament interwoven with his paraphrase which, in the case of the Gospels, harmonizes the words of the four evangelists into a single narrative. Surrounding it are critical notes of commentary, translation, and interpretation, and passages of 'improvement' containing Doddridge's suggestions for meditations and extempore prayer.[34] The title of *The Family Expositor* emphasized Doddridge's hope that it would be used in domestic settings, perhaps being read out loud by the head of the household. Its complex textual apparatus surrounded the New Testament with learned, practical, and emotionally affective additions, and the site of the page invited and guided a range of responses to the Gospels and Epistles. In the preface to the first volume, Doddridge introduced this design and his

[32] Orton, *Memoirs*, 143.   [33] *Calendar* 527.
[34] For a detailed account of the structure of *The Family Expositor*, see Isabel Rivers, 'Philip Doddridge's New Testament: *The Family Expositor* (1739–56)', in *The King James Bible After Four Hundred Years: Literary, Linguistic, and Cultural Influences*, ed. Hannibal Hamlin and Norman W. Jones (Cambridge, 2010), 124–45.

intentions in terms of improvement and candour. The first of these terms, as well as being the name he gave the sections of 'pressing Exhortations', recurs throughout the preface: the text will improve the scriptural understanding of its readers, the process of making the translation improved Doddridge's own understanding of the text and his stylistic facility, and the work as a whole has been improved by the suggestions of his friends.[35] The work itself is presented as a monument to 'growing Candour' on the part of some Church of England clergy and an 'engagement to cultivate' that candour on the part of moderate dissenters. Both groups are named 'Friends' by Doddridge, who frames the entire project as something that both promotes unity and requires liberality by claiming that 'if read with Impartiality and Seriousness' the New Testament would 'inlighten and adorn the Mind' and 'animate and transform the Heart'.[36] The intellectual, political, and social purposes of Bible reading are presented as having evangelical outcomes and enhancing personal piety.

The Family Expositor was often reprinted from its publication in 1739 until the middle of the nineteenth century.[37] But it was not as straightforwardly a Doddridge 'work' as the six volumes of similar bulk and consistent presentation in terms of title pages, prefaces, and indexes set out to suggest, for at the time of Doddridge's death in 1751 only the first three volumes (of six) had been published by the dissenting booksellers Richard Hett and James Waugh. In his lifetime, Doddridge oversaw every stage from composition to publication. He treated each volume of the work as a separate enterprise, perhaps because the complexity of the text meant each took a long time to complete, and he feared his health would not last. He told Samuel Clark before any of it had been published that:

> My Family Expositor goes on almost every Day & I press on ye faster in it that I may leave that on ye Evangelists compleat if w^t I have great Reason to expect God should call me speedily away. If I live I will give it a very attentive Review after you S^r & some other Friends have examined this rough & very imperfect Draught of it.[38]

The work took shape amid his schedule of lectures, pastoral visits, and preaching, and its content developed partly out of these tasks, for sections of the text began life in the academy lecture room. It was also formed out

---

[35] *The Family Expositor* (1739), I, v.   [36] *The Family Expositor* (1739), I, vii and i.

[37] John Guyse published a similar work entitled *A Practical Expositor* at almost the same time as Doddridge's, but it was not such a success. See G. F. Nuttall, 'Philip Doddridge, John Guyse and their Expositors', in *Kerkhistorische Opstellen Aangeboden aan Prof. Dr. J. van den Berg*, ed. C. Augustijn, P. N. Holtrop, et al. (Kampen, 1987), 102–13.

[38] Philip Doddridge to Samuel Clarke, 1 January 1736/7. DWL MS NCL L.1/10/20; *Calendar* 452.

of personal and intellectual association. Doddridge's comments indicate
that Clark and 'other Friends' were invited to act as trusted early readers,
among them the Presbyterian minister and biblical scholar Nathaniel
Lardner, whose *Credibility of Gospel History* (1727) was an important
contribution to the study of the New Testament. Lardner offered historical information and gave his preferred translation of some terms,
agreed with points where Doddridge questioned the authenticity of the
text, and suggested books that Doddridge might read to clarify points of
interpretation.[39]

Doddridge not only asked existing friends to help him improve the
work but used its composition to extend his intellectual circle further by
corresponding with scholars from the established church such as the
religious controversialist William Warburton, George Costard (Fellow of
Wadham College, Oxford), and Thomas Hunt of Hertford College.[40]
From them he sought advice on matters of translation and biblical
scholarship, and they offered him their knowledge and resources.[41] He
may also have hoped that their involvement would recommend the work
to university and established church associates.[42] The epistolary exchanges
these men conducted were sometimes registered in Doddridge's published
works. Warburton suggested an alternative interpretation of Jesus' words
in Luke 20:8, for example, which Doddridge incorporated into volume II
of *The Family Expositor*. He credited the suggestion to a 'very accurate and
learned Friend', though he did not name Warburton.[43] In return, Warburton acknowledged Doddridge for material he used in his own work.[44]

[39] *Calendar* 1433; Humphreys, V, 98–101.
[40] *Calendar* 457, 501, and 582. Hunt became Professor of Arabic in 1738, and of
Hebrew in 1747. Costard, also an expert in oriental languages, was primarily known as a
writer on ancient astronomy.
[41] Doddridge apparently asked to borrow a copy of Maimonides, *De jure pauperis et
peregrini apud Judaeos* (Oxford, 1679), for in a letter dated 2 August 1745, Hunt offered to
consult the work (a parallel text in Hebrew and Latin) in the Bodleian Library on
Doddridge's behalf. Humphreys, IV, 427; *Calendar* 1083.
[42] William Warburton gathered subscribers to *The Family Expositor*, including Philip
Yonge, Fellow of Trinity College, Cambridge, whom he described as 'the principal tutor in
his college'. William Warburton to Philip Doddridge, 15 August 1739. *Calendar* 558;
Humphreys, III, 394.
[43] *The Family Expositor*, II, 325. Earlier, he had characterized Warburton as 'An
excellent Person, justly celebrated in the Learned World' (49). For Warburton's suggested
interpretation, see Humphreys, III, 394–6. Doddridge's reason for not naming Warburton
may have been to conform to his strict code of propriety, for he says in the preface to
volume I that he had referenced everything except the particular contributions of living
friends 'where such Acknowledgement would not have been agreeable'. *The Family Expositor* (1739), I, iii.
[44] Warburton told Doddridge: 'I had occasion to quote a paragraph of yours of a passage
in the evangelists,' 2 February 1740/1. *Calendar* 659; Humphreys, III, 530.

The process of writing and publishing *The Family Expositor* introduced Doddridge into a circle of scholars who alluded to their personal, learned exchanges in print and letters.

Though Doddridge may have hoped that the intellectual prestige of *The Family Expositor* would be bolstered by these associations and his own reputation among these scholars assured by the work, his relations with writers and ministers from outside the dissenting community were not characterized by perfect equality. William Warburton was an eager reader of *The Family Expositor* and gathered some subscriptions for Doddridge, but he asserted his higher social standing and greater personal prestige at points in their correspondence both through his words (by dropping into his letters tales to illustrate his close personal associations with Pope, for example, who was a favourite secular author of Doddridge's) and his actions; or rather, his inactions. It is notable that he did not seek to introduce Doddridge to Pope, and that he responded to Doddridge's public (if unnamed) acknowledgement of his assistance with an acknowledgement of his own intellectual debt in a letter but not in print. Producing *The Family Expositor* brought Doddridge into friendly contact with scholars and well-connected establishment figures, but it did not secure him equal and easy friendship with them.

The composition of *The Family Expositor* was ongoing throughout the 1730s and 1740s and publication fell into several distinct phases. A sustained drive for subscribers meant that the first volume, published early in 1739, had a waiting audience of 1,600 subscribers. Throughout 1739 and 1740 correspondents enquired about the progress of volume II: that summer, William Warburton was impatient for its publication.[45] Volume II was published in September 1740 and priced at one guinea. At this stage, Doddridge expressed dissatisfaction with the quality of Richard Hett's materials and work. He was, he told his wife, 'a little chagrined to see how much [volume II] is disgraced by the bad Paper & Letter on which the Preface is done'.[46] A longer delay came between volumes II and III, which was eventually published in 1748, by James Waugh rather than Richard Hett. An agreement between Doddridge and Waugh in 1751 was for one thousand copies of volume IV to be printed, and both he and Waugh were anxious that printing should begin immediately.[47]

---

[45] *Calendar* 615.
[46] Philip Doddridge to Mercy Doddridge, 9 September 1740. *Calendar* 641. This criticism is particularly significant as the quality of the letter and paper of the first volume were two features specifically mentioned by Doddridge in his first preface: Doddridge, *The Family Expositor*, I, vii.
[47] Philip Doddridge to Mercy Doddridge, 12 June 1751. *Calendar* 1742.

Doddridge died before this happened. The fourth volume was not pub-lished until 1753 and volumes V and VI both appeared in 1756.

The model of gathering subscriptions instituted by Doddridge for the three volumes published in his lifetime was followed for the volumes published posthumously.[48] Volume IV (1753) attracted over a thousand subscribers.[49] Though this was far fewer than the 1,600 subscribers to volume I, it was approaching ten times the 136 listed in Watts's *Works* published in the same year, indicating that the number of purchasers committed to the project remained high in comparison to other publica-tions.[50] In keeping with its title, many family names from the lists in the first two volumes of *The Family Expositor* recur in the later ones.[51] For example, Miss Elizabeth Abney subscribed to volume IV, her mother having subscribed to volume I. The subscriber lists also provide evidence for Doddridge's growing international reputation. Volume II lists 'The Reverend Mr. Benion, Minister of the French Church at Rotterdam', 'The Reverend De-la-fay, D.D. Minister of the English Church at Utrecht' and 'The Reverend Monsieur Du-Mont, Professor of Ecclesias-tical History, and Minister of the French Church at Rotterdam'; volume IV lists merchants from Rotterdam among its subscribers, indicating that the appeal of the work had spread beyond the clergy of that city, and 'Mr Edward Brown, of Lisbon', where Doddridge had died. A short supplementary list of subscribers appears in volume V, which includes 'Reverend Samuel Davies, A.M. of Hanover, Virginia' as well as numerous booksellers, peers, and high-ranking cathedral clergy.[52] Subscribers to *The*

---

[48] A few copies of *Proposals for Printing by Subscription, in three volumes in Quarto, The Family Expositor, on the Epistolary Part of the New Testament, with The Book of the Revelation* survive, dated 1751 and 1752. The way *The Family Expositor* is defined in this document makes it clear the subscription is for volumes IV–VI (volumes I–III contained the four evangelists and the Acts of the Apostles). The original subscription drive for this phase was interrupted by Doddridge's death, and was resumed in 1752.

[49] 'Of the total of 2,800 about 1,600 subscribed when the first volume appeared in 1739, a further 150 on publication of the second volume in 1740, and another 1,035 in 1753 and 1756, when the last two volumes were issued after Doddridge's death.' Alan Everitt, 'Streams of Sensibility: Philip Doddridge of Northampton and the Evangelical Tradition', in *Landscape and Community in England* (London and Ronceverte, 1985), 209–46 (229).

[50] The decline in the number of subscribers to *The Family Expositor* might indicate that the volumes on the Gospels were of more interest to purchasers than the later volumes on the Epistles and Book of Revelation that make up the rest of the New Testament.

[51] Evidence of Doddridge's friends collecting subscriptions can be found in his corres-pondence, see *Calendar* 596, 604, and 663.

[52] *The Family Expositor*, II, vii; IV, vii–viii; V, sig. a4. For information about English and Scottish congregations in the Low Countries, see William Stevens, *The History of the Scottish Church, Rotterdam* (Edinburgh, 1832). Davis met Mercy Doddridge on 12 August 1754, see George William Pilcher (ed.), *The Reverend Samuel Davies Abroad: The Diary of a Journey to England and Scotland, 1753–55* (Urbana, Ill., 1967), 119.

Family Expositor in the 1730s, 1740s, and 1750s clearly saw the work as a scholarly resource suitable for the next generation of clergy. The number of female and lay subscribers indicates the work found its way into homes, perhaps being used for the family reading the title encouraged.

5. PUBLISHING VOLUMES IV–VI OF *THE FAMILY EXPOSITOR* (1752–1756)

Doddridge's will suggests that he envisioned the publication of the remaining volumes of *The Family Expositor* as a collaborative enterprise among his associates. He appointed his wife Mercy to be his executrix, and left her the manuscript of *The Family Expositor*. He requested that Job Orton and Nathaniel Neal 'by their prudent Advice [will] assist my dear Wife in the many difficulties which she must of course meet with in her Affairs', instructed Orton and Caleb Ashworth to 'get [*The Family Expositor*] Transcribed under their direction', and suggested that 'it may be published by a Subscription to be opened as soon as possible after my death'.[53] In 1752, Mercy Doddridge set in motion the publication of the remaining three volumes.[54] Her principal assistants were Job Orton, Caleb Ashworth, and Samuel Clark, the son of Doddridge's mentor. The latter two were the tutors of Daventry academy and all three had been students at Northampton. They completed the task of transcribing Doddridge's manuscript from shorthand to longhand, organized the proof-reading, and assisted Mercy Doddridge in her negotiations with the booksellers.

As well as the manuscript being transcribed and the proof sheets corrected, materials had to be supplemented and revised. Samuel Clark, in a letter agreeing to check the proofs in 1754, had said, 'I think wth Mr Godw[in]. that Mr Fourn[eaux]. sh^d by all means write the Introduct^ns. both for the reason you mention, & that they may all appear alike', indicating that consistency of tone across all the published volumes was desired.[55] Soon after, Clark wrote to Mercy Doddridge from London with information about the extent of corrections already undertaken and to tell her that Philip Furneaux had declined to write introductions to the

---

[53] TNA: PRO PROB 11/791, sig. 332.

[54] In Doddridge's lifetime Mercy Doddridge had played a role in the preparations for the publication of *The Family Expositor*. during a visit to London in 1740, she had passed on Doddridge's request that Edward Godwin draw up an index to the first three volumes, and conveyed the preface to volume II to Godwin to be checked. See DWL MS NCL L1/1/16; *Calendar* 620. See also *Calendar* 621.

[55] Samuel Clark to Mercy Doddridge, 25 July 1754. DWL MS NCL L.1/4/193.

commentaries on the books of the New Testament included in volumes V and VI.[56] Furthermore, in September 1755, Clark was having trouble finding someone to draw up the indexes.[57] It seems that persuading people to contribute to the publishing effort could be difficult despite the shared commitment to dissenting intellectual pursuits articulated in their letters. Furneaux did in the end agree to help, and in 1756 he wrote to Mercy Doddridge describing the sections he had contributed to *The Family Expositor*.[58]

While Clark and Furneaux contributed to the editorial effort, Caleb Ashworth negotiated with booksellers about accounting issues and Job Orton coordinated the process of completing the book. Orton did not find the task an easy one, and in particular found Edward Godwin's slow pace of work difficult to bear. He told Mercy Doddridge: 'I am astonished at your Intelligence of Mr Godwyn's transcribing &c ye 5th Volume as it was all transcribed by ye Dr & most of it had been reviewed and corrected by him.'[59] He followed this up some weeks later: 'I know not what can be done with Regard to Mr Godwyn. What he is doing occasions a very great & improper Delay to the Work, & will I apprehend add little or nothing to its Acceptance and Usefulness.'[60] Orton did not want to approach Godwin directly, however: he claimed the two men could not discuss the matter in person because he and Godwin did not live near each other, but a letter would not afford him the space to anticipate and answer Godwin's concerns with due politeness. Better, he suggested, for Nathaniel Neal or Philip Furneaux to pay a personal visit.[61] Completing Doddridge's work required the collaboration of a group of dissenters who did not necessarily know one another well or share the same view of how best to enact Doddridge's wishes. They had all been friends with Doddridge, but in some cases this was the only connection and without his presence they did not form a united group. Throughout the publishing process, Orton grappled with the niceties of social relations and the pragmatics imposed by geographical restrictions, and sought to activate personal connections among dissenters to sustain the project.

[56] Samuel Clark to Mercy Doddridge, 4 August 1754. DWL MS NCL L.1/4/194.
[57] DWL MS NCL L.1/5/8.
[58] Northampton Public Library MS DO/01/233. Earlier, Furneaux had written to Mercy Doddridge assuring her that his work on volume IV was nearly complete: see DWL MS NCL L.1/5/184.
[59] Job Orton to Mercy Doddridge, 29 October 1753. DWL MS NCL L.1/7/182.
[60] Job Orton to Mercy Doddridge, 3 December 1753. DWL MS NCL L.1/7/183.
[61] 'I know not how to write to him upon this Subject as he will certainly know I am urged to it by you or Mr Waugh—I think it would be very easy & natural for Mr Neal or Mr Furneaux to wait upon him.' Job Orton to Mercy Doddridge, 3 December 1753. DWL MS NCL L.1/7/183.

Orton was also concerned about the conduct of revising the text for publication. He took personal responsibility for improving, polishing, and checking the manuscript, and carefully devised an editorial procedure which followed Doddridge's own words and practices, in order to bring the process, as well as the completed work, as close to Doddridge as possible. For example, Orton requested that Samuel Clark consult books in the Daventry academy library that had come from Doddridge's own library to identify references that in the manuscript were unclear:

> I must give you some further trouble about the Expositor, which is, to consult 'Vitringa's Obs.' where he observes 'that there was an officer in the synagogue who had the name of *Angel*, to illustrate *Rev.* i.20. ii.1, &c. The Doctor in his MS Note about the Dragon in the Revelation, mentions one in the Royal Society's repository ___ feet long. Have you any book in the library out of which you can supply that blank?[62]

Orton saw Doddridge's library as a resource which could resolve questions raised while editing the manuscript. He considered it important to use Doddridge's own copies of particular works in order to preserve the integrity of the project. The exactitude of his practice of following Doddridge's methods and using his own books meant that the final work could be attributed to Doddridge alone. This was important to Orton because the slow circulation of information and changes made to the text contributed to delays in the publication of the work, and he feared that the longer after Doddridge's death the volumes appeared, the greater the suspicion might be that the work was not authentic. Time and reputable names (as with Watts's wish that Doddridge and Jennings would identify themselves as editors) were factors thought to allay readers' doubts about a work's legitimacy.

This completion and publication of *The Family Expositor* was a collective process, and by no means a painless one. Each member of the group had to deal with others (often far away) to complete his tasks, all developments had to be reported to Mercy Doddridge and all decisions approved by her. While the process of completing *The Family Expositor* relied on the collective activities of Doddridge's intellectual community, in print *The Family Expositor* was consistently and deliberately presented to its readers as wholly and solely Doddridge's work. The published volumes reveal very little of the overlapping involvement of different individuals involved in the work's construction.

---

[62] Job Orton to Samuel Clark, 22 December 1752: Palmer, *Letters to Dissenting Ministers*, I, 14–15. Palmer adds a footnote: '*The length is about twenty-three feet. See the Doctor's Note on *Rev.* xii. 3, as thus completed' (15). Doddridge's copy of the work referred to, in which volumes from two different editions are bound together, is held at DWL, shelfmark 3007.E.8. Campegius Vitringa, *Observationum sacrarum*, 2 vols (Amsterdam, 1721 and Franeker, 1723).

Job Orton and Mercy Doddridge corresponded over this carefully considered decision. Orton was particularly worried about how to present the final volume, which was the part of the work containing the most material from hands other than Doddridge's. In a letter to Mercy Doddridge a year before publication, Orton articulated some of his difficulties over presenting the work in print. The issues concerning him were whether (or indeed how) to explain who had done what to the work, how closely what was done reflected Doddridge's wishes, and how, therefore, to acknowledge that the words were not exclusively Doddridge's without on the one hand leaving the work open to criticism and, on the other, implying that he, Orton, was responsible for all the changes. To Orton, it was important to do all of this while presenting himself as the only editor. Orton claimed he did not want to take the credit from others, saying, 'it will be assuming to myself and taking from ye other Gentlemen an Honour y^t belongs to them'. Nor did he wish to be assumed to be responsible for changes with which he was unhappy:

> tho there have been, as I observed, no alterations in the Sentim^t, there have been some in the Style, especially in y^t part I transcribed, & some of them much for the worse, particularly some obscure words put instead of some plain ones—words which no common Reader will understand, & which the Author never used in writing or preaching.[63]

This particular criticism echoes Orton's complaints to Mercy Doddridge that Godwin was making unnecessary changes. Orton also complained that the duties of an editor require that:

> where other of his Friends propose Corrections & Alterations, he must submit to them tho in some Instances, contrary to his Judgm[en]t, or bear the Censure of being self sufficient & conceited.[64]

Orton's personal anxieties about the role of the editor in assessing other contributors' efforts and taking public responsibility for them were expressed in his uncertainty over how to present the work to readers. He wrote, 'If you can direct me how to express myself in a Preface, so as to keep to the Truth, & satisfy ye Publick, I will do w^t I can.'[65] Throughout the letter, he avoided explicitly naming the members of the group

---

[63] Job Orton to Mercy Doddridge, 3 February 1755. DWL MS NCL L.1/8/3. This criticism of Godwin echoes Watts's recommendation to Doddridge that he 'sink' the style of *The Rise and Progress of Religion in the Soul*: see *Calendar* 948. Watts expressed relief that Doddridge had been 'perswaded to reduce the Language into easier words and plainer periods': see *Calendar* 963.

[64] Job Orton to Mercy Doddridge, 3 February 1755. DWL MS NCL L.1/8/3.

[65] Job Orton to Mercy Doddridge, 3 February 1755. DWL MS NCL L.1/8/3.

responsible for the various elements of the final version of *The Family Expositor*. In his discussion of how Doddridge's prose had been shaped the work of one man slips into that of another and it is not clear who has done what. For example, Orton wrote, 'he ought to be ye best judge of the Author's Style Manner and Design', and the indeterminate pronoun is representative of the lack of clarity throughout this part of the letter. These elisions and evasions reflect the problematic nature of the idea that Orton was struggling to articulate: that the final volumes were a collective enterprise but that the aim was to produce a work as close to Doddridge's intentions as possible.

The sixth volume (published in 1756) commences with an 'Advertisement to the Reader by the Editor' signed by Orton which begins by quoting from Doddridge's will: 'I desire that it may be transcribed, as far as it goes, by Mr. *Orton*; and that he would add such Notes, as he shall judge most proper, from my written critical Notes.'[66] Orton uses Doddridge's own words to publicly endorse his own status as editor in an attempt, in Genette's terms, to bring the allographic preface closer to an authorial one. This is punctuated by the date on which Doddridge left the instruction: 'Jan. 1, 1746/7'. Orton then details the work Doddridge had done towards the final three volumes at the time of his death with the justification that 'it is therefore incumbent upon me to inform the Subscribers what Progress the *Author* had made in this Work, and what has been done to it since his Death, in Order to remove those Suspicions, which often arise concerning the Authenticity of posthumous Works'.[67]

Despite his claim most of the processes of construction are effaced in Orton's preface. He outlines the approach he took when deciding whether to extend or eliminate certain notes and describes a group of Doddridge's former students transcribing the work from shorthand, overseen by himself. Yet none of the other editorial participants is acknowledged: all the additional work done to *The Family Expositor* is contained in the figure of Orton. This streamlines the multiple and contested processes of production and does so in accordance with Doddridge's will. A final example of the imperfect reality of the work's construction is introduced in the preface when Orton recounts the anecdote of the manuscript of *The Family Expositor* being burned by a fallen candle in Doddridge's study

[66] The 'Advertisement' is dated 21 November 1755. An advertisement in the *Public Advertiser* on 26 January 1756 announces that volumes V and VI 'which complete the Work' will be sent to subscribers on 23 February. An advertisement on 25 February 1756 notes the publication of volumes V and VI and says that complete sets of six volumes can be purchased for four guineas bound.
[67] *The Family Expositor*, VI, v.

in June 1750.[68] In his letter to Mercy Doddridge, Orton had questioned whether the story ought be made widely known and wondered 'whether any Thing sh'd be said a^{bt} the Accident wch happened to some of [the] MSS by Fire'. The way it is mentioned in the 'Advertisement' suggests that the story was already circulating and Orton wished to counter rumours. Orton is careful to emphasize the providentialism Doddridge associated with the event:

> Being an Eye-witness of the Danger and Deliverance, I record this Account of it, partly for the Satisfaction of the Subscribers with Regard to the exaggerated Report, but Chiefly as it seems to denote a particular Care of Providence in Preserving this Work, and a favourable Omen, that GOD intends it for extensive and lasting Usefulness.[69]

Orton's interpretation of the event situates himself as an eyewitness, consolidating his claim to be the trusted amanuensis to Doddridge even now that he is dead. The 'Advertisement' is a carefully constructed attestation that the author's wishes have been carried out and that *The Family Expositor* is the work of scholarly and devotional utility planned by Doddridge.

6. *THE FAMILY EXPOSITOR* AFTER 1756

The completion of the first edition of *The Family Expositor* in 1756 was followed by discussions about how to develop future editions of the work. Mercy Doddridge negotiated, via her agents, with several publishers on matters including printing further impressions of the first two volumes of *The Family Expositor*, developing a version of the work to be published in parts, selling the right to print one edition, and selling the copyright to all of Doddridge's works while making specific demands about how the works should be treated. It also opened up the possibility of changing publisher, as Doddridge had done when he moved his business from Richard Hett to James Waugh.

Mercy Doddridge had to decide whether to sell the full copyright to Doddridge's works (which would leave the publisher to shoulder all the financial risk but consequently to benefit from the full profits) or to sell the right to publish an edition while retaining a commercial interest in the production and sale of the books. Ashworth wrote to Mercy Doddridge outlining his preferred course (the first) and contrasting it with Orton's

[68] Doddridge described this event in a letter dated 26 June 1750, *Calendar* 1630. Part of the scorched manuscript survives today: see DWL MS NCL L.143.
[69] *The Family Expositor*, VI, vi–vii.

suggestion (the second). While he was careful to articulate the implications of each strategy, Ashworth reaffirmed that everyone's intentions were the same: to establish 'the most certain way of spreading the Works'.[70]

Doddridge's associates did not believe his reputation ought to reside only in expensive publications, and Orton's priority was ensuring that the agreement allowed for flexibility over the form in which a work was published. Orton suggested that Mercy Doddridge should offer Waugh and another dissenting bookseller, James Buckland, the opportunity to share in the purchase of the copyright (set at £800) and put forward the idea of reissuing *The Family Expositor* 'in small volumes': in keeping with Doddridge's own plans and presumably intended to attract less wealthy purchasers.[71] The final decision lay with Mercy Doddridge, and it was not James Buckland, the dissenting bookseller and reliable personal friend recommended by Orton and Ashworth, that she approached. The day after Orton's letter, she drafted a proposal to a very different bookseller: James Rivington.

Today, James Rivington is notorious for his bankruptcies and questionable business practices. In 1759, he would have been known to Mercy Doddridge as the son of Charles Rivington, the respectable Anglican theological bookseller, and as a successful bookseller in his own right. It seems that Rivington approached Mercy Doddridge via an intermediary (Doddridge's friend the Anglican clergyman Dr James Stonhouse) expressing interest in publishing Doddridge's works.[72] Perhaps Rivington had enquired who owned the copyright, for Mercy Doddridge established her sole ownership of the entire copyright to Doddridge's works from the outset of the negotiations, instructing Stonhouse to tell Rivington 'that the property of Every copy of the Dear Deceas'd Writings is intirely vested in my self'. Mercy Doddridge stated the conditions under which she was prepared to sell to Rivington:

> I am very willing to dispose of my copy right either of all the six volumes of ye Family Expositor alone or of all ye copys together—if I can secure a consideration for ym equal to what either my self or friends think they are worth.

She left open the possibility of selling the copyright to *The Family Expositor* separately. Perhaps because of its size and complicated *mise-en-*

---

[70] Caleb Ashworth to Mercy Doddridge, 17 January 1759. DWL MS NCL L.1/3/206. For full details about the publishing processes and bookseller negotiations, see Tessa Whitehouse, 'The Family Expositor, the Doddridge Circle, and the Booksellers', *The Library*, 7th ser., 11 (2010), 321–44.
[71] Job Orton to Mercy Doddridge, 10 March 1759. DWL MS NCL L.1/8/32.
[72] According to a letter from Rivington dated 27 April 1759, Nathaniel Neal suggested Stonhouse act as a mediator between Rivington and Mercy Doddridge. DWL MS NCL L.63/11. Mercy Doddridge wrote to Job Orton that 'an application had been made to me from a very unexpected quarter', 1 May 1759. NCL MS L.63/12.

page it was the work which most needed a bookseller to take on the responsibility of publication. Mercy Doddridge particularly wished to secure an agreement that Rivington would purchase the physical copies of volumes I and II recently printed by Waugh along with the copyright to *The Family Expositor*.[73]

Mercy Doddridge framed her concern about selling all the copyrights not in terms of hunger for profits, but of anxiety about assuring circulation. She requested that the terms of any agreement include:

> ye further security I had in case I shd part with my copy right that none of ye smaller tracts may be Losd to the world by Lying out of print and that I may have ye Liberty of having what Number I pleas of ye smaller pieces at ye lowest price they are ever Sold to Bookselers—in this I have No view to make any personal advantage of ym to my self only to bear to my self ye right of having ym on as easy te terms as I can in case I shd see fitt at any time to give any Number of ym away.[74]

The situation described here is one in which self-publishing could be more appealing than relinquishing control to a bookseller. If the primary concern was for works to circulate continually and widely rather than necessarily to generate profit, the author (or his representative) might prefer to retain the responsibility for publishing a work in order to be free to reprint it as and when he or she wished. Mercy Doddridge understood that one implication of selling the copyright was that a bookseller had no obligation to keep works in print if they were not profitable. She therefore sought to prevent this happening by stipulating that she wished to be provided with works on demand. She offered all the extant copies of Doddridge's works and the copyright to everything (published and unpublished) to James Rivington for £1,200.[75] James Rivington's affirmative reply followed promptly on 9 April 1759.[76]

---

[73] 'I shall expect ye person yt purchais my copy right will also purchase all the printed copies of ye several editions Now in Hand.' Mercy Doddridge to James Stonhouse, 1 March 1759. DWL MS NCL L.63/5.

[74] Mercy Doddridge to James Stonhouse, 1 March 1759. DWL MS NCL L.63/5. The MS reads 'losest', which has been corrected to 'lowest' in the transcription above.

[75] Mercy Doddridge to James Rivington, 6 April 1759. DWL MS NCL L.63/8. The sum was more than double that suggested by William Warburton: 'If for these [printed copies] and the right of reprinting 500 of the last 4 V:s of the family expositor the Bookseller would give you 500*l*. I think it would be a better bargain than 650*l*. for all the printed Copies & the whole copy right together. As Dr Doddridge's works are chiefly practical, the copy right must be worth something considerable', William Warburton to Mercy Doddridge, 8 May 1759 in Nichol, *Pope's Literary Legacy*, 130. The letter is dated after Mercy Doddridge's negotiations with Rivington; perhaps she had hoped to receive Warburton's advice sooner.

[76] James Rivington to Mercy Doddridge, 9 April 1759. DWL MS NCL L.63/10.

Rivington understood that the market for religious books responded to different trends and influences according to geographical region and the religious sensitivities of the intended audience. His project to maximize the sale of *The Family Expositor* centred on making it simultaneously more appealing to both 'persons of the first Taste' and 'the lower class of churchgoers' in the Church of England and evangelical Calvinists in Scotland and America. In a letter to Stonhouse of 27 April 1759, Rivington gave more detailed comments on publishing a new edition of *The Family Expositor*. He determined to publish additional copies of each of the final four volumes of *The Family Expositor* so that owners of volumes I and II (which had been reprinted twice) could complete their sets. He also planned to enhance the value of the work by including engraved illustrations of scenes from the life of Christ:

> It will cost me 600£ to engrave the sett & I am resolved upon doing it, for I am confident I can sell five times as many of the Expositor with the help of these plates as I could do without them, for they are so elegant[.][77]

Another strategy for maximizing the sale of the work was to publish it with a recommendation from the popular evangelical writer James Hervey in Scotland and New England 'as all the religious in those Countries are great admirers of Mr Hervey' and his recommendations had advanced the sales of other religious authors.[78] Rivington also proposed to issue the work in weekly parts to make it affordable.[79] As part of his comprehensive marketing strategy for developing the reach of the work, he claimed he would:

> have four or five hundred thousand proposalls published directed & dispersed with the utmost diligence in every part where Our Language is known & on some Saturday Evening before the first Number appears I shall procure proper

---

[77] James Rivington to James Stonhouse, 27 April 1759. DWL MS NCL L.63/11. Extant volumes of the 1761–1762 edition of *The Family Expositor* contain images, with more than seventy plates distributed through the first three volumes. The £600 cost of commissioning the images appears plausible given the prices cited in Tim Clayton, 'Book Illustration and the World of Prints', *CHBB*, V, 230–47 (236).

[78] James Rivington to James Stonhouse, 27 April 1759. DWL MS NCL L.63/11. James Hervey was an evangelical Church of England clergyman who described himself as a moderate Calvinist and enjoyed a successful literary career.

[79] The work was issued in 155 weekly parts first advertised in September 1759, commencing 1 November 1759 (*London Evening Post*, 27–9 September 1759; *London Chronicle*, 1–3 November 1759). It was also published in six volumes in Edinburgh (1772) and the same edition with a new title page was sold in South Carolina (1773). See Calhoun Winter, 'The Southern Book Trade in the Eighteenth Century', in *A History of the Book in America: The Colonial Book*, ed. Amory and Hall, 224–46 (237–8).

persons in Every City town Village &c to put one of the Proposals in every pew in each Church and Meeting of protestant Dissenters in these several Kingdoms.[80]

The global scale of his ambition for the work was matched by his boldness in targeting places of religious worship as advertising spaces and his plans for market saturation.

Rivington may have been similarly audacious in other promotion methods. Although lists of subscribers did not appear in the printed volumes of the 1760–1761 edition of *The Family Expositor*, correspondence between Samuel Richardson and Mark Hildesley (Bishop of Sodor and Man, and a correspondent of Doddridge) suggests that the lists were published separately in order to promote the work. Hildesley wrote that 'seeing two such respectable names as Dr. Young's and Mr S. Richardson's, among the subscribers to Dr. Doddridge's *Family Expositor*, inclines me to hope that work commands some share of your approbation and esteem'.[81] Richardson replied, however:

> I cannot say that I have read the Expositor. I have been exceedingly ill in what I may call the paralytic way... and had not given directions to the proprietors of the work, to put me down as a subscriber to it. It was a spontaneous act of their own: and so (for ought I know) it is with regard to our Welwyn friend; for though I know that Dr. Young greatly respected Dr. Doddridge, for some of his former writings, I never heard him mention this. But your high opinion of it, will not suffer me, for my part, to be long without it.[82]

His mild response notwithstanding, Richardson's remarks suggest that Rivington's advertising tactics may have included subterfuge.

The ways in which Rivington promoted *The Family Expositor* certainly met with opposition from Doddridge's own supporters. Some months after Rivington described his plans to Stonhouse, Caleb Ashworth wrote Mercy Doddridge a long letter beginning with a detailed description of how James Rivington had been publicizing the planned reprinting of *The Family Expositor*. Ashworth was clearly concerned that James Rivington's aggressive marketing strategies would do *The Family Expositor*, and the dissenting cause, a disservice. He wrote: 'If there is any thing will lessen

---

[80] James Rivington to James Stonhouse, 27 April 1759. DWL MS NCL L.63/11.

[81] Mark Hildesley to Samuel Richardson, 26 August 1760. *The Correspondence of Samuel Richardson*, ed. Anna Letitia Barbauld, 6 vols (London, 1804), V, 135. 'Dr. Young' was the poet Edward Young.

[82] Samuel Richardson to Mark Hildesley, 10 September 1760. *The Correspondence of Samuel Richardson*, V, 138–9. No subscriber lists naming Richardson or Young have been located.

the Credit of F.E. 'tis in my opinion the zeal with which it is pressed.'
From Ashworth's description, it seems the plans Rivington described to
Stonhouse were no exaggeration. Ashworth reported that posters soliciting
subscriptions had been indiscriminately 'pasted up on sign posts, Town
pumps, & Barbers shops'. Rather than attacking Rivington, Ashworth
chose to emphasize that while he agreed with Rivington's opinion that *The
Family Expositor* was so important a work that it deserved to be widely
promoted, he considered the responsibility for instituting a personal,
focused, and carefully planned marketing strategy to lie with dissenters.
'I really think if M^r R[ivington] is not assisted in urging the Subscription,'
he wrote, 'he will alone take as vigorous methods to spread it as are
consistent with the Credit of the work.'[83] Ashworth made a distinction
between being involved in the content of the work itself and in the
methods of promotion of this new edition. He expressed reservations
about the methods currently being used when he wrote, 'if any Dissenter
be suspected of having had a hand in it, I think it w^d. somewhat prejudice
the Church against it'. He concluded his opinion by drawing a distinction
between the conduct expected of a bookseller and the social scrutiny under
which dissenters operated, observing that 'a Bookseller may take a variety
of ways to forward the Sale of a Book without any reflexion, because it is
known to be his Interest and his Business; But others are very apt to be
suspected of party, how good soever their motives may be'.[84] Even though
Doddridge had himself avowed the cross-denominational aspects of the
work, Ashworth was anxious not to provoke negative responses from
members of the establishment. He considered that the dissenters would
be held accountable for any perceived lack of propriety in the way *The
Family Expositor* was promoted—on 'every pew' of Church of England
places of worship, for example, or by inventing famous subscribers—and
his alarm indicates that concern over dissenters' social status persisted long
after Toleration, and even at times of no particular political unrest.[85]

   These observations from Caleb Ashworth register a negative side to
Mercy Doddridge's decision to take Doddridge's works to a bookseller who
was both from the Church of England and from a well-known bookselling
family. Rivington had offered a convincing and inviting marketing

---

[83]   Caleb Ashworth to Mercy Doddridge, 12 December 1759. DWL MS NCL L.63/14.
[84]   Caleb Ashworth to Mercy Doddridge, 12 December 1759. DWL MS NCL L.63/14.
[85]   As John Smail observes with reference to an earlier period, anxieties regarding
religious and political differences were a question not only of high politics, but of local
experience. See John Smail, 'Religion, Culture and Politics in Oliver Heywood's Halifax', in
Protestant Identities: Religion, Society, and Self-Fashioning in Post-Reformation England, ed.
Muriel C. McClendon, Joseph P. Ward, and Michael MacDonald (Stanford, Calif., 1999),
234–48.

programme for the new edition of *The Family Expositor*, promising editions in Scotland and America as well as England, which suited Mercy Doddridge's purpose of spreading Doddridge's works widely. Yet the reality was that his marketing strategies were feared to be distastefully aggressive, did not consider the nature of the work, and put its reputation (and by association, that of the dissenters) at risk. Given their marginal status—within the learned world, in this case, but not secure there—they could not risk being accused of misconduct in book marketing.

Even more dangerous to the success of *The Family Expositor* were Rivington's dubious business practices and his shaky financial position. Rivington had grown up apprenticed to his father Charles, and had been in partnership with his brother John until 1756. Upon the formal dissolution of this partnership (the formality of which indicates a serious disagreement), he worked with James Fletcher junior, a bookseller in Oxford. Most of their output was legitimate publishing, but Rivington also pirated the books of other London booksellers for the growing American market. In 1757, prior to any dealings with Mercy Doddridge, he had orchestrated a complicated sale of copyrights. The London book trade sought redress for the business they lost as a result of his underhand dealings. They brought injunctions against him, which resulted in the dissolution of his partnership with Fletcher in January 1760 and the sale of their stock on 3 April 1760, at which other booksellers purchased his stock and shares in the copyrights he owned.[86] Thomas Longman's annotated copy of the sale catalogue notes that the sale made just over £3,500, and that the wholesaler William Johnston purchased all the shares of Doddridge's works, divided into eight lots, for £1,200.[87] Not only did the £1,200 bid for Doddridge's works and copyright constitute almost a third

---

[86] For an account of James Rivington's business practice and in particular a summary of the events surrounding his bankruptcy, see Patricia Hernlund, 'Three Bankruptcies in the London Book Trade, 1746–61: Rivington, Knapton, and Osborn', in *Writers, Books and Trade: An Eighteenth Century English Miscellany for William B. Todd*, ed. O. M. Brack Jr (New York, 1993), 77–122. For a clear outline of James Rivington's practices in America, how they made him money, and why they enraged the London booksellers, see James N. Green, 'English Books and Printing in the Age of Franklin', in *A History of the Book in America*, ed. Amory and Hall, 248–98 (279–83).

[87] *A Catalogue of Copies, and Shares of Copies, of Messrs. James Rivington and James Fletcher* is catalogue 101 in the BL collection of Longman's trade sale catalogues, shelfmark Cup.407.e.6. Johnston is described as 'the prominent wholesaler' by Terry Belanger in 'Booksellers' Sales of Copyright: Aspects of the London Book Trade 1718–1768' (unpublished doctoral dissertation, Columbia University, 1970), 135. Caleb Ashworth (in London to gather information) reported to Mercy Doddridge: 'He intends to sell shares of it to some other Booksellers, Mr Buckland intends to have a share—I hear that Mr Waugh is not to have.' Caleb Ashworth to Mercy Doddridge, 4 July 1760. DWL MS NCL L.1/3/212.

of the money generated by the sale, but also it matched exactly the amount Mercy Doddridge had requested when selling the copyright.

James Rivington's bankruptcy delayed the publication of the new edition of *The Family Expositor* and resulted in its copyright entering the open market, and coming to be owned by an increasingly disparate group of booksellers. *The Family Expositor* was regularly republished, and retained the same six-volume quarto format in all the eighteenth-century editions that Doddridge had chosen for it. Whether Mercy Doddridge received all of the promised £1,200 from Rivington, and, if not, whether the booksellers who purchased the copyrights to Doddridge's works honoured that agreement, is not known. It is notable that Mercy Doddridge's authority for the publication is recorded on the title pages of editions published after the sale of James Rivington's property, when she had no financial connection with the booksellers or the edition. These volumes were advertised as being published 'by Assignment to the Author's widow'.[88] Though Doddridge's widow and her associates had relinquished control over the copyright to his works, the booksellers saw that much of the power of Doddridge's image derived from his place in the dissenting community, and the works themselves attest to the strength of that community. Mercy Doddridge and Job Orton were especially certain about what they wanted the publication of *The Family Expositor* to achieve: it was to present Doddridge, and through him dissent generally, as learned, polite, and pious.

7. MONUMENTS, CANONIZATION, AND COLLABORATION

Michael Anesko calls the publication of a collected edition 'an extraordinary publishing event' that, though it is a commodity, seeks to display its significance in cultural terms. Such an edition 'implies that the writer so distinguished has achieved unusual status among his contemporaries'.[89] This understanding of the function of *Works* (which Anesko argues still pertains today) has a long history. The evidence presented in this chapter supports the contention that eighteenth-century authors and editors assumed that a *Works* raised authorial status and declared the canonicity

---

[88] An 'Assignment' was a document that signed over a property (in this case, literary property), and any profits arising from the future sale of it, from one party to another. Collections of these survive: see BL Add. MSS 38, 728–30.

[89] Michael Anesko, 'Notes Towards the Redefinition of Culture', in *The Culture of Collected Editions*, ed. Andrew Nash (Houndmills, Basingstoke, 2003), 69–79 (69).

of a body of work, even if the methods required to construct such an edition posthumously might in fact lessen the author's presence within those texts.

Personal factors affecting editing such as friendship, a sense of duty, and personality clashes intertwine (sometimes uncomfortably) with practical and intellectual procedures for ensuring an authoritative and accurate edition. Furthermore, the histories of such publications are commercial as well as ideological. What booksellers were doing—how they financed editions, who they worked with, how they marketed publications, what risks they took—is as important to understanding the way posthumous works looked and how they were received as the editorial labours, but it is often more difficult to narrate, let alone analyse. The attempt to place trade-side activities alongside analysis of editorial process wherever possible here is intended to give a full picture of all the impulses, concerns, and contributions that went into the making of these texts.

The chapter has presented evidence about editors' intentions and how personal feeling and community identity affected their work. The information for this comes from correspondence and the appearance of the published volumes: the bibliographical codes and sites of discourse that the books and pages embodied. But the interpretations or conclusions about those intentions that can be made are tentative given the fragmentary nature of the evidence that is available. This challenge (one always animating discussions of how books came to be made) is complicated when the book in question is a collected works, and especially so when it is posthumously published. Once an author has gone and an editor has taken charge, power is dispersed among different interested parties and the sense of a unified body of work may be lost.

As well as being significant events in the (after)life of a particular author, collected editions have a place in broader narratives about the development of a national culture. Dissenting ministers, editors, and booksellers produced works that unambiguously declared high-profile dissenting authors to be memorable figures, worthy of substantial commemorative publishing projects. The editions of Watts's *Works* and Doddridge's *Family Expositor* in the 1750s and 1760s made confident, public declarations that these dissenting authors were pious, modern writers deserving a place in an English Protestant canon.

Finally, it must be remembered that these expensive monuments that placed dissenting writers in elite social and literary company were by no means the only forms in which Watts and Doddridge survived posthumously. Both men supported the circulation of small-format versions of their works as inexpensive editions easily given away, and these practices were sustained by their successors. There was an economic dimension to this efflorescence of small-format editions, certainly: the owners of Watts's copyright took out a patent in 1758 to protect the individual titles of his works rather than the six-volume edition of them all because they thought it financially expedient to do so.[90] But it is possible also to interpret the preference of dissenting editors, copyright holders, and readers for smaller books in terms of the humility that both men associated with true piety, and the care they expressed for readers and listeners of all stations in life. While the grand editions discussed in this chapter fitted the elegant surroundings of a gentleman's library or the industrious atmosphere of dissenting academies, and while those editions may have helped establish Watts and Doddridge in high literary culture, dissenting textual culture did not reside only or primarily in such sites and formats. Ongoing publication of individual works in small formats reanimated the pious and educative presence of these authors for new generations of readers decade after decade and into the nineteenth century.

---

[90] A patent was a publishing industry mechanism for restricting the possibility of works being reprinted without the copyright owner's permission. See Shef Rogers, 'The Use of Royal Licences for Printing in England, 1695–1760: A Bibliography', *The Library*, 7th ser., 1 (2000), 133–92. Rogers lists a licence issued to James Buckland, James Waugh, John Ward, Thomas Longman, and Edward Dilly 'for the works of Isaac Watts', 11 March 1758 (182). His collected works were next published in 1801.

Conclusion

Dissent and the World of Books

This concluding chapter, which has two parts, starts and ends at the turn of the century to present key aspects of dissenting textual culture in the period of transition between the 1760s and the 1800s. It will account for how Watts and Doddridge were imagined and presented by a new generation of successors at the century's end with reference to the practices of rational piety and paradigms of polish, improvement, and candour that have animated this book. From the late 1770s, the label 'dissenter' was being loaded with more strongly radical connotations than it had carried during the middle decades of the century, and the first half of the chapter charts the ways in which that shift was resisted by certain self-appointed heirs to Watts and Doddridge, who mobilized their textual practices to present alternative identities for dissent. The second half restates and amplifies the central arguments of the book as a whole and supplements these with further examples of collective textual endeavour. Together, the two halves argue that associative activities among dissenters created conservative cultural forms, and characterize the complex nature of that conservative project at a time when 'there was no essential coherence underpinning the large and growing body' of dissent.[1]

1. DISSENTERS IN NATIONAL LITERARY CULTURE

In 1790, the first stand-alone edition of Doddridge's correspondence was published, presented by its editor as conforming to the expectations and tastes of the time which 'appears to relish publications of this kind'. Comparing the present work to the recent publication of the correspondence of Thomas Herring, Archbishop of Canterbury from 1747 to

---

[1] Seed, *Dissenting Histories*, 131.

1757—'in which nothing is said that can offend'—the editor expressed satisfied confidence that readers would find it 'as little exceptionable as possible'. Not only Doddridge but each of his correspondents were 'friends of virtue, piety, and moderation' on the evidence of the letters presented here. Indeed, the publication itself took on the positive attributes of the people and their letters that constituted it; designed, the editor claimed, 'to serve the cause of truth and virtue, charity and moderation' as well as to provide funds for 'the venerable relict' Mercy Doddridge.[2]

The insistence on the unexceptionable qualities of the man, his friends, their letters, and the volume as a whole might seem to sit slightly oddly with the implicit comparison of Doddridge to an archbishop, given Doddridge's commitment to his dissenting community and the historical resistance to episcopacy that characterized his Congregationalist denomination. In the context of its publication moment, it may be seen as an attempt to distance Doddridge from radical associations being formed among some sections of the dissenting community at the start of what Jon Mee has termed 'the turbulent years of the 1790s'.[3] The peritextual apparatus to the volume downplayed the dissenting identity of the principal author in a number of ways, including the dedication to Rowland Wingfield (a Shropshire squire) and the prominent title page position for the name of the editor, who was not one of Doddridge's friends or former students but the 'Vicar of St Chad's, Shrewsbury': a clergyman of the established church with an MA to attest to his university attendance.

Geographically and culturally, this editor is at a distance from the Midlands and London suburbs where Doddridge's dissenting friends and associates had clustered as they published his other works. Nor had he known Doddridge personally. The letters had come to him second hand from an unnamed 'worthy and excellent Friend' who had allegedly hesitated at the suggestion of publishing them. Fortunately for the reading public of 1790, Stedman had prevailed and the letters were available, at the rather high price of six shillings.

Stedman's edition strongly asserts national, cross-denominational appeal for an acceptably polite religious author whose example in life could be considered as edifying as his practical and instructive writings. But as well as marking continuity—in terms of ongoing interest in Doddridge forty years after his death—the particular moment of the letters' publication is also a striking instance of intervention in dissenting

---

[2] Stedman, 'Preface', in *Letters to and from … Doddridge*, v–viii.
[3] Jon Mee, *Dangerous Enthusiasm: William Blake and the Culture of Radicalism in the 1790s* (Oxford, 1992), 226.

culture that is indicative of the process by which moderate, mid-century dissent was made to align with establishment values of conservatism and conformity. Principles of liberty (especially liberty of conscience) and liberality that characterized religious dissent were, in the months after the storming of the Bastille and during debates about the repeal of the Test and Corporation Acts, opened up to politically challenging capacities once more. Moderate nonconformists and their friends sought to differentiate their traditions of doctrinally orthodox religious dissent from the varieties of radicalism increasingly associated with the label by both friends and foes.[4] As the Stedman correspondence edition shows, continued efforts at inserting Doddridge and his correspondent Watts into a polite culture of letters while attempting to contain the radical potential of principles they had espoused—such as freedom of enquiry—took various forms and relied on networks of affinity that could be surprising.

The final decade of the eighteenth century and first decade of the nineteenth were a rich and active period in the literary afterlives of Watts and Doddridge. In the complicated political, religious, and literary climate of an era characterized at the time and retrospectively in terms of radicalism, division, and contention, the two authors were established as national authors and religious figureheads for posterity.[5] They were strenuously written into contemporary literary history by men within their tradition and outside it. This occurred across a spectrum of textual activities including correspondence editions, new and complete multi-volume collected works (for both men), the ongoing publication of their individual works (particularly Watts's hymns and educational books, and Doddridge's biography of James Gardiner and *The Rise and Progress of Religion in the Soul* which became key texts in evangelical movements), and, in the case of Doddridge, fresh editions of *The Family Expositor* and *A Course of Lectures* with supplementary materials. The presence of both men animated the low-cost participatory principles of magazines and tract societies but as authors they were also enshrined in monumental testaments to national culture such as the *Lives of the Poets* and *Biographia Britannica*.

Increasing numbers of new titles and republished editions produced by dissenting authors, editors, and booksellers are a striking counterpoint to the demographic context of 'persistent, unremitting decline' in numbers

---

[4] Seed, *Dissenting Histories*, 143–9.

[5] For the building political and cultural tensions in the period, see Jon Mee, *Romanticism, Enthusiasm and Regulation: Poetics and the Policing of Culture in the Romantic Period* (Oxford, 2003), ch. 2; Marilyn Butler, 'The Arts in the Age of Revolution: 1760–1790', in *Romantics, Rebels and Reactionaries* (Oxford, 1981; repr. 1985), 11–38.

of congregations and ministers in the period.[6] James E. Bradley rightly cautions against equating declining numbers with decreasing political importance, and contends that dissenters' 'repertoire of deferential postures did not, on the whole, decrease their political significance'.[7] In publishing too, small numbers and rhetorics of humility belie a significant and enduring influence. Surveying the bibliographic record indicates that any assumption that falling numbers lessened dissenters' engagement in the world of letters or their impact upon it cannot be proved. It may even be that shrinking congregations or the reduced need for assistant ministers drove dissenters to write. In that case, declining numbers might have acted as a spur to new and renewed engagements in the world of letters.

The work of Samuel Palmer may be understood in those terms. He was, as Seed says, 'one of the most important figures in the work of preserving... [dissenting] heritage'.[8] As well as the political functions of recovering seventeenth-century writing that Seed delineates, Palmer asserted the religious and literary significance of evangelical moderation as exemplified by Watts, Doddridge, Orton, and other dissenters of the eighteenth century in his efforts to construct a coherent tradition for orthodoxy. A dedicated minister who published a number of sermons, supported local endeavours (such as a new burial ground at St Thomas's in Hackney), and participated in larger-scale charitable associations, it was through books that he made a significant contribution to preserving his own religious inheritance. He used print to celebrate, disseminate, and narrate a history of orthodox dissent which sought to establish a canon of ministerial writers (primarily Presbyterian and Congregationalist) across a series of books. Palmer styled himself 'publisher' of a number of titles, most of which were adaptations or new editions of canonical authors of his particular dissenting tradition.[9] There was a steady flow of them from the 1760s into the nineteenth century. Examples include an edition of Doddridge's translation of the New Testament in 1765, which detached one of the original components of *The Family Expositor* from the interwoven paraphrase, harmony, improvements, and critical commentaries of the full edition. Its existence was justified in the language of utility and accessibility: 'To such as cannot reach the price of the larger work this will be a

[6] James E. Bradley, *Religion, Revolution and English Radicalism: Nonconformity in Eighteenth Century Politics and Society* (Cambridge, 1990), 92. Bradley's example is London and Middlesex in the period from 1727 to 1776 and refers not to individual dissenters, but to the number of congregations and of ministers in employment.
[7] Bradley, *Religion, Revolution and English Radicalism*, 106.
[8] Seed, *Dissenting Histories*, 133.
[9] See the advertisement leaves which list 'Books published by S. Palmer and sold by J. Buckland' at the end of *A Collection of Family Prayers* (London, 1783).

cheap and valuable abridgement, and to such as are possessed of that excellent commentary, this will be an useful Vade-Mecum for the pocket.'[10]

Advantages of piety, utility, and convenience were the watchwords for Palmer's publications throughout the 1760s, 1770s, and 1780s. These included *The Nonconformist's Memorial* which brought Edmund Calamy's early eighteenth-century accounts of ejected ministers up to date with information about subsequent ministers, *The Protestant Dissenter's Catechism* aimed at children and indebted to Watts's texts promoting piety and education, and *A Collection of Family Prayers* (1783).[11] This last work explicitly identified a tradition of worthy ministerial writers on its title page: Richard Baxter, Matthew Henry, John Willison (included, wrote Palmer, at the particular request of 'a pious lady'), Robert Bennett, Watts, and Doddridge. Together, these men and the particular works chosen for inclusion represented Presbyterian and Congregationalist customs (both English and Scottish) at their most practical and least overtly political and the conjunction of their names styled a line of devotional writers that began in the seventeenth century, ran through the eighteenth century, and reached to the period of the book's publication, a time at which 'there seemed particularly to be a want of further assistance [in family prayer] for Protestant Dissenters of an evangelical cast'.[12] Thus the writers of the past could provide energy and guidance for devotional activities in the present. Recognition of one's religious heritage was not solely a matter of factual knowledge of dead ministers, but also a spur to participate in a vibrant, ongoing tradition, and Palmer conveyed this principle in writings of different kinds.

As well as using print to resource an active and historically aware contemporary religious culture among evangelical dissenters, Palmer mobilized it to intervene in the establishment literary world. Two examples—one concerning letters and Thomas Stedman, the second biography and Samuel Johnson—illustrate the range of concerns Palmer had, the forms in which he expressed them, and the significance of genre in the positioning of Watts, Doddridge, and their associates in the literary landscape at the turn of the century.

The context to the first of these interventions is the edition of Doddridge's letters published by Stedman in 1790. Though Stedman did not identify the 'venerable possessor' of the correspondence he printed,

---

[10] Samuel Palmer, 'Preface', in *A New Translation of the New Testament* (London, 1765), sig. A.5.

[11] For the first two of these see Seed, *Dissenting Histories*, 133–7, 163.

[12] Palmer, *Family Prayers*, v.

surviving letters to Miss Mercy Doddridge (daughter of Philip and Mercy) from Stedman indicate that Doddridge's widow was the possessor to whom he referred, though it was Orton who held a run of early letters written in shorthand. Of these, Stedman reported to Doddridge's family:

> I have examin'd ye manuscripts left by Mr Orton, & can find only one Book of Letters written by Dr Doddridge; upon which there is ty'd a Slip of Paper, on which paper Mr Orton hath written as follows—This is a Collection of Dr Doddridge's Letters in early Life, in which there are many that are truly excellent. I made use of them in ye History of his Life, & as some of them are not fit to be seen except by his Relations & especially his children, I desire they may be return'd to Mrs Doddridge or her Daughter Mercy, who I suppose is ye only child of his which can read them.

Stedman sought permission for these letters to be sent to him in Shrewsbury so he could include them in the edition already in progress, assuring Miss Doddridge 'that nothing shall be printed but what shall do their excellent Writer Credit'.[13] Stedman's facility at reading shorthand—which qualified him to report to Doddridge's family on the content of Orton's bundle of letters—was the result of his acquaintance with Orton in the 1770s. The connection made through Doddridge's friend James Stonhouse (the rector of the living to which Stedman was appointed curate) extended into a later generation and, in a personal way, the influence beyond dissent into establishment culture that Doddridge had cultivated in his own lifetime.

During the preparations for the Doddridge edition, Stedman told the younger Mercy Doddridge that 'As to ye Letters of our good Friend Mr Orton, of which I had made a valuable Collection on ye Pastoral Care, I am advis'd to suppress them, at least for ye present.'[14] There are no indications as to the reason for this or who gave the advice, but only a year later *Letters to a Young Clergyman* was issued in two volumes: one of letters Thomas Stedman had received from James Stonhouse, and the other of his correspondence with Job Orton. This publication in the early 1790s of letters from the 1770s formalized and publicly broadcast the long-standing close connections between evangelical clergy in the established church and those dissenters who thought of themselves as moderates and who, by the late 1770s, sought to distance themselves from politically more radical dissenters, as some of Orton's letters included in the collection make clear. As such the collection can be seen as a mild,

---

[13] Thomas Stedman to Mercy Doddridge junior, 24 October 1789. DWL NCL MS L.1/8/179.

[14] Thomas Stedman to Mercy Doddridge junior, 19 February 1789. DWL NCL MS L.1/8/174.

non-sectarian, and non-oppositional counterpart to political narratives that constructed more inflammatory histories for dissenters by looking back to the puritan regicides and the Gordon riots, for example.[15]

Despite the generative cross-confessional friendliness that both of Stedman's letter collections represented in their form and content, not all dissenters were at ease with a Church of England clergyman editing dissenting ministers' correspondence. When Stedman issued an updated version of *Letters to a Young Clergyman* in 1805, Samuel Palmer was quick to respond with his own edition of Orton's letters in 1806. Its title page made several pointed claims: *Letters to Dissenting Ministers, and to Students for the Ministry, from the Rev. Mr. Job Orton, Transcribed from his original Short-Hand, with Notes, Explanatory and Biographical.* Advertising the inclusion of 'explanatory and biographical' notes promised a collection that would be as comprehensible to readers beyond the circle of 'ministers and students for the minister' as it would be edifying for those within it. The plural 'ministers' in contrast to the individual 'young clergyman' of Stedman's collection invokes a community of dissenters. In terms of these deliberately emphasized points of comparison and the declaration of dissenters' collective literary and religious culture, Palmer's edition is not so much in conversation with Stedman's as a challenge to it.

Even the declaration about shorthand makes a point about the traditions of dissent in competition with Stedman's edition. The advantages of shorthand correspondence were articulated in many of the letters in Stedman's collection, which tracked Orton's encouragement of Stedman's developing facility in the practice. It was also, as described in Chapter 2, central to dissenting academy life and one of the first skills new students developed, as Doddridge detailed in his 'Life of Steffe'.[16] By presenting a complete collection of shorthand letters, Palmer indicates that that aspect of the letters is one of their characteristically dissenting features. This suggestion is articulated more fully in his note on a letter Orton wrote him about a bundle of Doddridge's letters in shorthand which had apparently been circulating among a group of dissenting ministers in the 1770s, perhaps in a similar manner to Doddridge's own letters on education in the 1720s. Orton wrote:

> I beg you will send me 'Dr. DODDRIDGE's letters*' by the first safe hand. I want them very much, that I may destroy some and select others to be kept. Though I know not how they may be made useful, it is a pity they should be all destroyed. You will be pleased with his Letters to Dr. WRIGHT, who was

[15] Seed, *Dissenting Histories*, 156–60 and 175–9.
[16] Doddridge, 'Life of Steffe', xiv.

always very much his friend. I have seen many worse Letters in print than in the whole collection.

In a footnote, Palmer remarked:

> *Mr. ORTON had favoured me with the perusal of the copies of a great number of the Doctor's Letters to his correspondents. Mr. STEDMAN afterwards published a volume of 'Letters to and from Dr. Doddridge,' but I presume none, or few, of these.[17]

On this evidence, Orton's desire to manage all aspects of the circulation and reception of Doddridge's work extended beyond his manuscripts for publication to his personal correspondence. Palmer's comment makes no mention of Orton's editorial practice but highlights his own connection to the letters. He places himself closer to the centre of the circle around Orton than Stedman, who did not publish Doddridge's letters until after Palmer and other dissenters had seen them. The dissenters' view is especially privileged: because of their shared educational histories they have personal associations and technical skills that allow them sight of letters unseen by others. This is particularly important to Palmer as a third-generation legacy-holder for moderate dissent. He had not known Doddridge personally, but can claim a closer connection to him than Stedman could and a richer connection too. Stedman knew Doddridge as a dissenter only via Orton whereas Palmer was from the same educational tradition as Doddridge and could read his letters without difficulty.

Palmer sought to protect and champion a distinctive and enduring dissenting heritage that could stand apart from general culture on one side and radical varieties of rational dissent on the other and which would outlast current squalls. His edition of Orton's letters gave extensive details about Orton's opinions on educational practices, books and authors, and the political activities of those around him. Orton was a prickly man, but not a figure who courted controversy; as one reviewer put it, he was 'dear to the Dissenters' and 'THE LAST OF THE PURITANS.'[18]

When it came to Isaac Watts, the problems Palmer faced were more complex, for Watts was both very well known and subject to considerable scrutiny regarding the orthodoxy of his views on the Trinity. He was a hero to readers and writers outside his own tradition too, as Samuel Johnson's choice to include Watts in his series of biographical prefaces attests. Johnson's brief entry on Watts in *The Lives of the Poets* (first published in 1781) deals succinctly with his life and prose works. Watts's

---

[17] Job Orton to Samuel Palmer, n.d. ('It must have been in Jan. 1778'), in *Letters to Dissenting Ministers*, I, 201–2.
[18] *Monthly Repository*, 1 (1806), 257–61.

religious culture receives perfunctory treatment, and the rudeness sup-
posed by Johnson to be characteristic of nonconformist writers is emphasized by noting that any learning they might possess 'was commonly
obscured and blunted by coarseness and inelegance of style'.[19] Johnson
dismisses devotional poetry as an inferior type of verse and concludes by
stressing the limits to Watts's exemplarity:

> Happy will be that reader whose mind is disposed by his verses, or his prose,
> to imitate him in all but his non-conformity, to copy his benevolence to
> man, and his reverence to God.[20]

Palmer responded to Johnson within *The Life of the Rev. Isaac Watts, D.D.
By the Late Dr. Samuel Johnson, with Notes* (1785). This piece reproduces
Johnson's 'Life of Watts' along with extensive notes and other materials
including a 'Supplement to Dr. Gibbons's Character' of Watts and 'An
Authentic Account of Dr. Watts's last avowed sentiments concerning the
Doctrine of the Trinity.'[21] The work thus separates Watts from the
company of poets and places him back in a dissenting context. The nature
of this recontextualization is made explicit by the inclusion of the additional materials. Watts should be known primarily by his religious
identity, this volume reminds readers, while setting the terms in which
that memory should be constructed.

Palmer's principal purpose in the *Animadversions and Additions* is to
improve on Johnson's biography. He claims to enhance Johnson's factual
content by including a full list of the pieces published in Watts's *Works*
(1753) and attempts to secure Watts's literary legacy differently, noting
that Johnson neglects Watts's practical divinity writings and questioning
his assessment of Watts's poetry.[22] Motivating Palmer's *Animadversions
and Additions* is his concern that Johnson has misunderstood both Watts
and dissent. The crux of Palmer's disagreement with Johnson is the latter's
presentation of Watts as exemplary 'in all but his non-conformity'. Palmer
asks, 'Is not this exception, and even the mention of this circumstance,
a striking proof of Dr. Johnson's bigotted attachment to the national

---

[19] Johnson, 'Life of Watts', 107. Johnson gives a more extensive account of his views on
'pious poetry' in the 'Life of Waller', in *The Lives of the Most Eminent English Poets*, ed.
Lonsdale, I, 109–14.

[20] Johnson, 'Life of Watts', 110.

[21] Samuel Palmer, *The Life of the Rev. Isaac Watts, D.D. By the Late Dr. Samuel Johnson,
with Notes. Containing Animadversions and Additions Relating to Dr. Watts's Character,
Writings, and Sentiments, particularly on the Trinity* (London, 1785), hereafter referred to
as *Animadversions and Additions*. There was a second edition in 1791 with a new preface
and appendix. Each version of the work will be identified in these notes by the year of
publication.

[22] Palmer, *Animadversions and Additions* (1785), 11–12, 20, and 25.

established mode of worship?', and over three pages discourses on belief in freedom of conscience being a reasonable basis for refusal to conform to the Articles of the Church of England, and the illogical nature of Johnson's attack on nonconformity.[23] He offers an alternative final sentence to the 'Life of Watts':

> Dr. Johnson therefore had much better have said, 'Happy indeed is the reader who is disposed by his verses or his prose, to imitate him in his impartial enquiry after truth, and in following the dictates of his own conscience, in his reverence towards God and his benevolence to men, whether he be a conformist or a Nonconformist.'[24]

Palmer positions the impartial yet individual enquiries after truth that Watts undertook in the *Philosophical Essays*—and the guidance he offered to students on how to conduct such enquiries themselves in his educational works—at the centre of his religious and pedagogical project. Johnson's attempt to separate Watts's legacy into some elements suitable for everyone and other aspects only of interest to nonconformists was, to Palmer, a nonsense.

Palmer's rewriting of Johnson at the close of his *Animadversions and Additions* developed into a hydra-like textual project in which he addressed writings on the Trinity, on freedom of conscience, and on Watts from across the ecclesiological spectrum from high Anglican to Unitarian. The Johnson–Palmer work was repackaged for a new edition in 1791 which added a fresh preface and a third 'Appendix' of 'an additional account of *Dr Watts's Manuscripts*, and an Abstract of a Correspondence between him and the *Rev. Martin Tomkins*, on the Worship of the Holy Spirit, and on Trinitarian Doxologies'. It represents a renewed attempt to secure Watts's reputation as liberal yet orthodox at a time when the proposed repeal of the Test and Corporation actions forced the status of dissenters and questions about liberty of conscience into the limelight, and its existence reflects the increasing politicization of liberality as a principle in the 1790s.[25]

The first part of this appendix uses Stedman's edition of Doddridge's correspondence to summarize letters from Nathaniel Neal to Doddridge, to establish the corpus of Watts's work at the time of his death, and to show that Watts had not written anything new on the subject of the Trinity after 1746 (when Watts made his will). Palmer uses the chronology of the

---

[23] Palmer, *Animadversions and Additions* (1785), 25.

[24] Palmer, *Animadversions and Additions* (1785), 32.

[25] For the political background to this debate in 1789–90, see Watts, *The Dissenters*, II, 349, 379 and Thomas W. Davis, 'Introduction', in *Committees for Repeal of the Test and Corporation Acts: Minutes 1786–90 and 1827–8* (London, 1978), vii–xxvi.

manuscripts to show that Watts did not compose any pieces expressing changed views subsequent to his epistolary exchanges with Martin Tomkins in 1738, in which he propounded his view that 'Christ is a divine person in consequence of the in-dwelling of the Father, and that the Holy Spirit is God, as being the power, or active energy, of the Deity.'[26]

Given that Palmer's project in this publication was partly to protect Watts's reputation from the claims of his anti-trinitarianism made by the more heterodox wing of dissent, one might expect him to be as hostile to them as he was to Johnson and other establishment figures. On the contrary, he uses his preface to the second edition as an opportunity to celebrate the unity rather than dissonance of dissenters' voices:

> The Rev. Mr. *Lindsey*, in his *Second Address to the Students at Oxford and Cambridge* (a work in which he strongly testifies his disapprobation of some of Dr. Watts's opinions which the author of the *Notes* has favoured) is pleased to express himself, with regard to the work in general, in the following candid and respected terms, P. 3 'The public, who wish thoroughly to know Dr. Watts's character and sentiments, and who have no opportunity of perusing his voluminous works, are under great obligations to the ingenious author of *The Life of the Rev. Isaac Watts, D.D. By the late Dr. Samuel Johnson, with Notes*, containing animadversions and additions. From this publication the citations are here made.' Such testimonies from gentlemen whose sentiments are so different from his own (however obnoxious to some of his friends) he considers as more favourable to his work, than any from persons in his own scheme of divinity, and he takes this opportunity of expressing his obligations for their candour.[27]

Watts is used as a conduit for demonstrating dissenting harmony to the world. Including Theophilus Lindsey's statement allows Palmer to publicly announce his gratitude to Lindsey while maintaining his own—and Watts's—distance from the Unitarians around Lindsey. It evokes the idea of a community among dissenters and demonstrates the courteous conduct of disagreement between them which contrasts, in Palmer's description, with the shrill attacks of members of the Church of England. Palmer presents an example of dissenting cooperation that transcends religious differences and embodies the survival of a positive sense of the word 'candour'.

As well as affirming the opportunities for unity among dissenters of different groups, *Animadversions and Additions* resituates Watts within a broad dissenting literary tradition. In response to Johnson's claim that,

---

[26] Palmer, *Animadversions and Additions* (1791), sig. c 4v.

[27] Palmer, *Animadversions and Additions* (1791), sig. b2; Theophilus Lindsey, *A Second Address to the Students of Oxford and Cambridge, Relating to Jesus Christ* (London, 1790).

before Watts, dissenters' writings were 'obscured and blunted by coarseness and inelegance of style', Palmer asks:

> What occasion had Dr. Johnson for this sarcasm? If the Dissenters had universally been as destitute of the graces of language as he supposes, surely they might have learnt something from the more polished compositions of the established clergy, to whose works they were not utter strangers.[28]

Palmer constructs his defence of dissenting elegance both as a component of learning and as a historical point. He does not accept Johnson's restatement of the argument about the rudeness of dissenting literary style relative to that of establishment writers, and he firmly situates the debate in terms of the writings of ministers and not poets: 'Divines of all parties at that period were less attentive to the graces of language that they have been since,' he says, resisting Johnson's portrayal of Watts as an isolated genius. He even claims that 'there is no evidence that they afterwards owed their improvement to Dr. Watts', adding, 'Nor indeed does it appear that Dr. Watts's style altogether deserves the encomium here passed on it.'[29] Palmer's preferred exemplar of a graceful dissenting writer is not Watts but the ejected minister William Bates, and Watts's contemporaries Benjamin Grosvenor, John Evans, and James Foster are identified as being just as significant to the dissenting literary tradition as Watts. As well as the text of the 'Life of Watts' being placed within a collection of dissenting sources about his life, Watts the writer is recontextualized into a richer and less isolated literary history than that provided by Johnson.

2. MANUSCRIPT, PRINT, AND REPUTATION

Notwithstanding Palmer's anxieties about Watts's status as a national poet of unimpeachable orthodoxy, his reputation in other areas was quite secure. While religious magazines provided a forum for debates about the orthodoxy of his views on the Trinity, his standing as a hymnodist and educational writer was not at risk of being brought down. Several chapters of this book have shown how Watts was a connecting figure in the popular, polite, and orthodox educational culture that was burgeoning in the anglophone world in the second half of the eighteenth century. As Brian Young, Jonathan Sheehan, and Jonathan Yeager have all argued, and as this book has shown, developments in intellectual practices within

---

[28] Palmer, *Animadversions and Additions* (1785), 12.
[29] Palmer, *Animadversions and Additions* (1785), 13.

religious communities and for spiritual purposes contributed to the widespread willingness to adopt new methods of scholarship and the associated broadening knowledge of the world that can also be characterized as 'enlightened'. These themes can be understood through Watts's works which encouraged diverse means of developing rational habits of thought guided by religious understanding. But Watts was not, as Palmer sought to make clear, an isolated genius. His work was embedded in an intellectual culture with a rich heritage.

It also flourished in new settings. From early in his publishing career, Watts's works had found a place in America. This was partly thanks to his own efforts: he regularly sent copies of books to Benjamin Colman and other acquaintances as personal gifts to be distributed to individuals and institutions in New England. Harvard library catalogues of 1723, 1773, and 1790 show that all of his texts were held, sometimes in multiple copies, as discussed in Chapter 5.[30] Yale students also repeatedly borrowed and commented on Watts's books.[31] American readers in relative isolated situations such as Devereux Jarrett in Virginia (later an Episcopalian clergyman) and young Jonathan Edwards were familiar with books written and promoted by Watts.[32]

As well as finding clerical audiences, works such as *Divine Songs* and *The Improvement of the Mind* were significant texts in various forms of female education. Catherine Kelly has observed that American women evinced 'participation in a transatlantic community of letters' by sewing and writing extracts from good authors on samplers; in this culture, mottoes taken from Watts were especially popular.[33] Distinct from its place in the repertoire of feminine accomplishments, knowledge of Watts formed part of rigorous intellectual training for women. *The Improvement of the Mind* was the basis of the course at the Female Seminary in Connecticut, for example.[34] Joseph Emerson, a committed evangelical—who was

---

[30] As the entire library was destroyed by fire in 1764, most (or all) of the copies of Watts's texts would not be ones donated by him.

[31] Pratt notes that 'Copies of Watts's *Logick* in the Yale Library, provide evidence that this work was a text book in the College until the early nineteenth century. One edition has inscribed in it a succession of names and students identified as members of the classes of 1782, 1783, and 1784, and another bears the inscription "Roger S. Skinner, Yale College, 1809"', *Isaac Watts and his Gift of Books*, 68–9.

[32] David D. Hall and Elizabeth Carroll Reilly, 'Practices of Reading: Introduction', in *A History of the Book in America: The Colonial Book*, ed. Amory and Hall, 377–80 (378); Edwards, *Catalogue of Books*, ed. Thuesen, 199, 222, 270, and 275.

[33] Catherine E. Kelly, 'Reading and the Problem of Accomplishment', in *Reading Women: Literacy, Authorship, and Culture in the Atlantic World, 1500–1800*, ed. Heidi Brayman Hackel and Catherine E. Kelly (Philadelphia, 2008), 124–44 (131).

[34] 'Watts had been long studied in his school, and my brother had also studied it much before', Ralph Emerson, *Life of Rev. Joseph Emerson, Pastor of the Third Congregational*

persuaded by reading Hannah More that educating women was his vocation—founded a line of women's colleges which pioneered the provision of a thorough intellectual, practical, and religious education for young women. His students Zilpah Grant and Mary Lyon founded Ipswich Female Seminary and Mount Holyoke Female Seminary respectively. These related institutions borrowed heavily from Emerson's curriculum and *The Improvement of the Mind* was a set text at all three.[35] A copy of Emerson's *Questions and Supplement, to Watts on the Improvement of the Mind* from Ipswich Female Seminary in Massachusetts shows how one student underlined certain passages and filled in answers to various questions about recommended reading techniques in the margins of Emerson's book.[36] Watts's text, diligently read in this particular instance, was used in training American women to become missionaries. It thereby played a significant role in shaping a world of learning within the revival of piety in nineteenth-century America.[37] The comparison between Watts and John Erskine, who 'propagated books because he loved ideas', is again striking and these examples further support Yeager's contention that evangelicalism should not be seen as an anti-intellectual movement.[38]

In England too, encounters with Watts went on beyond the environments described in his prefaces or familiar to dissenting academies. The efforts of Anglican evangelicals such as More and Sarah Trimmer ensured the continued use of his educational works.[39] This pattern of use for Watts's books at the end of the eighteenth century continued his own earlier efforts to promote practical religion through the free distribution of works such as those by John Reynolds. Such habits were well embedded in

---

Church in Beverly, MS. and subsequently Principal of a Female Seminary (New York, 1834), 364.

[35] For evidence that *The Improvement of the Mind* was a set text at Mount Holyoke, see Amanda Porterfield, *Mary Lyon and the Mount Holyoke Missionaries* (Oxford, 1997), 43.

[36] Joseph Emerson, *Questions and Supplement, to Watts On the Improvement of the Mind* (Boston, 1831), British Library shelfmark 8403.b.47/3.

[37] Porterfield, *Mary Lyon*, 8.

[38] Yeager, *Enlightened Evangelicalism*, 12.

[39] Lists of the Cheap Repository Tracts and the publications of the Society for Promoting Christian Knowledge show that *Divine Songs* was a regular title for each society at the turn of the nineteenth century. See also Sarah Trimmer, *An Easy Introduction to the Knowledge of Nature* (London, 1780), where she locates the origins of the work in Watts's 'Essay on the Education of Children and Youth', also *The Servant's Friend* (London, 1787) and *A Comment on Dr. Watts's Divine Songs for Children, with Questions* (London, 1789); Hannah More, *Strictures on the Modern System of Female Education*, 2 vols (2nd edn, 1799), I, 179. Anna Letitia Barbauld drew on Watts in her own children's works, see William McCarthy, 'How Dissent Made Anna Letitia Barbauld, and What She Made of Dissent', in *Religious Dissent and the Aikin-Barbauld Circle*, ed. James and Inkster 52–69 (64).

this clerical culture by the 1750s, when the Society for Promoting Religious Knowledge Among the Poor became a significant force in the non-commercial distribution of religious materials. It was a society to which many of the figures in this book belonged and its foundation act was a gift of books sent to Doddridge by a London minister for distribution around Northampton.

The Society became a characteristic field of textual endeavour for moderate dissenters educated by Doddridge. Orton, Ashworth, and Kippis were early members of the Society and Kippis preached the annual sermon in 1762. Other dissenting ministers from their wider group who belonged to the Society included Philip Furneaux, Samuel Morton Savage, and Samuel Palmer, who delivered the annual sermon in 1781. The membership was not exclusively dissenting, however. Evangelicals such as Selina Hastings, George Whitefield, and John Newton joined, as did Samuel Davies, the American minister who toured Britain and subscribed to *The Family Expositor*. Nor was it entirely clerical: lay members made up a high proportion of the one thousand or more subscribers in 1792, according to the annual sermon for that year.[40] It is an example of a charitable and educational counterpart to the dissenting and low church alliances Bradley has identified as a method for securing representation on matters of shared political interest at a local and national level.[41] It is in this wider context that particular personal connections (such as Stedman's with Orton) may be understood.

Significant too is the point that the efforts of many individuals to open up and sustain cross-denominational cooperation were a striking feature of English life even at politically tense points in time such as the 1790s. Understanding this may lead to a revision of strong views like those of Paul Keen, whose account of the 'expansionary dynamics' of print culture and corresponding societies emphasizes radical dissent as the locus for reforming schemes of the period and presents the reactionary moves of the *Gentleman's Magazine* and publications of Hannah More as the only significant alternative. But 'literature as a public sphere' was not only imagined as such by activists at political extremes, nor was the political agency of literature understood only in a narrow sense by participants in the moderate, enlightened, but godly culture presented in this book.[42] Indeed the foregoing chapters have all shown that collective action across

[40] Isabel Rivers, 'Society for Promoting Religious Knowledge among the Poor (act. 1750–1920s)', *Oxford Dictionary of National Biography*.

[41] Bradley, *Religion, Revolution and English Radicalism*, 113–14.

[42] Paul Keen, *The Crisis of Literature in the 1790s: Print Culture and the Public Sphere* (Cambridge, 1999), 37.

denominational boundaries, religious commitment, preaching, letters, and optimism about the transformative power of books were all qualities of a moderate and polite dissenting culture of improvement that was both rational and evangelical.

The founding principles of the Society for Promoting Religious Knowledge Among the Poor were marked by those commitments and attested by its patterns of activity throughout the second half of the eighteenth century, which was its most active period. The Society is an example of the ways in which dissenting cultural life continued to be shaped by Watts and Doddridge in the generation following their deaths as their friends and pupils worked for general projects or specific societies the men had endorsed, and used those societies to perpetuate the widespread distribution of texts written by the men in a manner that followed their example. The continuities in publishing and associative practices in the second half of the eighteenth century among those who were committed to inter-denominational life and to education meant that principles at the heart of moderate dissenting culture continued to exert a broad influence.

In the Society for Promoting Religious Knowledge Among the Poor, the method of selecting titles to be distributed followed a democratic rule. The result of this, says Rivers, was a conservative list which changed little over the century. Watts's hymns and the version of Reynolds's *Christian Address* that he edited and introduced remained on the list of approved titles for decades. Rivers characterizes the type of books distributed as a traditional Calvinist canon of seventeenth-century nonconformists and eighteenth-century dissenters, along with bibles. As an outlet for the non-commercial distribution of texts written by men in the Watts–Doddridge tradition (such as Baxter and Henry before them, and Orton and Palmer later), Tract Society practices partly account for the strong, enduring, and disproportionate dissenting influence in the world of books. The process of preserving older texts and reanimating them by presenting them to new audiences served also to connect puritan, nonconformist, and dissenting authors into a long and coherent literary tradition and present it to readers and listeners as such, as Doddridge had done for his students through the recommendations he made in the 'Lectures on Preaching'.

The circulation of texts and stories from the (recent) past was animated by participatory forms of print such as magazines. The evangelical *Gospel Magazine* was among the earliest of these, and by the end of the eighteenth century there were dozens, representing the spectrum of religious opinion.[43] These magazines all contained biographies, theological and

---

[43] Mineka, *The Dissidence of Dissent*, 27–97; Josef L. Altholz, *The Religious Press in Britain 1760–1900* (New York, 1989), 57–78.

philosophical discourses, book reviews, accounts of missionary activities, descriptions of meetings, lively correspondence exchanges, and information about newly uncovered manuscripts such as the extracts from Doddridge's 'Lectures on Preaching' in the *Universal Theological Magazine*.

While the *Universal Theological Magazine* and its successor the *Monthly Repository* were denominational journals associated with rational dissent (though not confined to them, given Palmer's appearance in the pages of the latter), others such as the *Evangelical Magazine* (1793–1864) and the *Protestant Dissenter's Magazine* (1794–1799) sought to cross sectarian boundaries while maintaining a clearly defined character.[44] The *Protestant Dissenter's Magazine* explicitly dissociated itself from recent political activity around the campaigns to repeal the Test and Corporation Acts which had, argues Michael Watts, engendered 'growing hostility to dissent'. It declared in its first preface that:

> To prevent any wrong construction of our design, in this undertaking, it is proper to inform the public, that it is not the work of the Dissenters as a Body, and that the individuals engaged in executing the plan, which was formed some years ago, never had the most distant intention to interfere in any political contests; much less to introduce any thing that might tend to inflame the minds of readers against any measures of government; but that, on the contrary, it was our wish, as loyal subjects of the KING, and true friends to our country, and the present constitution, to contribute our part towards promoting peace and good order.[45]

The defensive opening sentence anticipates public criticism, but also a public of readers beyond dissent. The preface as a whole sets out the publication's position as a politically peaceable organ characterized by loyalty at a volatile time.

It also invited debate with voices from outside dissent:

> Though we shall think it right to vindicate ourselves against any unjust censures, we shall be equally ready to admit sober and candid animadversions on whatever may appear exceptionable, in dissenters, or any thing that may tend to correct or improve them in respect to doctrine, worship, discipline, or general conduct.

The disavowal of any intention to 'inflame the minds' of readers is connected to another purpose: self-regulation through 'sober and candid animaderversions'. In this configuration, free enquiry does not create

---

[44] The range of religious opinion represented in these magazines is surveyed by Stephen Burley, ' "In this Intolerance I Glory": William Hazlitt (1737–1820) and the Dissenting Periodical', *Hazlitt Review*, 3 (2010), 9–23 (11–12).

[45] *Protestant Dissenter's Magazine*, 1 (1794), sig. A2v. Watts, *The Dissenters*, I, 486.

heterodoxy or political dissension but provides a mechanism for ensuring 'improvement'.[46] The principles that structured Watts's and Doddridge's efforts are activated in this invitation to debate, by which the magazine suggests the particular qualities a dissenting periodical can bring to critical discourse.

The opening preface defines the dissenting community in broad terms (not divided into denominations, or by doctrinal commitment) and situates it within the nation but explains its purpose as being an internal cultural record. The content of the magazine over its six-year run reflects this priority. As the title page announces, it comprised: 'biographical memoirs; ecclesiastical history; sacred criticism; doctrinal and practical divinity; a review of theological publications; devotional poetry; miscellaneous essays and articles of intelligence'; within the magazine itself this latter category was confined to 'religious intelligence' concerning ordinations and funerals of ministers.

Reader contributions facilitated one of the cultural purposes of magazines, which in this instance was to record and transmit materials from dissent's recent past so that readers could see the continuities and changes from the seventeenth and earlier eighteenth centuries to their own time. Examples include John Evans writing to the *Monthly Repository* to announce that he had located a shorthand copy of Doddridge's theological lectures, letters written by Doddridge being reprinted which establish his doctrinal position or reveal—in the words of the magazine—'a curious specimen of the religious taste of a former age', and an account of a dream Doddridge had following a conversation with Samuel Clark about the nature and knowledge of the soul after death.[47] The cumulative effect of publishing these items was to make the memory of Doddridge available to late eighteenth- and nineteenth-century readers of these magazines, and to accumulate a body of materials representative of that memory in ways which also kept alive dissenting commitments to constructive debate. As Roger Chartier has written, 'pasts are always, in some fashion, still-living presents' and commitment to that humanistic belief animated, in informal and amateur ways, the many dissenting contributors to these magazines who thereby participated in the ongoing construction of their culture.[48]

---

[46] *Protestant Dissenter's Magazine*, 1 (1794), sig. A2v.

[47] *Monthly Repository*, 13 (1818), 37–8. See also *Monthly Repository*, 1 (1806), 341–4 (a letter from Doddridge to Samuel Bourn dated 12 December 1741 in which Doddridge denies he is an Arian) and 568 (a letter from Doddridge to William Glover dated 14 September 1742 concerning the text for a funeral sermon on Song of Songs 2:14); *Protestant Dissenter's Magazine*, 6 (1799), 424.

[48] Roger Chartier, 'Listen to the Dead with your Eyes', in *The Author's Hand and the Printer's Mind*, tr. Lydia G. Cochrane (Cambridge, 2013), 3–26 (24).

The interconnection of the different genres and endeavours discussed in this concluding chapter is a significant aspect of the collaborative literary culture encouraged by moderate dissenters and their associates. Reviews of new books appeared in periodicals, and not only those periodicals associated with a particular group. For example, Palmer's edition of Orton's letters was positively reviewed in both the Unitarian *Monthly Repository* and the establishment *Critical Review*, which found it 'an acceptable service'.[49] But more striking even than the overlapping content and purpose of different print genres is the sustained mutual enrichment of manuscript and printed texts in this milieu. In the case of the textual culture delineated here manuscript culture was not only enduring but also vibrant, because it enabled important aspects of dissenting intellectual life to be protected and transmitted. But the different modes of transmission did not do entirely separate work. Just as often as manuscripts provide information about printed texts (such as Mercy Doddridge's correspondence about publishing her husband's posthumous works) so printed works trace, transcribe, debate, and annotate materials long kept in manuscript. Palmer's correspondence editions not only make letters available in print but also provide information about the circulation and destruction of manuscripts from the 1720s in the 1770s and 1780s; contributors to magazines such as Evans tell of the manuscripts they have found—particularly letters and lectures—and compare these to printed copies.

There were practical dimensions to the interrelations of print and manuscript, such as the method for soliciting contributions and advertising his project considered by Thomas Stedman, who told Mercy Doddridge junior, 'I sometimes think of inserting an address to ye public in ye Gentleman's Magazine, mentioning my intended publication, & requesting ye favor of a Communication of Letters.'[50] Stedman's letters to Mercy Doddridge junior contain several directions about gaining press coverage as well as reports of statements and questions he has noted in the press, such as a Mr John Pope's request that the successors of Doddridge and David Jennings confirm or deny whether all Watts's final manuscripts were indeed published.[51] This third example points to a kind of intellectual cross-fertilization, whereby questions raised or debates begun in the pages of periodicals were later addressed in individual books. Of course, dissenters did not invent these practices. The specific nature of the

---

[49] *Monthly Repository*, 1 (1806), 257–61, 301–5; *Critical Review* 8 (1806), 304–15 (312).
[50] Thomas Stedman to Mercy Doddridge junior, 14 November 1789. DWL LNC MS L.1/8/181.
[51] DWL NCL MS L.1/8/184–7.

questions they worried over—who should be responsible for safeguarding a reputation? How should the personal papers of public figures best be represented in print?—were often answered through and by a technology and literary forms that were not uniquely theirs. The ways in which dissenting writers adapted genres and methods to suit their expressive needs (sometimes public facing, at others more internally directed; sometimes celebratory, at others defensive; usually harmonious but sometimes divisive) was in some respects typical of their age, but was also edged with a knowledge of their liminal status and this meant that dissenters' relation to national and international literary, educational, and intellectual culture was complex.

The literary projects surveyed in this book have ranged from the ambitious to the minute, from expansive, cross-denominational action to defiant and pedantic expressions of dissent's unique culture. What they have all shared is their educational aims. The epigraphs to Palmer's version of Doddridge's New Testament translation are extracts from Rousseau and from Locke, a paratextual move that encapsulates the approach to education that has been presented here. The choice of epigraphs succinctly notes the enduring influence of Lockean experiential epistemologies, attests to a committed willingness to engage with new ideas (which includes, in the case of Rousseau, an author unknown to Watts and Doddridge) and thereby celebrates and enacts the synthesis of different traditions. Self-reflexive recognition of the importance of dissent's own heritage is fundamental to many of these educational projects. Watts and Doddridge are repeatedly used to frame endeavours in different ways ranging from textual means such as epigraphs and invocation in magazine articles, to organizational structures like tract societies and charitable trusts for education provision.

Through its presence in the world of books, dissent contributed to larger intellectual patterns too. Their habits of mind and action included circulating letters containing ideas, news, and introductions, exchanging visits and books, and pursuing friendship with people not yet met, all of which they inherited from the seventeenth century and earlier and adapted to fit contemporary social paradigms. Dissenting endeavours had a distinctively humanist aspect which the eighteenth-century writers, ministers, and editors discussed here absorbed into their own undertakings. The engagements of moderate, orthodox dissenters in projects for improvement were expansive and various. These included: writing texts on many topics, disseminating those texts in a range of formats, anticipating readers, among them children (both wealthy ones with tutors and those at charity schools), servants, and apprentices, academy, college, and university students, women, and ministers from across the spectrum of Protestant belief in Britain, Europe, and America, and promoting the books of other authors. These dissenters moved beyond the insularity of denominational identity and, along with many of their peers, 'celebrated knowledge' in a manner that optimistically asserted the transformative yet sustaining potential of books.[52]

[52] Keen, *The Crisis of Literature*, 30.

APPENDIX

Biographical Notes

These short entries provide relevant details about the subjects of this book, most of whom were dissenting ministers within Doddridge's circle. One woman and two members of the Church of England are also included. The entries supplement material in the *Oxford Dictionary of National Biography* and incorporate information in *Dissenting Academies Online: Database and Encyclopedia* where appropriate. Other sources are given in the entries.

CALEB ASHWORTH (*c.* 1722–1775)

Ashworth was educated at Northampton academy from 1739 and worked as divinity tutor at Daventry academy from 1752 to 1775. He corresponded with Mercy Doddridge about the establishment of the academy, the progress of her son Philip (a student at Daventry), and about various publication matters.

Sources: Alexander Gordon, 'Ashworth, Caleb (d. 1775)', rev. W. N. Terry, *ODNB*; *Dissenting Academies Online* database, person id 593.

SAMUEL CLARK SENIOR (1684–1750)

Minister at St Albans, an early teacher of Doddridge, and his long-standing correspondent. He was descended from two venerable Samuel Clark(e)s: his maternal grandfather was the biblical commentator and his paternal great-grandfather was the biographer and compiler of Protestant history. Clark founded a charity school in 1716.

Sources: *Calendar*, W. G. Blaikie, 'Clarke, Samuel (1684–1750)', rev. M. J. Mercer, *ODNB*.

SAMUEL CLARK JUNIOR (1727–1769)

The eldest son of the above. Clark was educated at Northampton academy by Doddridge and became his assistant tutor in 1750. He led the academy during Doddridge's final illness and worked under Caleb Ashworth in its early years at Daventry until his departure in 1757 to minister to a congregation in Birmingham. He and his sister Elizabeth were both long-standing correspondents of Mercy Doddridge.

Sources: *Calendar* 1649, 1770, 1778; *Dissenting Academies Online* database person id 956.

MERCY DODDRIDGE (1709–1790)

Little is known of Mercy Doddridge's early life and education. She met and married Philip Doddridge in 1730 and they had nine children, five dying in infancy and only three outliving their mother. During Doddridge's lifetime she assisted him in the management of the academy and after his death she corresponded extensively with his friends and former students. She was instrumental in the programme of posthumous publications of his works and is also thought to have offered informal advice on ministerial appointments in the Midlands.

Sources: *Calendar*; W. N. Terry, 'Doddridge, Mercy (1709–1790)', *ODNB*; Whitehouse, '*The Family Expositor*, the Doddridge Circle, and the Booksellers.'

PHILIP DODDRIDGE (1702–1751)

Orphaned in his teenage years, Doddridge was mentored by Samuel Clark senior who encouraged him to train for the dissenting ministry. Despite an offer from the Duchess of Bedford to support his education at one of the English universities, he chose at the age of seventeen to join John Jennings's academy where he remained for four years. He then ministered to the rural congregation of Kibworth while pursuing a diligent programme of reading and study and making plans to develop Jennings's academy course. He began teaching in 1729 and relocated his academy to Northampton when he accepted the invitation of a congregation there. The course of studies he developed took five years, and he employed assistant tutors (among them Job Orton and Samuel Clark) to teach the younger students. He stopped work at Northampton academy in July 1751 in order to travel to Lisbon, where he died in October. As well as his teaching and ministerial work, Doddridge published a great deal.

Sources: Orton, *Memoirs*; Kippis, 'Doddridge (Philip)', in *Biographica Britannia*, V; Isabel Rivers, 'Doddridge, Philip (1702–1751)', *ODNB*; *Dissenting Academies Online* database person id 645.

PHILIP FURNEAUX (1726–1783)

Furneaux trained for the ministry in London, first with John Eames at Moorfields and then with David Jennings at Wellclose Square. He was minister to the Congregationalists at Clapham, a Trustee of several dissenters' educational and charitable funds from the 1760s, and a political campaigner. He assisted Mercy Doddridge by undertaking editing work for *The Family Expositor* and was associated with the literary circle of nonconformist women writers in the West of England. From 1777 he was confined to a private mental institution in Hoxton.

Sources: Alan Ruston, 'Furneaux, Philip (1726–1783)', *ODNB*; Marjorie Reeves, *Female Education and Nonconformist Culture*, 27–8; *Dissenting Academies Online* database person id 2124.

THOMAS GREAVES (d. 1798)

Educated at Northampton academy (where he was funded by the Coward Trust) from 1740 to 1746, he worked as a minister in Palgrave from 1746 before moving to Rotterdam in 1752 where he was assistant to Benjamin Sowden. Greaves took over from Sowden in 1778, a position in which he served until his own death in 1798. His relations with Sowden were not good, and some hints of their discord are revealed in Sowden's correspondence with Mercy Doddridge. He did, however, preach the funeral sermon for Sowden's wife in 1763. Greaves published a Dutch edition of Doddridge's 'Lectures on Preaching' and subscribed to the Dutch edition of *A Course of Lectures*.

Sources: van den Berg and Nuttall, *Philip Doddridge (1702–1751) and the Netherlands*, 60, 80–1; *Dissenting Academies Online* database person id 3458.

JOHN JENNINGS (1687/8–1723)

Son of an ejected minister, Jennings was educated at Attercliffe academy by Timothy Jollie and took over his father's former congregation at Kibworth in 1709. He founded his own academy in around 1715 and continued to work as a tutor until his death in 1723. His daughter Jane married John Aikin (a student of Philip Doddridge and later tutor at Warrington academy); their daughter was Anna Letitia Barbauld.

Sources: David L. Wykes, 'Jennings, John (1687/8–1723)', *ODNB*; Tessa White-house, 'John Jennings (1687/8–1723)' and 'John Jennings's Academy, Kibworth Harcourt and Hinckley, *c*.1715–1723', *Dissenting Academies Online: Database and Encyclopedia* (2011); *Dissenting Academies Online* database person id 15.

DAVID JENNINGS (1691–1762)

Brother of John Jennings, educated at Moorfields academy, divinity tutor at Wellclose Square academy, and author of several published works including sermons, lectures, and educational guides. The academy was supported by the Coward Trust who, following Jennings's death, appointed his former student Samuel Morton Savage to lead a new academy in Hoxton Square. Jennings's son married a sister of Nathaniel Neal.

Sources: *Calendar* 1006; Alan Ruston, 'Jennings, David (1691–1762)', *ODNB*; Tessa Whitehouse, 'Jennings, David (1691–1762)' and 'David Jennings's Academy, Wellclose Square, 1744–1762', *Dissenting Academies Online: Database and Encyclopedia* (2011); *Dissenting Academies Online* database person id 919.

ANDREW KIPPIS (1725–1795)

First encouraged in his education efforts by Samuel Merivale, later divinity tutor at Exeter academy. He entered Doddridge's academy in 1741 and took up his first ministerial appointment in 1746, to the Presbyterian congregation of Boston, Linconshire. From 1753 he lived in Westminister, where he was minister. In 1762 he was appointed philological tutor at Hoxton academy, where he taught William Godwin. He resigned his post in 1784 and soon became a founding governor and tutor of New College Hackney, though he resigned from this post in 1791. He was an active participant in the metropolitan world of letters and contributed to and edited numerous works and periodicals including *The New Annual Register* and the second edition of *Biographia Britannica*, which was incomplete at his death.

Sources: Alan Ruston, 'Kippis, Andrew (1725–1795)', *ODNB*; Stephen Burley, 'Andrew Kippis (1725–1795)', *Dissenting Academies Online: Database and Encyclopedia* (2011); *Dissenting Academies Online* database person id 977.

NATHANIEL NEAL (d. 1765)

Son of the celebrated historian of dissent Daniel Neal, and nephew of the biblical scholar Nathaniel Lardner, Nathaniel Neal (d. 1765) was a lawyer in London and a Coward Trustee. He knew Watts and Doddridge well. The first known letter he wrote to Doddridge is dated April 1738.

Source: *Calendar* 640, 887, 1495, 1637, 1796.

JOB ORTON (1717–1783)

After an early education at grammar schools in his hometown of Shrewsbury and in Warrington, Orton began his studies at Doddridge's academy in 1734. He was appointed assistant tutor in 1739 (later being paid in this position by the Coward Trust) and preached in the local area. He returned to Shrewsbury at the invitation of two congregations (Presbyterian and Congregationalist) in 1741, where he united the two churches. Despite declining health, Orton continued his ministerial duties and in the 1750s accepted the task of editing Doddridge's posthumous works (principally the hymns and the final volumes of *The Family Expositor*; he was also Doddridge's first biographer). Orton retired in 1765 and moved to Kidderminster in 1766 where he concentrated on his own writing, which included an Old Testament expositor. Orton, who never married, corresponded with many dissenting ministers and other clergy, and part of his correspondence was published after his death. He encouraged both Thomas Stedman and Samuel Palmer in their literary work.

Sources: *Calendar* 575; Kippis, 'Orton (Job)' within 'Doddridge (Philip)', in *Biographia Britannica*, V; David L. Bates, 'Orton, Job (1717–1783)', *ODNB*; *Dissenting Academies Online* database person id 1453.

SAMUEL PALMER (1741–1813)

Born in Bedford, Palmer was trained for the ministry at Daventry academy under Caleb Ashworth between 1758 and 1762. He spent most of his career with the congregation of Mare Street, Hackney, and operated a boarding school for many years. His work as an editor of dissenting works and biographer of dissenting ministers was his main activity, however. He preached Caleb Ashworth's funeral sermon.

Sources: Alexander Gordon, 'Palmer, Samuel (1741–1813)', rev. S. J. Skedd, *ODNB*; *Dissenting Academies Online* database person id 2125.

BENJAMIN SOWDEN (d. 1778)

Sowden's education at Northampton was supported by the Coward Trust from 1740 to 1743. He was ordained in 1746 and settled at the English Church in Rotterdam by 1749. Despite some discussions about moving back to England, and difficulties with his assistant Thomas Greaves, he remained in Rotterdam for the rest of his life. He corresponded with Mercy Doddridge and his letters included news about Dutch editions of Doddridge's works. He also held the manuscript of Mary Wortley Montagu's letters written during her husband's embassy to Turkey.

Sources: *Calendar* 1511; van den Berg and Nuttall, *Philip Doddridge (1702–1751) and the Netherlands*, 80–7; *Dissenting Academies Online* database person id 3442; Doddridge Family Correspondence, DWL NCL MSS L1/9.

THOMAS STEDMAN (1775–1826)

Educated at Pembroke College, Oxford (where he matriculated 1768 and graduated MA 1787), Stedman was curate at Little Cheverell and Cheverell Magna in Wiltshire (where James Stonhouse was rector), rector at Wormington from 1775 to 1791, and vicar at St Chad's, Shrewsbury, from 1783 until his death in 1826. Wormington lay within the jurisdiction of William Warburton as Bishop of Gloucester until his death in 1779. Stedman knew Job Orton, who urged him to study shorthand and lent him a collection of Doddridge's letters. Stedman corresponded with Mercy Doddridge junior and published editions of the correspondence of Doddridge, Orton, and Stonhouse.

Sources: Doddridge Family Correspondence, DWL NCL MS L1/8; Stedman, *Letters to a Young Clergyman*; *Clergy of the Church of England Database* person id 19914.

JAMES STONHOUSE (1716–1796)

James Stonhouse, a physician living in Northampton, became a Church of England clergyman in 1754 having been influenced by Doddridge's sermons and personal friendship in the mid-1740s. His surname was spelled variously as 'Stonhouse' and 'Stonehouse'. John and James Rivington had published Stonhouse's *A Friendly Letter to a Patient* in the later 1740s, and several of Stonhouse's tracts were later published by the Society for Promoting Christian Knowledge, of which the Rivingtons were the official booksellers. He held several livings in the Church of England, and Thomas Stedman was his curate for some years.

Sources: *Calendar*; Amanda Berry, 'Stonhouse, Sir James, seventh and tenth baronet (1716–1795)', *ODNB*; *Clergy of the Church of England Database* person id 53898.

ISAAC WATTS (1674–1748)

Watts was born in penal times to a family of ardent nonconformists in Southampton. He trained for the ministry at the academy of Thomas Rowe, which was probably located in the City of London at the time Watts attended it (1690–1694). As well as ministering to the Mark Lane congregation in the City of London (associated with the Cromwell family and later located in Bury Street), Watts was a significant religious and educational author and a founding Trustee of the Coward Trust, established in 1738 for the provision of educational resources for ministers being trained in traditions of orthodox dissent. Though he did not work in dissenting academies, he tutored in the Hartopp and Abney households, which informed the content of several of his educational works. Much of his correspondence (which must have been very extensive) is lost, though materials remain in Dr Williams's Library, the Massachusetts Historical Society, and the Archiv Franckesche Stiftungen, Halle.

Sources: *Calendar*; Thomas Gibbons, *Memoirs of the Revd Isaac Watts D.D.* (1780); A. P. Davis, *Isaac Watts: His Life and Works* (1948); Isabel Rivers, 'Watts, Isaac (1674–1748)', *ODNB*; *Dissenting Academies Online* person id 933.

Bibliography

The bibliography consists of four parts:

  I. Unpublished material
    i. Manuscripts
    ii. Theses
 II. Primary material
    i. Periodicals
    ii. Books
III. Secondary material
IV. Electronic resources

I. UNPUBLISHED MATERIAL

i. Manuscripts
Bristol Baptist College Library
MS G 93, Philip Doddridge's 'Lectures on Preaching', David Jennings's
'The Christian Preacher', and John Lavington's 'Lectures on Preaching' (1779–1781)
[no call number], 'Cash Accounts of the Bristol Education Society, 1770'

British Library
Add. MSS 38728–30, assignments of literary property

Castle Hill United Reformed Church, Northampton
Blackmore MSS, Thomas Blackmore's lecture notes (1761–1762)
Doddridge MSS, Doddridge family correspondence
Watson MSS, Thomas Watson's lecture notes in shorthand (1746–1747)

Dr Williams's Library, London (DWL)
MS 24.179.11, Samuel Palmer's incomplete lecture notes (n.d.)
MSS 28.35–44, Samuel Henley's lecture notes in shorthand (1759–1761)
MS 28.117, John Jennings's 'Theologia, pars II' (n.d.)
MS 28.124, Timothy Davis's lecture notes in shorthand (1801)
MS OD68, Presbyterian Fund Board Minutes (1695–1722)
MS 69.21, incomplete copy of 'Lectures on Preaching', mostly in shorthand (n.d.)

Dr Williams's Library, New College Collection
MS NCL CT1, Coward Trust Minutes (1738–1778)
MS NCL L.1/1, Doddridge family correspondence
MS NCL L.1/3, Doddridge family correspondence
MS NCL L.1/4, Doddridge family correspondence

MS NCL L.1/5, Doddridge family correspondence
MS NCL L.1/7, Doddridge family correspondence
MS NCL L.1/8, Doddridge family correspondence
MS NCL L.1/9, Doddridge family correspondence
MS NCL L.63, Doddridge family correspondence
MSS NCL L.28/1–2, John Conder's theology lectures (1775–1778)
MS NCL L.28/3, 'Lectures on Preaching' (n.d.)
MS NCL L.28/5, 'Lectures on Preaching' (1780)
MS NCL L.29/11, John Conder's copy of Doddridge's lectures (n.d.)
MSS NCL L.29/12–16, theology lectures in shorthand (n.d.)
MS NCL L.29/20, Lectures on Preaching' and 'John Jennings's lectures on
    Oratory' in shorthand (n.d.)
MS NCL L.29/22, 'Lectures on the Composition & Delivery of Sermons
    Prayer ye Administration of ye Sacraments & other Branches of the Ministerial &
    Pastoral office by P. Doddridge' in shorthand (1744)
MS NCL L.29/23, 'Lectures on Preaching' in shorthand (n.d.)
MS NCL L.29/24, 'Lectures on Preaching' made by J. Stoddon (1779)
MS NCL L.102, Philip Doddridge's notes on Jewish antiquities in shorthand (n.d.)
MSS NCL L.113/1–2, 'Appendix to John Jennings's Algebra' in Philip Dod-
    dridge's hand (n.d)
MS NCL L.114, Philip Doddridge's notes on John Eames's lectures on Anatomy,
    in shorthand (n.d.)
MS NCL L.143, Philip Doddridge's 'Paraphrase & Notes on the Epistle to the
    Ephesians' in shorthand (1747)
MS NCL L.171, notes on mathematics and astronomy (1744)
MS NCL L.185, John Jennings's notebook, also owned and used by Doddridge
    and owned by Thomas Belsham (n.d.)
MS NCL L.227/1, John Jennings's 'Arithmetica' with Philip Doddridge's add-
    itions (n.d.)
MSS NCL L.559/1–12, miscellaneous lecture notes by Philip Doddridge, mostly
    in shorthand (n.d.)

Harris Manchester College Library, Oxford
MS Belsham 7, 'Lectures on Preaching' in shorthand (1768)
MS Belsham 8, theology lectures in shorthand (1768)
MS Heineken 6, 'Lectures on Divinity' in shorthand (n.d.)
MS Heineken 10, 'Lectures on Preaching By P. Doddridge D.D.' in shorthand (n.d.)
MS Orton 1, Job Orton's lecture notes in shorthand (1735–1739)

Northampton Public Library
MS DO/01/233, letter from Philip Furneaux to Mercy Doddridge (1756)

The John Rylands University Library, The University of Manchester
UCC MS B2, Thomas Stedman's transcription of Philip Doddridge correspond-
    ence (1791)

The National Archives
TNA: PRO PROB 11/776, sig. 509, Isaac Watts's will (1747)
TNA: PRO PROB 11/791, sig. 332, Philip Doddridge's will (1749)

The Roderic Bowen Library and Archives, University of Wales, Trinity Saint David
MS UA/TP/8, 'Lectures on Preaching' (n.d.)

ii. Theses
Belanger, Terry, 'Booksellers' Sales of Copyright: Aspects of the London Book Trade 1718–1768' (unpublished doctoral dissertation, Columbia University, 1970).
Burden, Mark, 'Academical Learning in the Dissenters' Private Academies, 1660–1720' (unpublished doctoral dissertation, University of London, 2012).
Mills, Simon, 'Joseph Priestley and the Intellectual Culture of Rational Dissent, 1752–1796' (unpublished doctoral dissertation, University of London, 2009).

II. PRIMARY MATERIAL

i. Periodicals
Critical Review
Evangelical Magazine
Gentleman's Magazine
Gospel Magazine
History of the Works of the Learned
London Chronicle
London Evening Post
Monthly Repository of Theology and General Literature
New Annual Register
Protestant Dissenter's Magazine
Public Advertiser
Universal Theological Magazine

ii. Books
An Alphabetical Catalogue of all the Books in the Library, Belonging to the Bristol Education Society (Bristol, 1795).
Addison, Joseph, and Richard Steele, *The Spectator*, ed. Donald F. Bond, 5 vols (2nd edn, Oxford, 1985).
Arnauld, Antoine, and Pierre Nicole, *Logique, ou l'art de penser* (Paris, 1662).
Arnauld, Antoine, and Pierre Nicole, *Logica, sive ars cogitandi* (London, 1674).
Bacon, Francis, *The Works of Francis Bacon*, 3 vols (London, 1753).
Baxter, Richard, *Practical Works*, 4 vols (London, 1707).
Beattie, James, *An Essay on the Nature and Immutability of Truth* (Edinburgh and London, 1770).

228   *Bibliography*

Bentham, Edward, *Reflexions Upon the Study of Divinity. To which are Subjoined Heads of a Course of Lectures* (Oxford, 1771).

Biographia Britannica: or, the Lives of the Most Eminent Persons who have Flourished... from the Earliest Ages, to the Present Times, 2nd edn, ed. A. Kippis, 5 vols (1778–95).

Biographie universelle ancienne et moderne, 85 vols (Paris, 1811–62).

Buddaeus, Johannes, *Compendium historiae philosophicae* (Halle, 1731).

Burnham, Richard, *Pious Memorials or, the Power of Religion upon the Mind in Sickness and at Death*, rev. and ed. George Burder (London, 1820).

A Catalogue of Books in the Library of the College of New-Jersey, January 29th 1760 (Woodbridge, Mass., 1760).

A Catalogue of Copies, and Shares of Copies, of Messrs. James Rivington and James Fletcher (London, 1759).

Cicero, *De amicitia*, tr. W. A. Falconer, Loeb Classical Library 154, Cicero vol. XXI (London and Cambridge, 1923).

Clap, Thomas, *The Annals or History of Yale-College, 1700 to 1766* (Boston, 1766).

Clarke, Samuel, *The Lives of Sundry Eminent Persons in this Later Age* (London, 1683).

A Catalogue of Copies, and Shares of Copies, of Messrs. James Rivington and James Fletcher (London, 1760).

[Defoe, Daniel], *An Essay Upon Projects* (London, 1697).

Doddridge, Philip, 'An Account of Mr Jennings's Method', in *Dissenting Education and the Legacy of John Jennings, c.1720–c.1729*, ed. Tessa Whitehouse, Dr Williams's Centre for Dissenting Studies, URL: <http://www.english.qmul.ac.uk/drwilliams/pubs/jennings%20legacy.html>.

Doddridge, Philip, *Free Thoughts on the Most Probable Means of Reviving the Dissenting Interest* (London, 1730).

Doddridge, Philip, *The Family Expositor*, 6 vols (London, 1739–1756).

Doddridge, Philip, 'Life of Thomas Steffe', in Thomas Steffe, *Sermons on Several Subjects* (London, 1742).

Doddridge, Philip, *The Rise and Progress of Religion in the Soul* (London, 1745).

Doddridge, Philip, *Paraphrastische Erklärung der sämmtlichen Schriften des Neuen Testaments* (Magdeburg, 1749).

Doddridge, Philip, *The Family Expositor*, 6 vols (London, 1760–1761).

Doddridge, Philip, *A Course of Lectures on the Principal Subjects of Pneumatology, Ethics and Divinity*, ed. S. Clark (London, 1763).

Doddridge, Philip, *Cours de lectures... du D. Doddridge*, 4 vols (Liège, 1768).

Doddridge, Philip, *Lessen over het Samensteelen en Uitspreken can Predikatien*, ed. Thomas Greaves (Rotterdam, 1770).

Doddridge, Philip, *Verzameling van Akademische Lessen*, 3 vols (Rotterdam, 1773).

Doddridge, Philip, *Letters to and from the Rev. Philip Doddridge, D.D.*, ed. Thomas Stedman (Shrewsbury, 1793).

Doddridge, Philip, *A Course of Lectures on the Principal Subjects of Pneumatology, Ethics and Divinity*, ed. A. Kippis, 2 vols (London, 1794).

Doddridge, Philip, *The Works of the Rev. P. Doddridge, D.D.*, ed. E. Williams and E. Parsons, 10 vols (Leeds, 1802–1805).

Doddridge, Philip, *Lectures on Preaching* (London, 1807).

Doddridge, Philip, *The Correspondence and Diary of Philip Doddridge*, ed. J. D. Humphreys, 5 vols (London, 1829–1831).

Doddridge, Philip, *The Devotional Letters and Sacramental Meditations of the Rev. P. Doddridge, with his Lectures on Preaching* (London, 1832).

Doddridge, Philip, *The Miscellaneous Works of Philip Doddridge, D.D.*, ed. Thomas Morrell (London, 1839).

Edwards, Jonathan, *A Faithful Narrative of the Surprizing work of God . . . In a Letter to the Revd. Dr. Benjamin Colman* (London, 1737).

Edwards, Jonathan, *The Works of Jonathan Edwards XXVI: Catalogue of Books*, ed. Peter J. Thuesen (New Haven, 2008).

Edwards, Jonathan, *The Works of Jonathan Edwards, IV: The Great Awakening*, ed. C. C. Goen (New Haven, 2009).

Emerson, Joseph, *Questions and Supplement, to Watts On the Improvement of the Mind* (Boston, 1831).

Emerson, Ralph, *Life of Rev. Joseph Emerson, Pastor of the Third Congregational Church in Beverly, MS and subsequently Principal of a Female Seminary* (New York, 1834).

Gibbons, Thomas, *Memoirs of the Rev. Isaac Watts D.D.* (London, 1780).

Gough, Strickland, *An Enquiry Concerning the Causes of the Decay of the Dissenting Interest* (London, 1730).

Grove, Henry, *A System of Moral Philosophy*, ed. Thomas Amory, 2 vols (London, 1749).

Hey, John, *Heads of a Course of Lectures in Divinity* (Cambridge, 1783).

Hey, John, *Lectures in Divinity*, 4 vols (Cambridge, 1796–1798).

Hutcheson, Francis, *Philosophiae moralis institutio compendiaria* (Glasgow, 1742).

Hutcheson, Francis, *A Short Introduction to Moral Philosophy* (Glasgow, 1747).

Jennings, David (ed.), *Instructions to Ministers* (London, 1744).

Jennings, David, *A Funeral Sermon Occasioned by the Death of the Late Reverend Isaac Watts* (London, 1749).

Jennings, David, *Jewish Antiquities, or a Course of Lectures on the First Three Books of Godwin's Moses and Aaron*, 2 vols (London, 1766).

Jennings, John, *Miscellanea in usum juventutis academicae* (Northampton, 1721).

Jennings, John, *Two Discourses: the First, of Preaching Christ; the Second, of Particular and Experimental Preaching*, 3rd edn (London, 1736).

Jennings, John, *Two Discourses: the First, of Preaching Christ; the Second, of Particular and Experimental Preaching* (Boston, 1740).

Johnson, Samuel, *Letters to and from the Late Samuel Johnson*, ed. Hester Piozzi, 2 vols (London, 1788).

Johnson, Samuel, *The Lives of the Most Eminent English Poets: With Critical Observations on their Works*, ed. Roger Lonsdale, 4 vols (Oxford, 2006).

Lampe, Friedrich Adolphus, *Synopsis historiæ sacræ ecclesiasticæ ab origine mundi ad præsentia tempora* (Utrecht, 1721).

Lardner, Nathaniel, *The Credibility of Gospel History*, 2 vols (London, 1727).

Law, William, *A Serious Call to a Devout and Holy Life* (London, 1729).

Le Clerc, Jean, *Logica, sive ars ratiocinandi* (London, 1692).

Lindsey, Theophilus, *A Second Address to the Students of Oxford and Cambridge, Relating to Jesus Christ* (London, 1790).

Locke, John, 'Of the Conduct of the Understanding', in *Posthumous Works of Mr John Locke* (London, 1706).

Locke, John, *Some Thoughts Concerning Education*, ed. John W. and Jean S. Yolton (Oxford, 1989).

Maimonides, *De jure pauperis et peregrini apud Judaeos* (Oxford, 1679).

Mason, John, *Select Remains* (London, 1736).

Mather, Samuel, *The Life of the very Reverend and Learned Cotton Mather D.D. & F.R.S.* (Boston, 1729).

Newbery, John, *Circle of the Sciences*, 7 vols (London, 1745–1748).

Newton, Richard, *Rules and Statutes for the Government of Hertford College* (London, 1747).

Orton, Job, *Memoirs of the Life, Character and Writings of the Late Philip Doddridge, D.D.* (Shrewsbury, 1766).

Orton, Job, *Letters to Dissenting Ministers, and to Students for the Ministry*, ed. Samuel Palmer, 2 vols (London, 1806).

Palmer, Samuel, *A Defence of the Dissenters Education in their Private Academies* (London, 1703).

Palmer, Samuel, *A New Translation of the New Testament of our Lord and Saviour Jesus Christ. Extracted from the Paraphrase of the Late Philip Doddridge, D.D. and Carefully Revised*, 2 vols (London, 1765).

Palmer, Samuel, *The Nonconformist's Memorial*, 2 vols (London, 1775).

Palmer, Samuel, *A Collection of Family Prayers* (London, 1783).

Palmer, Samuel, *The Life of the Rev. Isaac Watts, D.D. By the late Dr. Samuel Johnson, with Notes. Containing Animadversions and Additions Relating to Dr. Watts's Character, Writings, and Sentiments, Particularly on the Trinity* (London, 1785).

Palmer, Samuel, *The Life of the Rev. Isaac Watts, D.D. By the late Dr. Samuel Johnson, with Notes. Containing Animadversions and Additions Relating to Dr. Watts's Character, Writings, and Sentiments, Particularly on the Trinity*, 2nd edn (London, 1791).

The Polite Student (London, 1748).

Pope, Alexander, *The Works of Alexander Pope*, ed. William Warburton, 9 vols (London, 1751).

Priestley, Joseph, *A Course of Lectures on the Theory of Language* (Warrington, 1762).

Priestley, Joseph, *A Syllabus of a Course of Lectures on the Study of History* (Warrington, 1765).

Priestley, Joseph, *A Course of Lectures on Oratory and Criticism* (London, 1777).

Proposals For Printing by Subscription, In three Volumes in Quarto, The Family Expositor, On the epistolary part of the New Testament, with The Book of the Revelation (London, 1751).

Proposals for Printing by Subscription in Weekly Numbers . . . Dr. Doddridge's Family Expositor (London, 1759).

Rees, Abraham, *A Sermon Preached . . . Upon Occasion of the Much Lamented Death of the Rev. Andrew Kippis* (London, 1795).

Reynolds, John, *A Practical Discourse of Reconciliation between God and Man* (London, 1729).

Richardson, Samuel, *The Correspondence of Samuel Richardson*, ed. Anna Letitia Barbauld, 6 vols (London, 1804).

Ripa, Cesare, *Iconologia: or, Moral Emblems* (London, 1709).

Stedman, Thomas, *Letters to a Young Clergyman*, 2 vols (2nd edn, 1805).

Steele, Richard, and Joseph Addison, *The Tatler*, ed. D. F. Bond, 3 vols (Oxford, 1987).

A Supplement to Dr. Harris's Dictionary of Arts and Sciences (London, 1744).

Tillotson, John, *The Works of the Most Reverend Dr. John Tillotson, Archbishop of Canterbury*, ed. Thomas Birch, 3 vols (London, 1752).

Vitringa, Campegius, *Observationum sacrarum*, 2 vols (Amsterdam, 1721 and Franeker, 1723).

Voltaire, *Letters Concerning the English Nation* (London, 1733).

Waterland, Daniel, *Advice to a Young Student. With a Method of Study for the Four First Years* (London, 1730).

Watts, Isaac, *Hymns and Spiritual Songs* (London, 1707).

Watts, Isaac, *Divine Songs Attempted in Easy Language for the Use of Children* (2nd edn, 1716).

Watts, Isaac, *An Essay Towards the Encouragement of Charity Schools* (London, 1728).

Watts, Isaac, *A Short View of the Whole Scripture History* (London, 1732).

Watts, Isaac, *Questions Proper for Students in Divinity* (London, 1741).

Watts, Isaac, *The Works of the Late Reverend and Learned Isaac Watts, D.D.*, ed. P. Doddridge and D. Jennings, 6 vols (London, 1753).

Watts, Isaac, *The Posthumous Works of the Late Reverend Dr. Isaac Watts containing the Second Part of the Improvement of the Mind* (London, 1754).

Watts, Isaac, *The Beauties of the Late Revd. Dr. Isaac Watts* (London, 1782).

Watts, Isaac, 'Letters to Benjamin Colman', in *Proceedings of the Massachusetts Historical Society*, Massachusetts Historical Society, *Proceedings*, 2nd ser., 20 vols (1884–1907), IX (1894–1895), 331–410.

Watts, Isaac, 'Reply to Doddridge's, "Account"', in *Dissenting Education and the Legacy of John Jennings, c.1720–c.1729*, ed. Tessa Whitehouse, Dr Williams's Centre for Dissenting Studies (2nd edn, 2011). URL: <http://www.english.qmul.ac.uk/drwilliams/pubs/jennings%20legacy.html>.

Wesley, John, *Works, Volume 25: Letters I*, ed. Frank Baker (Oxford, 1980).

Wesley, Samuel, *A Letter from a Country Divine to his Friend in London. Concerning the Education of the Dissenters* (London, 1703).

Williams, Edward, *The Christian Preacher: or, Discourses on Preaching* (Halifax, 1800).

Williams, Edward, *A Syllabus of Lectures on the Most Important Subjects in Theology* (Rotherham, 1812).

III. SECONDARY MATERIAL

Achinstein, Sharon, *Literature and Dissent in Milton's England* (Cambridge, 2003).

Altholz, Josef K., *The Religious Press in Britain 1760–1900* (New York, 1989).

Altman, Janet Gurkin, *Epistolarity: Approaches to a Form* (Columbus, Oh., 1993).

Aston, Nigel, 'Rationalism, the Enlightenment, and Sermons', in *The Oxford Handbook of the British Sermon 1689–1901*, ed. Keith A. Francis and William Gibson (Oxford, 2012), 390–405.

Axtell, James, *The School Upon a Hill: Education and Society in Colonial New England* (New Haven, 1974).

Bach, Thomas P., 'G. A. Francke and the Halle Communication Network: Protection, Politics and Piety', in *Pietism and Community in Europe and North America, 1650–1850*, ed. Jonathan Strom (Leiden, 2010), 95–110.

Bailyn, Bernard, *Education in the Forming of American Society* (New York, 1960).

Baker, Frank (ed.), 'Introduction' to *The Works of John Wesley (Letters I: 1721–39)* (Oxford, 1980), 1–140.

Barchas, Janine, *Graphic Design, Print Culture, and the Eighteenth-Century Novel* (Cambridge, 2003).

Barker, Nicolas (ed.), *A Potencie of Life: Books in Society* (London, 1993).

Bator, Robert, 'Out of the Ordinary Road: John Locke and English Juvenile Fiction in the Eighteenth Century', *Children's Literature*, 1 (1972), 46–53.

Belanger, Terry, 'Booksellers' Trade Sales, 1718–1768', *The Library*, 5th ser., 4 (1975), 281–302.

Benedict, Barbara, *Making the Modern Reader: Cultural Mediation in Early Modern Literary Anthologies* (Princeton, 1996).

Bennett, G. V., 'University, Society and Church 1688–1714', in *The History of the University of Oxford Volume V: The Eighteenth Century*, ed. L. S. Sutherland and L. G. Mitchell (Oxford, 1986), 359–400.

Bergamasco, Lucia, 'Évangelisme et Lumières', in *Revue française d'études américaines*, 92 (2002) 22–46.

Bigold, Melanie, *Women of Letters, Manuscript Circulation and Print Afterlives in the Eighteenth Century: Elizabeth Rowe, Catharine Cockburn and Elizabeth Carter* (Houndmills, Basingstoke, 2013).

Bishop, Selma L., *Isaac Watts's Hymns and Spiritual Songs (1707): A Publishing History and a Bibliography* (Ann Arbor, Mich., 1974).

Black, Jeremy, *Eighteenth-Century Britain, 1688–1783*, 2nd edn (Houndmills, Basingstoke, 2008).

Blair, Ann, 'An Early Modernist's Perspective', *Isis*, 95 (2004), 420–30.

Blair, Ann, 'Student Manuscripts and the Textbook', in *Scholarly Knowledge: Textbooks in Early Modern Europe*, ed. Emidio Campi, Simone De Angelis, Anja-Silvia Goeing, and Anthony Grafton (Geneva, 2008), 39–74.

Bond, W. H., and Hugh Amory (eds), *The Printed Catalogues of the Harvard College Library 1723–1790* (Boston, 1996).

Bradley, James E., *Religion, Revolution and English Radicalism: Nonconformity in Eighteenth Century Politics and Society* (Cambridge, 1990).

Brant, Clare, *Eighteenth Century Letters and British Culture* (Houndmills, Basingstoke, 2006).

Bremer, Francis, *Congregational Communion: Clerical Friendship in the Anglo-American Community, 1610–1692* (Boston, 1994).

Brewer, John, *The Pleasures of the Imagination: English Culture in the Eighteenth Century* (London, 1997).

Broderick, Francis A., 'Pulpit, Physics and Politics: The Curriculum of the College of New Jersey, 1746–1794', *William and Mary Quarterly*, 3rd ser., 6 (1949), 42–68.

Brunner, Daniel L., *Halle Pietists in England: Anthony William Boehm and the Society for Promoting Christian Knowledge* (Göttingen, 1993).

Bryson, Anna, *From Courtesy to Civility: Changing Codes of Conduct in Early Modern Europe* (Oxford, 1998).

Burley, Stephen, '"In this Intolerance I Glory": William Hazlitt (1737–1820) and the Dissenting Periodical', *Hazlitt Review*, 3 (2010), 9–23.

Butler, Jon, *Awash in a Sea of Faith: Christianizing the American People* (Cambridge, 1990).

Butler, Marilyn, *Romantics, Rebels and Reactionaries* (Oxford, 1981; repr. 1985).

Calhoun, Craig (ed.), *Habermas and the Public Sphere* (Boston, 1992).

Carter, Philip, *Men and the Emergence of Polite Society, Britain 1660–1800* (Harlow, 2001).

Chartier, Roger, 'Listen to the Dead with Your Eyes', in *The Author's Hand and the Printer's Mind*, tr. Lydia G. Cochrane (Cambridge, 2013), 3–26.

Claeys, Gregory, 'Virtuous Commerce and Free Theology: Political Economy and the Dissenting Academies 1750–1800', *History of Political Thought*, 20 (1999), 141–72.

Clayton, Tim, 'Book Illustration and the World of Prints', in *The Cambridge History of the Book in Britain Volume V: 1695–1830*, ed. Michael F. Suarez, SJ and Michael L. Turner (Cambridge, 2009), 230–47.

Colley, Linda, *Britons: Forging the Nation 1707–1837* (New Haven, 1992; repr. 1996).

Cornwall, Robert D., and William Gibson (eds), *Religion, Politics and Dissent, 1660–1832: Essays in Honour of James E. Bradley* (Farnham, 2010).

Cremin, Lawrence A., *Traditions of American Education* (New York, 1977).

Cressy, David, *Literacy and the Social Order: Reading and Writing in Tudor and Stuart England* (Cambridge, 1980).

Darnton, Robert, 'What is the History of Books?', *Daedalus*, 111 (1982), 65–82.

Darnton, Robert, 'Two Paths Through the Social History of Ideas', in *The Darnton Debate: Books and Revolution in the Eighteenth Century*, ed. Haydn T. Mason (Oxford, 1998), 251–94.

Darnton, Robert, *George Washington's False Teeth* (New York, 2003).

Darnton, Robert, '"What is the History of Books?" Revisited', *Modern Intellectual History*, 4 (2007), 495–508.

Davie, Donald, *A Gathered Church: The Literature of the English Dissenting Interest, 1700–1930* (New York, 1979).

Davie, Donald, *Dissentient Voice* (Notre Dame, Ind., 1982).

Davis, A. P., *Isaac Watts: His Life and Works* (London, 1948).

Daybell, James, *The Material Letter in Early Modern England: Manuscript Letters and the Culture and Practices of Letter-Writing, 1512–1635* (Houndmills, Basingstoke, 2012).

DeMaria, Robert, *Johnson's Dictionary and the Language of Learning* (Oxford, 1986).

DeMaria, Robert, *Samuel Johnson's Life of Reading* (Baltimore, 1997).

Deacon, Malcolm, *Philip Doddridge of Northampton, 1702–51* (Northampton, 1980).

Deconinck-Brossard, Françoise, 'La Sténographie de Philip Doddridge (1702–1751)', *Bulletin de la Société d'Études Anglo-Américaines des XVIIᵉ et XVIIIᵉ Siècles*, 12 (1981), 29–43.

Deconinck-Brossard, Françoise, 'The Art of Preaching', in *Preaching, Sermon and Cultural Change in the Long Eighteenth Century*, ed. Joris van Eijnatten (Leiden, 2009), 95–130.

Dixon, Rosemary, 'The Publishing of John Tillotson's Collected Works 1695–1757', *The Library*, 7th ser., 8 (2007), 154–81.

Dunan-Page, Anne, and Clotilde Prunier (eds), *Debating the Faith: Religion and Letter–Writing in Great Britain, 1550–1800* (Dordrecht, 2013).

Eger, Elizabeth, Charlotte Grant, Clíona Ó Gallchoir, and Penny Warburton (eds), *Women, Writing and the Public Sphere 1700–1830* (Cambridge, 2001).

Escott, Harry, *Isaac Watts, Hymnographer: A Study of the Beginnings, Development, and Philosophy of the English Hymn* (London, 1962).

Everitt, Alan, 'Streams of Sensibility: Philip Doddridge of Northampton and the Evangelical Tradition', in *Landscape and Community in England* (London and Ronceverte, 1985), 209–46.

Ezell, Margaret, *Social Authorship and the Advent of Print* (Baltimore, 1999).

Ferch, David L., '"Good Books are a Very Great Mercy to the World": Persecution, Private Libraries, and the Printed Word in the Early Development of the Dissenting Academies, 1663–1730', *Journal of Library History*, 21 (1986), 350–61.

Foucault, Michel, 'What is an Author?', in *The Foucault Reader*, ed. Paul Rainbow (Harmondsworth, 1984), 101–20.

Gascoigne, John, *Cambridge in the Age of the Enlightenment: Science, Religion and Politics from the Restoration to the French Revolution* (Cambridge, 1989).

Genette, Gerard, *Paratexts: Thresholds of Interpretation*, tr. Jane E. Lewin (Cambridge, 1997).

Gingerich, Owen, *An Annotated Census of Copernicus' De revolutionibus (Nürnberg, 1543 and Basel, 1566)* (Leiden, 2002).

Goldgar, Anne, *Impolite Learning: Conduct and Community in the Republic of Letters 1680–1750* (New Haven, 1995).

Goldie, Mark (ed.), *John Locke: Letter on Toleration and Other Writings* (Indianapolis, 2010).

Goodman, Dena, *The Republic of Letters: A Cultural History of the French Enlightenment* (2nd edn, Ithaca, NY, 1996).

Gordon, Alexander, *Essays and Addresses, Biographical and Historical* (London, 1922).

Grayling, A. C., *Friendship* (New Haven, 2013).

Green, Ian, *Humanism and Protestantism in Early Modern English Education* (Farnham, 2009).

Green, James N., 'English Books and Printing in the Age of Franklin', in *A History of the Book in America: The Colonial Book in the Atlantic World*, ed. Hugh Amory and David D. Hall (Cambridge, 2000), 248–98.

Green, V. H. H., *Religion at Oxford and Cambridge* (London, 1964).

Gregory, Jeremy, '*Homo religiosus*: Masculinity and Religion in the Long Eighteenth Century', in *English Masculinities 1660–1800*, ed. Tim Hitchcock and Michèle Cohen (Harlow, 2001), 85–110.

Gregory, Jeremy, 'Religion in the Age of Enlightenment: Putting John Wesley in Context', *Religion in the Age of Enlightenment*, 2 (2010), 19–53.

Grenby, M. O., *The Child Reader 1700–1840* (Cambridge, 2011).

Habermas, Jürgen, *The Structural Transformation of the Public Sphere: An Inquiry into a Category of Bourgeois Society*, tr. Thomas Burger and Frederick Lawrence (Cambridge, Mass., 1989).

Hall, David D., *Printing and Society in Early America* (Worcester, Mass., 1983).

Hall, David D., 'Learned Culture in the Eighteenth Century', in *A History of the Book in America: The Colonial Book in the Atlantic World*, ed. Hugh Amory and David D. Hall (Cambridge, 2000), 411–33.

Hall, David D., and Elizabeth Carroll Reilly, 'Practices of Reading: Introduction', in *A History of the Book in America: The Colonial Book*, ed. Amory and Hall, 377–80.

Hamilton, James, *Christian Classics: Readings from the Best Divines, with Notices Biographical and Critical*, 4 vols (New York, 1859).

Hayes, Kevin J., *A Colonial Woman's Bookshelf* (Knoxville, Tenn., 1996).

Haykin, Michael A., and Kenneth J. Stewart (eds), *The Emergence of Evangelicalism: Exploring Historical Continuities* (Nottingham, 2008).

Hempton, David, 'Established Churches and the Growth of Religious Pluralism: A Case Study of Christianisation and Secularisation in England since 1700', in *The Decline of Christendom in Western Europe, 1750–2000*, ed. Hugh McLeod and Werner Ustorf (Cambridge, 2003), 81–98.

Hernlund, Patricia, 'Three Bankruptcies in the London Book Trade, 1746–61: Rivington, Knapton, and Osborn', in *Writers, Books and Trade: An Eighteenth Century English Miscellany for William B. Todd*, ed. O. M. Brack Jr (New York, 1993), 77–122.

Hindmarch, Bruce D., 'Reshaping Individualism: The Private Christian, Eighteenth-Century Religion, and the Enlightenment', in *The Rise of the Laity in Evangelical Protestantism*, ed. Deryck W. Lovegrove (London, 2002), 67–84.

Hindmarch, Bruce D., *The Evangelical Conversion Narrative: Spiritual Autobiography in Early Modern England* (Oxford, 2005).

Hood, Edwin Paxton, *Isaac Watts: His Life and Writings, his Homes and Friends* (London, 1875), 103.

Howe, Sarah, 'The English Author Portrait, 1500–1640', *Papers of the Bibliographical Society of America*, 102 (2008), 465–99.

Howsam, Leslie, *Old Books and New Histories: An Orientation to Studies in Book and Print Culture* (Toronto, 2007).

Hoyles, John, *The Waning of the Renaissance 1640–1740* (The Hague, 1971).

Hunter, Michael (ed.), *Archives of the Scientific Revolution: The Formation and Exchange of Ideas in Seventeenth-Century Europe* (Woodbridge, 1998).

Immel, Andrea, 'Children's Books and School-Books', in *The Cambridge History of the Book in Britain Volume V: 1695–1830*, ed. Michael F. Suarez, SJ and Michael L. Turner (Cambridge, 2009), 736–49.

Ingram, Robert G., 'William Warburton, Divine Action, and Enlightened Christianity', in *Religious Identities in Britain, 1660–1830*, ed. William Gibson and Robert G. Ingram (Farnham, 2005), 97–118.

Jackson, H. J., *Marginalia: Readers Writing in Books* (New Haven, 2001).

Jacob, W. M., *The Clerical Profession in the Long Eighteenth Century: 1680–1840* (Oxford, 2007).

James, Felicity, and Ian Inkster (eds), *Dissent and the Aikin–Barbauld Circle* (Cambridge, 2011).

Janowitz, Anne, 'Amiable and Radical Sociability: Anna Barbauld's "Free Familiar Conversation"', in *Romantic Sociability: Social Networks and Literary Culture in Britain, 1770–1840*, ed. Gillian Russell and Clara Tuite (Cambridge, 2002), 62–81.

Justice, George, and Nathan Tinker (eds), *Women's Writing and the Circulation of Ideas: Manuscript Publication in England, 1550–1800* (Cambridge, 2002).

Karian, Stephen, *Jonathan Swift in Print and Manuscript* (Cambridge, 2010).

Keeble, N. H., *Richard Baxter, Puritan Man of Letters* (Oxford, 1982).

Keeble, N. H., *The Literary Culture of Nonconformity in Later Seventeenth Century England* (Leicester, 1987).

Keeble, N. H., *'Loving and Free Converse': Richard Baxter in his Letters* (London, 1991).

Keen, Paul, *The Crisis of Literature in the 1790s: Print Culture and the Public Sphere* (Cambridge, 1999).

Kelly, Catherine E., 'Reading and the Problem of Accomplishment', in *Reading Women: Literacy, Authorship, and Culture in the Atlantic World, 1500–1800*, ed. Heidi Brayman Hackel and Catherine E. Kelly (Philadelphia, 2008).

Kernan, Alvin B., *Samuel Johnson and the Impact of Print* (Princeton, 1989).

Klein, Lawrence E., 'Coffeehouse Civility, 1660–1714: An Aspect of Post-Courtly Culture in England', *Huntingdon Library Quarterly*, 59 (1996), 30–51.

Klein, Lawrence E., 'Gender, Conversation and the Public Sphere in Early Eighteenth-Century England', in *Textuality and Sexuality: Reading Theories and Practices*, ed. Judith Still and Michael Worton (Manchester, 1993), 100–15.

Klein, Lawrence E., *Shaftesbury and the Culture of Politeness: Moral Discourse and Cultural Politics in Early Eighteenth Century England* (Cambridge, 1994).

Klein, Lawrence E., 'Politeness for Plebes: Some Social Identities in Early Eighteenth-Century England', in *The Consumption of Culture, 1600–1800: Image, Object Text*, ed. Ann Bermingham and John Brewer (London, 1995), 362–82.

Klein, Lawrence E., 'Sociability, Solitude, and Enlightenment', *Huntingdon Library Quarterly*, 60 (1997), 153–77.

Klein, Lawrence E., 'Politeness and the Interpretation of the British Eighteenth Century', *Historical Journal*, 45 (2002), 869–98.

Kleeman, Heather, 'The Matter for Moral Education: Locke, Newbery and the Didactic Book–Toy Hybrid', *Eighteenth-Century Studies*, 44 (2011), 223–44.

Knoles, Thomas, Rick Kennedy, and Lucia Zaucha Knoles, *Student Notebooks at Colonial Harvard: Manuscripts and Educational Practice* (Worcester, Mass., 2003).

Knudsen, Jonathan B., 'On Enlightenment for the Common Man', in *What is Enlightenment? Eighteenth-Century Answers and Twentieth-Century Questions*, ed. James Schmidt (Berkeley and Los Angeles, 1996), 270–90.

Lambert, Frank, 'The First Great Awakening: Whose Interpretive Fiction?', *New England Quarterly*, 68 (1995), 650–9.

Langford, Paul, 'The Uses of Eighteenth-Century Politeness', *Transactions of the Royal Historical Society*, 6th ser., 12 (2002), 311–31.

Lehmann, Hartmutt, 'Continental Protestant Europe', in *The Cambridge History of Christianity, VII: Enlightenment, Reawakening and Revolution 1660–1815*, ed. Stewart J. Brown and Timothy Tackett (Cambridge, 2006), 33–55.

Levy, Michelle, *Family Authorship and Romantic Print Culture* (Houndmills, Basingstoke, 2007).

Love, Harold, *Scribal Publication in Seventeenth-Century England* (Oxford, 1993).

Love, Harold, 'Oral and Scribal Texts in Early Modern England', in *The Cambridge History of the Book in Britain Volume IV: 1557–1695*, ed. Lotte Hellinga, D. F. McKenzie, John Barnard, J. B. Trapp, and David McKitterick (Cambridge, 2002), 97–121.

Lyell, James P. R., *Mrs. Piozzi and Isaac Watts* (London, 1934).

McCarthy, William, *Anna Letitia Barbauld: Voice of the Enlightenment* (Baltimore, 2008).

McCarthy, William, 'How Dissent Made Anna Letitia Barbauld, and What She Made of Dissent', in *Religious Dissent and the Aikin–Barbauld Circle, 1740–1840*, ed. Felicity James and Ian Inkster (Oxford, 2012), 52–69.

McGann, Jerome, *The Textual Condition* (Princeton, 1991).

McGrath, Thomas, 'Facing the Text: Author Portraits in Florentine Printed Books, 1545–1585', *Word and Image: A Journal of Verbal/Visual Enquiry*, 19 (2003), 74–85.

McKenzie, D. F., *Making Meaning: 'Printers of the Mind' and Other Essays*, ed. Peter D. McDonald and Michael F. Suarez, SJ (Amherst, Mass., and Boston, 2002).

McKitterick, David, *Manuscript, Print and the Search for Order* (Cambridge, 2003).

McLachlan, H., *English Education Under the Test Acts* (Manchester, 1931).

McLaverty, James, 'From Definition to Explanation: Locke's Influence on Johnson's Dictionary', *Journal of the History of Ideas*, 47 (1986), 377–94.

McLaverty, James, *Pope, Print and Meaning* (Oxford, 2001).

Marotti, Arthur, *Manuscript, Print, and the English Renaissance Lyric* (Ithaca, NY, 1995).

Mee, Jon, *Dangerous Enthusiasm: William Blake and the Culture of Radicalism in the 1790s* (Oxford, 1992).

Mee, Jon, *Romanticism, Enthusiasm, and Regulation: Poetics and the Policing of Culture in the Romantic Period* (Oxford, 2003).

Mee, Jon, *Conversable Worlds: Literature, Contention and Community 1762–1830* (Oxford, 2011).

Miller, Thomas P., *The Formation of College English: Rhetoric and Belles Lettres in the English Cultural Provinces* (Pittsburgh, 1997).

Mineka, Francis E., *The Dissidence of Dissent: The Monthly Repository, 1806–1838* (Chapel Hill, NC, 1944).

Monaghan, E. Jennifer, *Learning to Read and Write in Colonial America* (Worcester, Mass., 2005).

Moore, Susan Hardman, *Pilgrims: New World Settlers and the Call of Home* (New Haven, 2007).

Moretti, Franco, 'Network Theory, Plot Analysis', *New Left Review*, 2nd ser., 68 (2011), 80–102.

Nauert, Charles G., *Humanism and the Culture of Renaissance Europe* (2nd edn, Cambridge, 2008).

Nichol, Donald W., *Pope's Literary Legacy: The Book-Trade Correspondence of William Warburton and John Knapton, with Other Letters and Documents, 1744–1780* (Oxford, 1992).

Noll, Mark A., *Princeton and the Republic, 1768–1822: The Search for a Christian Enlightenment in the Era of Samuel Stanhope Smith* (Princeton, 1989).

Noll, Mark A., *The Rise of Evangelicalism: The Age of Edwards, Whitefield and the Wesleys* (Downers Grove, Ill., 2003).

Noll, Mark A., David W. Bebbington, and George Rawlyk (eds), *Evangelicalism: Comparative Studies of Popular Protestantism in North America, the British Isles, and Beyond, 1700–1900* (Oxford, 1994).

Novak, Maximilian E., *The Age of Projects* (Toronto, 2008).

Nuttall, G. F. (ed.), *Philip Doddridge, 1702–51: His Contribution to English Religion* (London, 1951).

Nuttall, G. F., *Richard Baxter and Philip Doddridge: A Study in a Tradition* (Oxford, 1951).

Nuttall, G. F., *New College London and its Library: Two Lectures* (London, 1977).

Nuttall, G. F., *A Calendar of the Correspondence of Philip Doddridge* (London, 1979).

Nuttall, G. F., *Handlist of the Correspondence of Mercy Doddridge 1751–1790* (London, 1984).

Nuttall, G. F., 'Philip Doddridge, John Guyse and their Expositors', in *Kerkhistorische Opstellen Aangeboden aan Prof. Dr. J. van den Berg*, ed. C. Augustijn, P. N. Holtrop, et al. (Kampen, 1987), 102–13.

Nuttall, G. F., *Philip Doddridge: Additional Letters* (London, 2001).

Nuttall, G. F., *Studies in English Dissent* (Weston Rhyn, 2002).

O'Brien, Susan, 'A Transatlantic Community of Saints: The Great Awakening and the First Evangelical Network, 1735–1755', *American Historical Review*, 91 (1986), 811–32.

O'Brien, Susan, 'Eighteenth-Century Publishing Networks in the First Years of Transatlantic Evangelicalism', in *Evangelicalism: Comparative Studies of Popular*

Protestantism in the North America, the British Isles, and Beyond 1700–1900, ed. Mark A. Noll, David W. Bebbington, and George A. Rawlyk (Oxford, 1994), 38–57.

Olsen, Mark, and Louis-Georges Harvey, 'Reading in Revolutionary Times: Book Borrowing from the Harvard College Library, 1773–1782', *Harvard Library Bulletin*, new ser., 4 (1993), 57–72.

Ong, Walter J., *Orality and Literacy: The Technologizing of the Word* (1982; repr. London, 2002).

Parker, Irene, *Dissenting Academies in England* (Cambridge, 1914).

Paul, Charles Kegan, *William Godwin, his Friends and Contemporaries*, 2 vols (London, 1876).

Pearsall, Sarah M. S., *Atlantic Families: Lives and Letters in the Later Eighteenth Century* (Oxford, 2008).

Pestana, Carla Gardina, *Quakers and Baptists in Colonial Massachusetts* (Cambridge, 1991).

Pestana, Carla Gardina, *Protestant Empire: Religion and the Making of the British Atlantic World* (Philadelphia, 2009).

Peters, Kate, 'Patterns of Quaker Authorship, 1652–56', in *The Emergence of Quaker Writing: Dissenting Literature in Seventeenth-Century England*, ed. Thomas C. Corns and David Lowenstein (London, 1995).

Peterson, Mark A., '*Theopolis Americana*: Boston and the Protestant International', in *Soundings in Atlantic History: Latent Structures and Intellectual Currents 1500–1830*, ed. Bernard Bailyn and Patricia L. Denault (Cambridge, Mass., 2009), 329–69.

Pilcher, George William (ed.), *The Reverend Samuel Davies Abroad: The Diary of a Journey to England and Scotland, 1753–55* (Urbana, Ill., 1967).

Piper, David, *The Image of the Poet: British Poets and their Portraits* (Oxford, 1982).

Plumb, J. H., 'The New World of Children in Eighteenth-Century England', in *The Birth of a Consumer Society: The Commercialization of Eighteenth-Century England*, ed. Neil McKendrick, John Brewer, and J. H. Plumb (London, 1982), 286–315.

Pocock, J. G. A., 'Post-Puritan England and the Problem of the Enlightenment', in *Culture and Politics from Puritanism to the Enlightenment*, ed. Perez Zagorin (Berkeley and Los Angeles, 1980), 91–112.

Pointon, Marcia, *Hanging the Head: Portraiture and Social Function in Eighteenth-Century England* (New Haven, 1993).

Porterfield, Amanda, *Mary Lyon and the Mount Holyoke Missionaries* (Oxford, 1997).

Pratt, Anne Stokley, *Isaac Watts and his Gift of Books to Yale College* (New Haven, 1938).

Prescott, Sarah, 'Provincial Networks, Dissenting Connections, and Noble Friends: Elizabeth Singer Rowe and Female Authorship in Early Eighteenth-Century England', *Eighteenth-Century Life*, 25 (2001), 29–42.

Rack, Henry, *John Wesley: Reasonable Enthusiast* (London, 1989).

Raven, James, *London Booksellers and American Customers: Transatlantic Literary Community and the Charleston Library Society, 1748–1811* (Columbia, SC, 2002).

Raven, James, *The Business of Books* (New Haven, 2007).

Raven, James, 'The Book as a Commodity', in *The Cambridge History of the Book in Britain Volume V: 1695–1830*, ed. Michael F. Suarez, SJ and Michael L. Turner (Cambridge, 2009), 85–117.

Reeves, Marjorie, *Female Education and Nonconformist Culture, 1700–1900* (2nd edn, London, 2000).

Richetti, John (ed.), *The Cambridge History of English Literature 1660–1780* (Cambridge, 2005).

Rivers, Isabel, *Reason, Grace, and Sentiment: A Study of the Language of Religion and Ethics in England 1660–1780*, 2 vols (Cambridge, 1991–2000).

Rivers, Isabel, *The Defence of Truth Through the Knowledge of Error: Philip Doddridge's Academy Lectures* (London, 2003).

Rivers, Isabel, 'The First Evangelical Tract Society', *Historical Journal*, 50 (2007), 1–22.

Rivers, Isabel, 'Society for Promoting Religious Knowledge among the Poor (*act.* 1750–1920s)', in *Oxford Dictionary of National Biography* (Oxford, 2007).

Rivers, Isabel, 'Writing the History of Early Evangelicalism', *History of European Ideas*, 35 (2009), 105–11.

Rivers, Isabel, 'Philip Doddridge's New Testament: *The Family Expositor* (1739–56)', in *The King James Bible After Four Hundred Years: Literary, Linguistic, and Cultural Influences*, ed. Hannibal Hamlin and Norman W. Jones (Cambridge, 2010), 124–45.

Rivers, Isabel (ed.), Mark Burden, assistant ed., *A History of the Dissenting Academies in the British Isles, 1660–1860* (Cambridge, forthcoming).

Rivers, Isabel, and David L. Wykes (eds), *Joseph Priestley: Scientist, Philosopher, and Theologian* (Oxford, 2008).

Robbins, Caroline, *The Eighteenth-Century Commonwealthmen: Studies in the Transmission, Development and Circumstance of English Liberal Thought from the Restoration of Charles II until the War with the Thirteen Colonies* (Cambridge, Mass., 1959).

Rogers, Shef, 'The Use of Royal Licences for Printing in England, 1695–1760: A Bibliography', *The Library*, 7th ser., 1 (2000), 133–92.

Roscoe, S., *John Newbery and his Successors, 1740–1814: A Bibliography* (Wormley, 1973).

Rosenblatt, Helena, 'The Christian Enlightenment', in *The Cambridge History of Christianity, VII: Enlightenment, Reawakening and Revolution 1660–1815*, ed. Stewart J. Brown and Timothy Tackett (Cambridge, 2006), 283–301.

Rummel, Erika, *Desiderius Erasmus* (London, 2004).

Rupp, Gordon, *Religion in England 1688–1791* (Oxford, 1986).

St Clair, William, *The Reading Nation in the Romantic Period* (Cambridge, 2004).

Schneider, Gary, *The Culture of Epistolarity: Vernacular Letters and Letter Writing in Early Modern England, 1500–1700* (Newark, Del., 2005).

Schuurman, Paul, 'Locke's Way of Ideas as a Context for his Theory of Education in *Of the Conduct of the Understanding*', *History of European Ideas*, 27 (2001), 45–59.

Searle, Alison, '"Though I am a stranger to you by face, yet in neere bonds by faith": A Transatlantic Puritan Republic of Letters', *Early American Literature*, 43 (2008), 277–308.

Searle, Alison, 'Writing Authority in the Interregnum: The Pastoral Letters of Richard Baxter', in *Debating the Faith: Religion and Letter-Writing in Great Britain, 1550–1800*, ed. Anne Dunan-Page and Clothilde Prunier (Dordrecht, 2013), 49–68.

Seed, John, 'History and Narrative Identity: Religious Dissent and the Politics of Memory in Eighteenth-Century England', *Journal of British Studies*, 44 (2005), 46–63.

Seed, John, *Dissenting Histories: Religious Division and the Politics of Memory in Eighteenth-Century England* (Edinburgh, 2008).

Sell, Alan P. F., *Philosophy, Dissent and Nonconformity 1689–1920* (London, 2003).

Shapin, Steven, and Simon Schaffer, *Leviathan and the Air-Pump: Hobbes, Boyle and the Experimental Life* (Princeton, 1985).

Sheehan, Jonathan, *The Enlightenment Bible: Translation, Scholarship, Culture* (Princeton, 2005).

Sheehan, Jonathan, 'Sacred and Profane: Idolatry, Antiquarianism and the Polemics of Distinction in the Seventeenth Century', *Past and Present*, 192 (2006), 35–66.

Sher, Richard B., *Church and University in the Scottish Enlightenment: The Moderate Literati of Edinburgh* (Edinburgh, 1985).

Sher, Richard B., *The Enlightenment and the Book: Scottish Authors and their Publishers in Eighteenth-Century Britain, Ireland, and America* (Chicago, 2006).

Siskin, Clifford, *The Work of Writing* (Baltimore, 1997).

Smail, John, 'Religion, Culture and Politics in Oliver Heywood's Halifax', in *Protestant Identities: Religion, Society, and Self-Fashioning in Post-Reformation England*, ed. Muriel C. McClendon, Joseph P. Ward, and Michael MacDonald (Stanford, Calif., 1999), 234–48.

Smith, Hannah, 'English "Feminist" Writings and Judith Drake's *An Essay in Defence of the Female Sex* (1696)', *Historical Journal*, 44 (2001), 727–47.

Smith, J. W. Ashley, *The Birth of Modern Education: The Contribution of the Dissenting Academies, 1660–1800* (London, 1954).

Snead, Jennifer, 'Print, Predestination, and the Public Sphere: Transatlantic Evangelical Periodicals, 1740–1745', *Early American Literature*, 45 (2010), 93–118.

Stanford, Charles, *Philip Doddridge, D.D.* (London, 1880).

Stephenson, William E., 'Isaac Watts's Education for the Dissenting Ministry: A New Document', *Harvard Theological Review*, 61 (1968), 263–81.

Stevens, William, *The History of the Scottish Church, Rotterdam* (Edinburgh, 1832).

Stewart, Larry, *The Rise of Public Science: Rhetoric, Technology and Natural Philosophy in Newtonian Britain* (Cambridge, 1992).

Stone, Lawrence (ed.), *The University in Society*, 2 vols (Princeton, 1974).

Stott, Anne, *Hannah More: The First Victorian* (Oxford, 2003).

Stott, Anne, 'Evangelicalism and Enlightenment: The Educational Agenda of Hannah More', in *Educating the Child in Enlightenment Britain: Beliefs, Cultures, Practices*, ed. Mary Hilton and Jill Shefrin (Farnham, 2009), 41–56.

Stoughton, John, *Philip Doddridge: His Life and Labours* (London, 1851).

Suarez, Michael F., 'Introduction', in *The Cambridge History of the Book in Britain Volume V: 1695–1830*, ed. Michael F. Suarez, SJ and Michael L. Turner (Cambridge, 2009), 1–35.

Suarez, Michael F., 'Publishing Contemporary English Literature, 1695–1771', in *The Cambridge History of the Book in Britain Volume V: 1695–1830*, ed. Michael F. Suarez, SJ and Michael L. Turner (Cambridge, 2009), 649–66.

Suarez, Michael F., 'Towards a Bibliometric Analysis of the Surviving Record', in *The Cambridge History of the Book in Britain Volume V: 1695–1830*, ed. Michael F. Suarez, SJ and Michael L. Turner (Cambridge, 2009), 39–65.

Tadmor, Naomi, *Family and Friends in Eighteenth-Century England: Household, Kinship, and Patronage* (Cambridge, 2001).

Taylor, J. H., 'Doddridge's "Most Considerable Work": *The Family Expositor*', *Journal of the United Reformed Church History Society*, 7 (2004), 235–52.

Thompson, John Handby, *A History of the Coward Trust: The First Two Hundred and Fifty Years 1738–1988* (London, 1998).

Topham, Jonathan, 'A View from the Industrial Age', *Isis*, 95 (2004), 431–42.

Tyacke, Nicholas, 'The "Rise of Puritanism" and the Legalizing of Dissent, 1571–1719', in *From Persecution to Toleration: The Glorious Revolution in England*, ed. Ole Peter Grell, Jonathan I. Israel, and Nicholas Tyacke (Oxford, 1991), 17–49.

van den Berg, J., and G. F. Nuttall, *Philip Doddridge (1702–1751) and The Netherlands* (Leiden, 1987).

van Eijnatten, *Liberty and Concord in the United Provinces: Religious Toleration and the Public in the Eighteenth-Century Netherlands* (Leiden, 2003).

Van Kley, Dale, *Religion and Politics in Enlightenment Europe* (Notre Dame, Ind., 2001).

Van Reyk, William, 'Christian Ideals of Manliness in the Eighteenth and Early Nineteenth Centuries', *Historical Journal*, 52 (2009), 1053–73.

Walsh, John, Colin Haydon, and Stephen Taylor (eds), *The Church of England, c.1689–c.1833: From Toleration to Tractarianism* (Cambridge, 1993).

Walsh, Marcus, *Shakespeare, Milton and Eighteenth-Century Literary Editing: The Beginnings of Interpretative Scholarship* (Cambridge, 1997).

Walsh, Marcus, 'Form and Function in the Eighteenth-Century Literary Edition: The Case of Edward Capell', *Studies in Bibliography*, 54 (2001), 225–42.

Ward, W. R., 'The Relations of Enlightenment and Religious Revival in the Early Eighteenth Century', in *Reform and Reformation: England and the Continent c.1500– c.1750*, ed. Derek Baker (Oxford, 1979), 281–305.

Ward, W. R., *The Protestant Evangelical Awakening* (Cambridge, 1992).

Ward, W. R., 'German Pietism, 1670–1750', *Journal of Ecclesiastical History*, 44 (1993), 476–505.

Warner, Michael, *Publics and Counterpublics* (New York, 2005).

Watson, J. R., *The English Hymn: A Critical and Historical Study* (Oxford, 1997).

Watson, J. R., 'The Hymns of Isaac Watts and the Tradition of Dissent', in *Dissenting Praise: Religious Dissent and the Hymn in England and Wales*, ed. Isabel Rivers and David L. Wykes (Oxford, 2011), 33–67.

Watts, Michael R., *The Dissenters*, 2 vols (Oxford, 1978–97).

Whelan, Timothy, *Nonconformist Women Writers 1720–1840*, 8 vols (London, 2011).

Whelan, Timothy, *Other British Voices: Women, Poetry and Religion 1766–1840* (Houndmills, Basingstoke, 2015).

White, Daniel E., 'The "Joineriana": Anna Barbauld, the Aikin Family Circle, and the Dissenting Public Sphere', *Eighteenth-Century Studies*, 32 (1999), 511–33.

White, Daniel E., *Early Romanticism and Religious Dissent* (Cambridge, 2006).

Whitehouse, Tessa, '*The Family Expositor*, the Doddridge Circle and the Booksellers', *The Library*, 7th ser., 11 (2010), 321–44.

Whitehouse, Tessa, 'Godly Dispositions and Textual Conditions: The Literary Sociology of International Religious Exchanges, c.1722–1740', *History of European Ideas*, 39 (2011), 394–408.

Whitehouse, Tessa, 'Intellectual and Textual Entrepôts: Moses and Aaron, Hermann Witsius and the International Transmission of Educational Texts', *English Studies*, 92 (2011), 562–75.

Whitehouse, Tessa, '"Upon Reading Over the Whole of this Letter I am Sensibly Struck": Affectionate Networks and Schemes for Dissenting Academies', *Lives and Letters*, 3 (2011).

Whyman, Susan, *The Pen and the People: English Letter Writers 1660–1800* (Oxford, 2009).

Winter, Calhoun, 'The Southern Book Trade in the Eighteenth Century', in *A History of the Book in America: The Colonial Book in the Atlantic World*, ed. Hugh Amory and David D. Hall (Cambridge, 2000), 224–46.

Wood, Paul, *The Aberdeen Enlightenment: The Arts Curriculum in the Eighteenth Century* (Aberdeen, 1993).

Wood, Paul (ed.), *Science and Dissent in England 1688–1945* (Aldershot, 2004).

Woodmansee, Martha, 'The Genius and the Copyright: Economic and Legal Conditions of the Emergence of Authorship', *Eighteenth Century Studies*, 17 (1984), 425–48.

Wright, John P., 'The Understanding', in *The Oxford Handbook of British Philosophy in the Eighteenth Century*, ed. James A. Harris (Oxford, 2013), 149–70.

Wykes, David L., 'The Contribution of the Dissenting Academy to the Emergence of Rational Dissent', in *Enlightenment and Religion: Rational Dissent in Eighteenth-Century Britain*, ed. Knud Haakonssen (Cambridge, 1996), 99–139.

Wykes, David L., '*To Revive the Memory of Some Excellent Men': Edmund Calamy and the Early Historians of Nonconformity* (London, 1997).

Yeager, Jonathan, *Enlightened Evangelicalism: The Life and Thought of John Erskine* (Oxford, 2011).

Yeo, Richard, *Encyclopaedic Visions: Scientific Dictionaries and Enlightenment Culture* (Cambridge, 2001).

Yolton, J. W., *Perceptual Acquaintance from Descartes to Reid* (Minneapolis, 1984).

Yolton, J. W., 'Schoolmen, Logic and Philosophy', in *The History of the University of Oxford Volume V: The Eighteenth Century*, ed. L. S. Sutherland and L. G. Mitchell (Oxford, 1986), 565–92.

Young, Brian, '"The Soul-Sleeping System": Politics and Heresy in Eighteenth-Century England', *Journal of Ecclesiastical History*, 45 (1994), 64–81.

Young, Brian, *Religion and Enlightenment in Eighteenth-Century England* (Oxford, 1998).

IV. ELECTRONIC RESOURCES

All accessed May 2015

The British Book Trade Index
   URL: <http://www.bbti.bham.ac.uk>

Clergy of the Church of England Database
   URL: <http://theclergydatabase.org.uk/>

Committees for Repeal of the Test and Corporation Acts: Minutes 1786–90 and 1827–8 (London, 1978), ed. Thomas W. Davis
   URL: <http://www.british-history.ac.uk/report.aspx?compid=38777>

Dissenting Academies: Historical Information
   URL: <http://www.english.qmul.ac.uk/drwilliams/academies.html>

Dissenting Academies Online
   URL: <http://www.english.qmul.ac.uk/drwilliams/portal.html>

Dissenting Education and the Legacy of John Jennings, c.1720–c.1729, ed. Tessa Whitehouse, Dr Williams's Centre for Dissenting Studies (2nd edn, 2011)
   URL: <http://www.english.qmul.ac.uk/drwilliams/pubs/jennings%20legacy.html>

English Short Title Catalogue
   URL: <http://estc.bl.uk>

Oxford Dictionary of National Biography
   URL: <http://www.oxforddnb.com>

Oxford English Dictionary
   URL: <http://www.oed.com>

The Reading Experience Database 1450–1945
   URL: <http://www.open.ac.uk/Arts/reading/>

The Surman Index Online, Dr Williams's Centre for Dissenting Studies
   URL: <http://surman.english.qmul.ac.uk/>

Index